OCR
ICT for A2

OCR
RECOGNISING ACHIEVEMENT

HODDER
EDUCATION

Official Publisher Partnership

- **Paul Long**
- **Glen Millbery**
- **Sonia Stuart**

DL DYNAMIC LEARNING

HODDER
EDUCATION
AN HACHETTE UK COMPANY

The Publishers would like to thank the following for permission to reproduce copyright material:

Photo credits:

p.10 © Winston Davidian/istockphoto.com; **p.11** ©Photodisc/Getty Images; **p.12** © Graça Victoria – Fotolia.com; **p.53** © Gareth Leung – Fotolia.com; **p.54** *t* © AP/PA Photos, *b* © TomTom, with permission; **p.78** © Kent Knudson/PhotoLink/Photodisc/Getty Images; **p.81** *t,* © Sergey Galushko – Fotolia.com, *b* © Aleksandr Ugorenkov – Fotolia.com; **p.82** © Comstock Images/Photolibrary Group Ltd; **p.83** © Andrzej Tokarski – Fotolia.com; **p.84** Joe Zambon/St Francis of Assisi Catholic Technology College; **p.85** *t* © Clément Contet/iStockphoto.com, *b* © SpbPhoto – Fotolia.com; **p.86** *t* © Tatiana Popova/ iStockphoto.com, *b* © Ola Dusegård – Fotolia.com; **p.91** © diego cervo – Fotolia.com; **p.93** © Supertrooper – Fotolia.com; **p.108** © StockTrek/Photodisc/Getty Images; **p.109** © TomTom, with permission; **p.124** Steve Connolly; **p.126** © Royalty-Free/Corbis; **p.127** © Sharpshot – Fotolia.com; **p.129** © Courtesy of It's a Wrap (N.E) Ltd.; **p.133** © Bill Bachman/Alamy; **p.138** ©2007/Ed Kashi/Corbis; **p.139** © Jupiter Images/ Creatas/Alamy; **p.140** © atmospheric – Fotolia.com; **p.157** © Konstantin Sutyagin – Fotolia.com; **p.175** © Monkey Business – Fotolia.com; **p.176** © Stockdisc/Stockbyte/Getty Images; **p.177** © Ken Pilon – Fotolia.com; **p.202** © AP/PA Photos; **p.205** © Photodisc/Getty Images; **p.206** © PHOTOTAKE Inc./Alamy; **p.207** © Andrew Twort/Alamy; **p.209** © Photodisc/Getty Images; **p.220** © Ingram Publishing (Superstock Limited)/Alamy; **p.227** © Ted Pink/Alamy; **p.230** © Michael Prince/Corbis; **p.231** © Jo Katanigra/Alamy; **p.233** © Andrew Gentry – Fotolia.com; **p.234** © keith morris/Alamy; **p.236** © face to face Bildagentur GmbH/Alamy; **p.238** © Hugh O'Neill – Fotolia.com.

Every effort has been made to trace all copyright holders, but if any have been inadvertently overlooked the Publishers will be pleased to make the necessary arrangements at the first opportunity.

t = top, *b* = bottom, *l* = left, *r* = right, *c* = centre

Although every effort has been made to ensure that website addresses are correct at time of going to press, Hodder Education cannot be held responsible for the content of any website mentioned in this book. It is sometimes possible to find a relocated web page by typing in the address of the home page for a website in the URL window of your browser.

Hachette's policy is to use papers that are natural, renewable and recyclable products and made from wood grown in sustainable forests. The logging and manufacturing processes are expected to conform to the environmental regulations of the country of origin.

Orders: please contact Bookpoint Ltd, 130 Milton Park, Abingdon, Oxon OX14 4SB. Telephone: (44) 01235 827720. Fax: (44) 01235 400454. Lines are open 9.00 – 5.00, Monday to Saturday, with a 24-hour message answering service. Visit our website at www.hoddereducation.co.uk

© Paul Long, Glen Millbery and Sonia Stuart 2009

First published in 2009 by
Hodder Education,
an Hachette UK Company
338 Euston Road
London NW1 3BH

Impression number   5 4 3 2 1

Year   2013 2012 2011 2010 2009

Cover photo © Duncan Walker/iStockphoto.com

Illustrations by DC Graphic Design Limited, Swanley Village, Kent

Typeset in Stone Sans 11pt by DC Graphic Design Limited, Swanley Village, Kent

Printed in Italy

A catalogue record for this title is available from the British Library

ISBN-13: 978 0340 966 518

Contents

The systems cycle

Introduction

This chapter covers the stages that should be followed when developing a system. The tools and techniques that could be used during these stages, many of which will be of use when you are completing the coursework element of the A2 course, are also covered in this chapter. You should also be able to apply your knowledge to a specified scenario.

This chapter covers:

■ The systems cycle
■ Project management
■ Process modelling

Describe the following stages of the system life cycle (definition of the problem, investigation and analysis, design, implementation, testing, installation, documentation, evaluation and maintenance) and how the stages relate to ICT systems

All projects, resulting in a solution to a problem, go through a number of stages before they are complete: the system life cycle. As the term cycle suggests there is no clear start or finish point but it may be useful to think that the start is when a new software system is being considered. It may be that the existing system is unable to cope with the demands of the end users or the volume of work has increased leading to a reduction in the efficiency of the current system.

The system life cycle is a continuous loop with each stage leading into the next.

Each stage within the life cycle has a dependency on the stages that occur immediately before and after it. For example, if you look at the diagram of the systems life cycle you can see that the installation stage will depend on the testing stage (the stage before) and the documentation stage will depend on the installation stage.

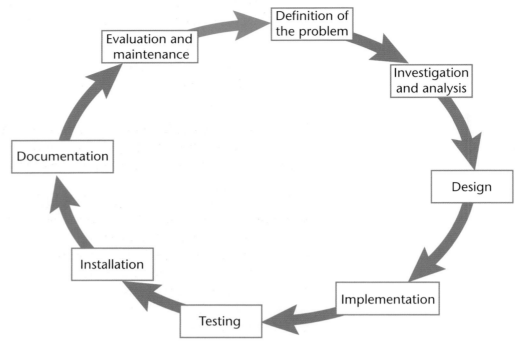

Figure 1.1 The system life cycle

▣ Problem definition stage

During this stage the feasibility of the proposed system is considered. This stage is also known as the feasibility stage. It is the initial look at the existing system to see how it can be improved or if it is possible to meet the needs of the end users. The result of this stage is a feasibility report.

This stage answers some very important questions:

- Can the need for a new software system be justified?
- Is it technically feasible and economically desirable to the end users?

During this stage a number of important questions may be asked. These include:

- Can the solution be designed and implemented within the given constraints of time-scale allocated and budget?
- Will the solution have a positive impact on the end users, and will the new system bring benefits?
- Will the solution fulfill all the needs and requirements of the end users?

For the project to continue the answer to all these questions must be 'yes': there is the time, money and resources, and the impact of the proposed solution will be positive.

The stage begins with an initial, brief investigation that involves the systems analyst obtaining some general information:

- The system currently being used, its benefits and limitations (i.e. why the existing system is not meeting its user's needs).
- The additional end user requirements of the new software system (i.e. the purpose of a new system).

The analyst needs to identify why the current system is not meeting the needs of the organisation, why a new software system is needed and what the purpose of the software system is.

There are many reasons why a new system may be required:

- An organisation wants to computerise a part of its operations that is current done manually.
- The capacity of the existing software system is too small to carry out the work now demanded of it.
- The existing system is now outdated and no longer suits the needs of the organisation.
- The existing system has come to the end of its life and needs to be replaced.

The analyst must be able to clearly identify the general reasons why a new software system is required and the specific needs given by the end users. The client will define process constraints to the analyst. The main process constraints are:

- time
- budget
- hardware choice
- software choice.

The feasibility report is written by an analyst for the management of the organisation needing the new software system. It is very important, therefore, that it is written, as far as possible, in non-technical language so that the contents of the report can be clearly understood. The feasibility report should describe the system from an end user perspective.

■ Investigation and analysis stage

This stage follows the definition of the problem and must be fully completed before moving to the design stage. This stage uses the feasibility report (the output from the previous stage) as its main input.

The full nature of the problem to be solved is investigated during this stage. The result of this investigation forms the basis for the analysis.

Different methods can be used for investigating the current system. These include:

- questionnaires
- interviews
- meetings
- document analysis
- observations.

(These investigation methods are discussed later in this chapter.)

The results of the investigation have to be fully analysed to gain a full understanding of the current system. If the investigation has been incomplete, then the new system may not cover all the inadequacies of the current system and will not bring any benefits to the organisation.

Towards the end of this stage the user requirements have to be defined. The user requirements are agreed with the client and will form the basis for the rest of the system life cycle. The agreed needs are the output of this stage: the requirements specification.

Once the user requirements have been agreed by the client and the analyst then, during the rest of the life cycle, it is important that these user requirements are constantly referred to. By doing this the analyst can be assured that the new system, once implemented, will meet all the user requirements.

If the requirements are not referred to, then the system may not fully, if at all, meet the needs of the end users. If this situation occurs, then the new system will not be useful to the organisation, thereby resulting in a waste of money.

It may be that some of the functions of the current system have to be incorporated into the new system although these functions may need to be updated. It is more likely, however, that new functions will need to be added to the new system to solve the previously identified problems with the current system.

Design stage

The design stage comes after the investigation and analysis stage has been completed. This stage must be completed before the implementation stage is started.

The design stage follows the set of objectives (the requirements specification) that have been defined in the investigation and analysis stage. It begins to develop the design of the system. The methods of data capture have to be considered to ensure that the format of the data capture and the methods of data capture to be used are compatible with the design of the processing to be used in the system.

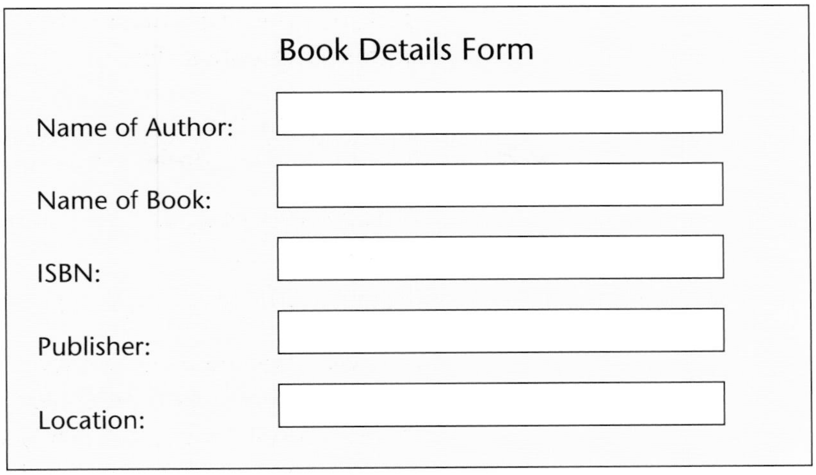

Book Details Form

Name of Author: _____

Name of Book: _____

ISBN: _____

Publisher: _____

Location: _____

Figure 1.2 Example of a screen form design

Leading on from this, the preparation, input and storage of the data must also be considered. This covers such activities as the design of the user interface and screen layout.

The structure of the data must be defined together with the processing and the validation routines that will be used. The development of any user feedback requirements (e.g. the creation of helpful error messages) should be linked with this.

The validation routines, structure of the data and the processing are likely to form the basis of test plans that are developed as part of this stage.

The design of the queries and reports that have been identified during the investigation stage will need to be considered. The reports may include documents and/or screen reports. The reports should follow, as far as possible, the existing house style of the organisation. The reports will be part of the design of the output that is required from the system. The output requirements should have been defined in previous stages of the system life cycle.

The design stage may also involve the development of a project plan. This must be developed in conjunction with the client who may have specified a deadline for the installation of the system.

The main output from this stage is the design specification.

Implementation stage

This stage is also known as the development stage. The implementation stage comes after the design stage has been completed and it must be completed before the testing stage is started. It uses the design specification (the output from the design stage) and is about taking the design forward and putting it into practice.

During this stage the programmers will create the code required for the software solution, including the development of the user interfaces and output. These will have been designed in the design stage, so the programmers will need to ensure that the code matches this. The programmers will also need to develop any macros, processing and queries that are required by the client. The back-up and storage of the data should be considered during the creation of the code.

A decision will need to be taken about the strategy to be taken. This is dependent on the system requirements. It may be that off-the-shelf software is purchased and either installed as it is or may be customised to fully meet the defined needs of the client. Software that is currently available will be much cheaper in terms of time and money than creating custom-written software. When making the decision about which strategy to take the budget constraint defined by the client should be considered.

The output from this stage will be working software code that is ready to be tested.

Testing stage

The testing stage comes after the implementation stage has been completed. The stage must be completed before the installation stage is started. It tests the output from the implementation stage (the software code).

There are two main functions of this stage. They are to find out:

- if there are any bugs or errors in the code
- if the system correctly meets the defined user requirements.

If a high quality and reliable solution is to be installed, then the testing must follow a well-defined and comprehensive test plan. It is acknowledged that the reliability of a software solution increases with the amount of testing completed. However, testing is generally time-consuming and expensive, so, in consideration of the budget set by the client, some compromise may need to be reached. Some software systems need to be more reliable than others and so the purpose of the software will also need to be a major factor when considering how much testing should be completed.

If all the previous stages of the system life cycle have been fully completed, then the software under test will be well-designed and so should be easier to test.

There are many types of testing that can be carried out at this stage. The type of testing must be appropriate to the purpose of the software.

The test plan to be followed should have been developed in previous stages of the life cycle. This test plan should be followed with the results being recorded. Finding faults with the software, however, may result in the software having to be returned to the previous stage. This demonstrates the iterative nature of the system life cycle.

Installation stage

The installation stage comes after the testing stage has been completed. It usually runs in conjunction with the documentation stage. This stage uses the output from the implementation and testing stages: the completed and tested software code.

The strategy of installation needs to be decided. There are four main strategies that can be taken when installing a new system. These are:

- parallel
- phased
- pilot
- direct.

These strategies are discussed in chapter 10.

When making a decision about which strategy to use the time scale for implementing the new system must be considered. Another consideration is the sensitivity of the data and the effect that any data loss will have on the organisation.

The training of the employees will need to be completed during this stage in the system life cycle.

Documentation stage

When the system has been implemented and the staff trained it is essential that documentation is given to the end users. Not all of this documentation will be used on a day-to-day basis, but it should be kept in a safe place in case it needs to be referred to at a later date. The documentation that is passed to the end user serves a number of purposes.

The documentation that may be passed to the end user includes:

- detailed program specifications
- recovery procedures
- operating procedures
- user manuals
- test plans, data and logs
- security details
- version details
- technical manuals for the associated hardware.

Detailed program specifications are given to the end user so that if any maintenance is needed at a later date, the programmer completing this maintenance will be able to see clearly how the system was constructed. It is unlikely, but not impossible, that the same team who developed the system will perform any required maintenance.

Security details should be handed over to ensure that the access rights initially set are maintained – staff changes will inevitably occur during the life of a system, so these details will ensure that the security of an organisation is not compromised.

Version details should be passed to the organisation to ensure that the organisation is holding and using the most up-to-date set of documents. As with any iterative activity, different versions of documentation are produced as changes are implemented. Version controls will ensure that changes made to the system can be tracked and that any maintenance performed uses the most recent set of documents.

Additionally, documentation can provide reference material for staff training. Each task and procedure covered by the system should be clearly detailed. This will also enable users to solve any minor issues or problems with the system once they are using it on a day-to-day basis.

The documentation should also provide a detailed explanation of how the system works. This will enable the people working with the system (e.g. technicians) to diagnose and solve day-to-day issues that may arise. The documentation should also contain detail that will help if any maintenance is to be carried out on the system at a later date.

< Activity >

Investigate and identify why the following pieces of user documentation should be passed to the end user. Explain how each piece of documentation may be used during the life of the system:

- Recovery procedures

- Operating procedures

- User manuals

Evaluation and maintenance stage

The final stage of the life cycle is the evaluation and maintenance stage. It may form the basis on which the decision is taken to begin the life cycle again. The linkage between this stage and the definition of the problem demonstrates the iterative nature of the life cycle.

The solution should be evaluated once it has been implemented. If the time scale of the life cycle has been long then it may be that some of the user requirements have changed. This can be identified during the evaluation and can be rectified through maintenance. Maintenance is the process of ensuring that a system continues to meet the needs of its users. Further details about maintenance can be found in chapter 5.

The inputs and outputs of stages of the system life cycle are shown in the following table.

Stage	Input	Output
Problem definition		Feasibility study
Investigation and analysis	Feasibility study	Requirements specification
Design	Requirements specification	Designs
Implementation	Designs	Completed system
Testing	Completed system / test plans	Working system / test logs
Installation	Working system	Installed system

QUESTION

Describe the following stages of the system life cycle:
1 Design
2 Implementation

Discuss different approaches an analyst might use when investigating a system: questionnaires, interviews, meetings, document analysis, observation

There are different methods that can be used to gather the information during the investigation and analysis stage of the system life cycle. They include:

- questionnaires
- interviews
- meetings
- document analysis
- observations.

The analyst will select the most appropriate method of investigation for the task. The choice will will depend on:

- the people involved
- the type of information being gathered
- the place in which the investigation is to be carried out.

Each method of investigation has benefits and limitations. Based on these, and the factors given above, the analyst may use more than one method during the investigation stage.

Questionnaires

Questionnaires are an excellent way of gathering information. However the questionnaire must be structured correctly, the return of the questionnaires must be strictly controlled and the questionnaire must be sent to relevant end users.

The questionnaire should be structured clearly and provide opportunities for short answers based on facts and figures and descriptive answers. The balance of type of questions will ensure that all the information required by the analyst will be gathered.

The return of a questionnaire may cause a problem to the analyst. One idea maybe to put a time constraint on the return or the questionnaire (e.g. 'Please return within five working days'). Another idea may be to distribute the questionnaires at a meeting and collect them in at the end of the meeting – this is not always feasible and this approach should be carefully considered.

Figure 1.3 Example questionnaire

When designing a questionnaire it is important to consider who the questionnaire is aimed at. End users of a system can interpret questions differently depending on their job role within the organisation.

Interviews/meetings

The analyst can clarify that the information already gathered is correct by interviewing, or holding meetings with, users. If the questions are well-planned, interviews can reveal new information and give the analyst the opportunity to understand the system with the end user's perspective. However, interviewing end users can be problematic if the organisation has a number of geographically distributed branches or offices.

The analyst should always carefully plan an interview. The questions to be asked must be unambiguous to ensure the information required is gathered.

One of the main benefits of interviewing is that the planned questions can be modified as the interview progresses. An answer

Figure 1.4 Interviewing an end user

might be given that raises some relevant and/or additional information that the analyst has not considered. If this occurs it may be beneficial for a checklist of points to be drawn up to ensure that all the points that need to be covered are covered.

Sometimes meeting and interviews do not go as planned. This may be because:

- people are unable or unwilling to answer the questions (e.g. the procedures defined by the management of the organisation are not being followed and staff do not wish to draw attention to it)
- irrelevant or unnecessary information may given in response to a question (e.g. it may be that the question is ambiguous and may need to be restructured, or a topic under discussion may lose its focus leading to irrelevant dialogue taking place)
- insufficient information may be given in response to the question
- inaccurate information may be given in response to a question. The interviewer may not be aware of any inaccuracy until the responses from other investigations are collated.

If the system to be designed is to meet the needs of the organisation, then it is important that the analyst has all the relevant information. This situation may mean that the interviewer has to ask more questions in order to gather the required information.

It is very important that the analyst talks to all different types of end user, from management to staff of all levels, and that the interviewee feels comfortable and at ease with the questioning. A good interview will enable a rapport to be developed between the interviewer and interviewee. This rapport may prove to be important if further interviews are needed or further information has to be gathered.

There are four factors that the analyst should consider when arranging interviews or meetings:

- Who to interview or invite to the meeting.
- Where and when to conduct the interview or meeting.
- What questions to ask.
- How to record the answers to the questions.

If all these points are carefully considered, then the interview or meeting will go well and all the information required by the analyst should be gathered.

Document analysis

The analysis of documentation used in the current system is a good way of identifying the format of the input, processing and outputs that occur in that system.

The drawback is that this method of investigation can only be used when the information flow is document based. This method can be used to clarify the information given by the end user and can also trace the source and recipients of a particular piece of information used by the current system. The analyst should collect copies of all documents used by the current system.

The most common documents analysed include invoices, purchase orders, goods received notes, receipts, stock records and customer records.

Figure 1.5 Example of documents used in a system

< Activity >

Identify **five** documents that might be used in systems in the following establishments, and that could be examined. Describe how an analyst might use the information.

- School or college

- Sports club

- Supermarket

- Hotel

Observation

If several activities are taking place in the system being investigated, then observation (or shadowing) may be the best methods for collecting the information.

Observing someone doing their job is better than asking someone to describe it. Over a period of time, the possibility of anything being forgotten or missed is reduced. Observation is suitable on a factory production line, for example, where there will not be much documentation for analysis and, because of the nature of the activity, interviewing or questionnaires are inappropriate.

The analyst observing a system will be able to identify all the processes that occur, how long the user takes to perform a specific task and what hardware, software (if any) and people are involved.

One thing the analyst must be aware of is that people are involved in a system. The analyst must always ask the permission of the people involved before beginning their observation or shadow. To ensure that the observation or shadow gathers the information required the following factors should be carefully considered:

- How the findings will be recorded.
- Where and when the observation/shadow will take place.
- What part of the current system will be observed.

QUESTIONS

1 Explain why an analyst might use the technique of observation?
2 Identify **two** situations when observation would be appropriate.

Discuss different approaches an analyst might use when investigating a system

Method	Benefits	Limitations
Questionnaires	■ Large numbers of people can be asked the same questions, therefore comparisons are easy to make (e.g. 72% of people said they were unhappy with the current system). ■ Cheaper than interviews for large numbers of people. ■ Anonymity may provide more honest answers. ■ Factual information required can be easily gathered.	■ Must be designed very carefully. Questions need to be unambiguous. ■ Cannot guarantee 100% return. ■ It is difficult to gain a realistic view of the use of a system.
Interviews	■ A rapport can be developed with the people who will use the system. ■ Questions can be adjusted as the interviews proceed – additional questions can be added to gather more information.	■ Can be time-consuming and costly. ■ Poor interviewing can lead to misleading or insufficient information being gathered. ■ It might be impossible to interview every relevant person in a large organisation.
Meetings	■ A group of people, possibly from a specific department, can attend a meeting. ■ Discussions can take place with different views being expressed. ■ Can be used to gather or give information. ■ Body language can be seen.	■ The discussions can lose focus resulting in the questions not being fully answered. ■ Some staff may not attend because jobs and tasks still need to be completed while the meetings are being held.
Document/record analysis and inspection	■ Good for obtaining factual information (e.g. volume of sales over a period of time, inputs and outputs of the system).	■ Cannot be used when input, output information is not document based.
Observation	■ The effects of office layouts and conditions on the system can be assessed. ■ Work loads, methods of working, delays and 'bottlenecks' can be identified. ■ Potential to experience all aspects of job role.	■ Can be time-consuming and costly. ■ Problems may not occur during observation. ■ Users may put on a performance when being observed.

QUESTIONS

1 Describe how interviews could be used as an investigative method.
2 What are the advantages of using meetings as an investigative method?
3 What are the disadvantages of using observation as an investigative method?

Describe the following software development methodologies: prototyping and rapid application development (RAD)

A major problem with the traditional structured life cycle model is the duration of the activities that have to take place. There is usually a long time delay between the definition of the problem and the implementation of the solution. In some cases this may mean that the delivered system does not fully meet the current requirements of the organisation it has been designed for.

This problem could be solved by using a different software development methodology.

Prototyping

Prototypes are a first attempt at a design which are then extended and enhanced through the use of iterations. The prototyping methodology stresses the early delivery to the end users of an incomplete, but working, system which can then be changed following feedback from the client. Typically, a prototype simulates only a few aspects of the software system and may be completely different from the final solution that is implemented.

The main purpose of a prototype is to allow the end users of the software to evaluate the proposals for the design of the software by actually trying them out, rather than having to interpret and evaluate the design based on descriptions.

Prototyping can take place at different stages of the development life cycle, but the use of this methodology must be planned to ensure maximum feedback is obtained from the end users of the system.

This methodology is popular because it can be used to verify that what the designer has conceptualised is what the end user requires, thereby fully meeting the need. End users can often find it difficult to define their exact requirements. This may be because they do not exactly know or find it difficult to imagine how, for example, the user interface will need to look when the solution has been completed.

Prototyping can also be used by end users to describe requirements that the designer may not have considered, so controlling the prototype can be a key factor in the relationship between the designer and the end users.

By creating a prototype, concepts can be demonstrated, design options can be tried out and problems with possible solutions can be investigated. For example, a prototype of a screen design for a user interface could be developed to test the appropriateness of the layout. It would not be necessary, in this case, to develop the data files that are queried or written to using the screens. However, when the screen design has been agreed, then the data files can be developed as a prototype to ensure that the end users are happy with the way they interact.

There are two main ways of prototyping:

■ Evolutionary
■ Throw-away.

Evolutionary prototyping is when an initial prototype of the system is developed and evaluated by the end users. Using the feedback from this a second prototype is developed and then evaluated. This process continues with each prototype and evaluation making the system closer to what the end users require. Finally, on the last evaluation, the system meets all the requirements.

Throw-away prototyping is when a working model of various parts of the system is developed after a short investigation. The prototype is developed and evaluated by the end user, but this prototype is not used in the final solution: it is thrown away! This enables the end users to give, and receive, quick feedback. This means that any refinements can be done early in the development. Making changes early in the development life cycle is cost effective because there is nothing to redo. If a project is changed after considerable work has been done, then small changes could require large efforts to implement since software systems have many dependencies.

QUESTION

Describe the evolutionary and throw-away prototyping methodologies.

■ Benefits of prototyping methodology

Reduced time and costs

Prototyping can improve the quality of requirements and specifications provided to developers. Changes cost exponentially more to implement as they are detected later in development, so early clarification of what the user really wants can result in faster development and less development costs.

Improved and increased user involvement

Prototyping requires the involvement of users. This enables them to see and interact with a prototype providing better and more complete feedback and specifications. Misunderstandings that can occur when each side believes the other understands what they said are fewer. The end users know the problem better than the designer, so increased user involvement can result in a better and more appropriate final product that is likely to satisfy the end users' needs in terms of look, feel and performance.

The designer can obtain feedback from the end users early in the project. This will, hopefully, ensure that the software made matches the software specification. This can also check that the deadlines proposed can be successfully met.

Disadvantages of prototyping methodology

Confusion between the prototype and the finished system

End users can think that a prototype, intended to be thrown away, is actually a final system that merely needs to be finished. This can lead them to expect the prototype to accurately match the final system. Users can also become attached to features that were included in a prototype for user evaluation and then removed from the final system.

Excessive development time of the prototype

The main aim of prototyping is that it is supposed to be done quickly. It is very tempting to develop a prototype that is too complex, leading to the development time being extended. This would also lead to an increase in the cost of the resources needed.

It would not be appropriate to use this methodology where user requirements are well established or the system is a standard one used by the organisation.

< Activity >

Investigate software systems that could be developed using the prototyping methodology.

Rapid application development (RAD)

Another approach to shortening the project duration is rapid application development (RAD). The RAD methodology is based on a life cycle that is both iterative and evolutionary.

One of the main aims of RAD is to produce a software solution within a relatively short duration. The typical duration of a RAD system is less than six months. This duration is generally considered to be the longest period over which user requirements will stay static.

Describe software development methodologies: prototyping and rapid application development (RAD)

The short duration, along with increased opportunities for user involvement, are the two main benefits of RAD. These will, hopefully, ensure that no changes to the end user requirements will appear towards the end of the development process. During the RAD process, there are a number of tools that can be used by the developers to build the graphical user interface (GUI) that can be seen and evaluated by the end user. The use of these tools will assist end users to visualise the GUI and to provide helpful feedback to the development team before the system is implemented.

RAD has two main features. The first is the use of joint development application (JAD) workshops. These are requirement gathering workshops which aim to develop a set of requirements that, hopefully, will not change before the system is implemented.

The second feature of RAD is timeboxing. This means that the requirements of the system are defined in small 'chunks', each of which is considered using a JAD. Each 'chunk' is allocated a specified timescale which must not be exceeded. At the start of each timebox the objectives are defined and, at the end of the timebox, these are evaluated. If requirements are not successfully completed, then they may be added to another timebox or dropped. The requirements that are not implemented are those with the lowest priority because they have been prioritised.

If the requirements of several consecutive timeboxes cannot be completed, then the overall system may need to be reviewed. This should ensure that the incomplete requirements do not pile up and cause excessive delays to the overall product.

RAD attempts to maintain overall control over the development process, but also provides continual feedback on the progress of a project. This means that if there is any slippage in the defined time schedule, then plans can be adjusted.

RAD is also helpful to the end users of the system being developed. They are party to the evaluations, which means they are continually involved. This involvement should ensure that the system, once developed and implemented, fully meets their defined requirements.

Benefits of RAD

- The end user is involved at all stages and the system is implemented within six months. These should ensure that the final system fully meets the defined requirements.
- End users do not have to define all the requirements of the system at the beginning of the process.

Disadvantages of RAD

- The solution developed may, on the surface, meet the end user requirements but the functionality may not be acceptable. For example, if the system is tested using a small number of users then it may not fully function when many end users try to use the system concurrently.
- The project manager, who is overseeing the development of the system, will need to keep very tight control over the whole development process and the team. The timescales defined must be adhered to otherwise the solution will not be developed within the six months deadline required by RAD.

QUESTION

Describe the RAD methodology.

Describe the purpose of test data and explain the importance of testing and test plans

When a system has been created (implemented) then it must be tested to ensure that, as far as possible, it is free from errors. Testing checks that a system works as intended.

There are set procedures that should be followed to ensure that a system works. These procedures are grouped together to form a test plan. Testing is important and should:

- make sure that the system (software) meets the design specification
- make sure that the system returns the correct results and actually works
- give confidence to the end users: they will have more faith and confidence in a new system if it has successfully completed and passed all the tests.

It is important to understand the difference between an error and a fault. An error is a human action that produces an incorrect result. A fault is a manifestation of an error in the system – these are also known as bugs or defects. A fault may cause a software failure, it is a deviation of the software from what is expected.

Reliability is also a key factor in testing. Reliability is the probability that the software will not cause the failure of the system for a specified time under specified conditions. Testing is about ensuring the software is reliable.

Errors occur with software because people are not perfect. While they are working under constraints, such as deadlines, they can, due to the stress and pressure, make mistakes.

The amount of testing that is carried out on a system depends on the risks that are involved. A safety critical system, which would cause more risk if it failed, would need more rigorous testing than, for example, a stock database.

Testing is about trying to identify faults and rectifying them. The reliability and quality of a system increases as faults are identified and rectified.

When carrying out tests, it is important to consider other factors that may have an impact on the system. These may include contractual (part of the handover of the system) or legal (industry standards) requirements.

It is sometimes difficult to determine how much testing should be carried out. However, it is unlikely that all the faults will be found during the testing process. Large software vendors release patches to solve any bugs found after the software has been released.

Test data

The data that is selected for testing is important and should cover:

- Normal data: The data that is used everyday. It is data that is correct and should not generate any errors on entry.
- Extreme data: The data that is also correct, but is at the upper and lower boundaries of tolerance. It should not generate any errors when entered because it is normal data.
- Erroneous data: The data that is incorrect. It may be outside the boundaries of tolerance or be of the wrong data type.

Test plans

A test plan has to be developed before testing is carried out. This is a formal document that lists the tests that will be carried out on the system.

The test plan should ensure that the tests cover:

- the requirements
- pathways
- validation routines
- a comparison of the actual performance against the design specification.

The test plan structure, as explained further in coursework chapter 10, is shown below.

Test number	Description of test	Type of test	Data used	Expected result

- Test number: a unique identifier for each test.
- Description of test: an everyday language description of what is being tested.
- Type of test: normal, extreme, erroneous (incorrect).
- Data used: the data that will be entered to run the test. It must be specific and if relevant, indicate where it will be entered. All data used must be given.
- Expected result: what you expect to happen when you run the test. For normal tests it should be a positive result. Incorrect data should result in an error message.

The format of the test plan is important because the test plan should be in sufficient detail to enable a third party to exactly recreate the tests and the actual results obtained. The test plan may also be included in the documentation that is passed over following the installation of the system.

The test plan aims to clearly document how each test will be carried out. The input data and expected output should be clearly defined. This will enable any discrepancies between the expected output and actual output to be clearly identified. Any tests where there is a difference between the actual and expected results will need to be re-tested once the remedial action has been taken to rectify the fault. These will need to be added to the test plan to ensure that it stays complete.

QUESTIONS

1 Describe the importance of a test plan.
2 When should a test plan be changed?
3 Explain the purpose of test data.

Describe the contents of the requirements specification, the design specification and the system specification, distinguishing between them

Requirements specification

The requirements specification is usually developed by the systems analyst. It will be developed following investigations that have been carried out on the system.

The requirements specification should clearly define what the system is to do and how this should be achieved. It should also describe all the interactions the users will have with the software.

The defined functional (what the end user wants the system to do) and non-functional requirements (the end user defined limitations relating to response time/hardware/software/ programming language) should also be included within the requirements specification.

The contents of a requirements specification will also include:

- the objectives/purpose of the system
- the scope of the system
- the proposed timescale for the project
- end-user defined constraints including budget, time, hardware and software choices
- a contract.

Design specification

The design specification is usually developed by the systems designer. The specification is usually created following the investigations. The contents of the design specification may have a different focus dependent on the type of system that is being developed. For example, if a website is being developed, then it would be appropriate to include the links between the webpage's and how these pages would be organised.

This would not be appropriate if a database system is being developed. However, both the website and the database might include data entry forms. The design for the data entry forms would be included in the design specification.

The design specification usually includes:

- the purpose of the system
- assumptions, limitations or constraints
- the inputs – documents and screens/interface
- the outputs – documents and screens/interface
- error messages
- the colours/fonts/sizes, including the consideration of the corporate image/house style, to be used
- validation rules
- processing requirements/queries
- data structures
- modelling diagrams (e.g. data flow diagrams, entity relationship diagrams and state transition diagrams)
- the hardware
- the software/programming language to be used
- test plan.

System specification

The system specification defines the requirements for the new system. These include, for example, the facilities and outputs that the new system should provide. The requirements are developed and formulated from the results of the investigation of the current system.

The system specification should include:

- operation requirements: what operations the system should carry out
- information requirements: what information the system should provide to the end users
- volume requirements: for example, how much volume of processing is to be handled
- general systems requirements: for example, the degree of data accuracy needed, security issues, the need for an audit trail, the flexibility of the system and its ability to adapt to growth and change etc.

> **QUESTION**
>
> Describe the contents of the design specification.

Describe the roles and responsibilities of the following members of the project team: project manager, systems analyst, systems designer, programmer and tester

Many people are involved in the development of a system, both at specific or all stages of the system life cycle.

The main members of the project team will be the project manager, systems analyst, systems designer, programmer and tester. Each member of the team has a different role and responsibility. If, however, the project team is small then it is possible that one person may take on more than one of these roles and responsibilities.

Project manager

The main role of the project manager is to plan and control the whole project. The project manager is, if required, responsible for identifying potential problems and issues, and if they arise, for rectifying them.

After consulting with the end user and other members of the project team, the project manager will set the deadlines for each stage of the project. This task is completed at the beginning of the project to ensure that the system being developed is delivered to the end user on schedule. This enables the project manager to have, at any given point during the development, an overall understanding of how the project is progressing. This may, if the project is falling behind the defined time schedule, involve the rescheduling of any tasks, and associated resources such as time, staff and money. One of the other associated roles of the project manager is to oversee the project team.

The budget allocated by the end user will need to be agreed at the start of the project. The project manager is responsible for ensuring that the budget is adhered to and that any slippage in costs is notified to the end user (i.e. the project manager should try to ensure that the project costs do not exceed those set by the end user).

The project manager must ensure that all the associated project reports and documentation are correctly completed during the project. This may involve consultation between all members of the project team to ensure that the documentation provides accurate and complete details.

The system life cycle is an iterative process, so the project manager is responsible for ensuring that each stage (and any associated tasks) of the life cycle is completed before the next stage is started. As each stage or task is completed the project manager should provide progress reports to the end user of the system.

Systems analyst

The main role of the systems analyst is to analyse the existing system. During the analysis the analyst will investigate the current system using appropriate investigative methods.

The results of the analysis will enable the systems analyst to assess the suitability of the current system for upgrading.

After the investigations, the systems analyst must develop a plan for developing the proposed system. As part of this the analyst must specify:

- the procedures involved (computerised and manual)
- how the data is to be captured
- the software required to process the data
- how the data is to be output
- the hardware that is required
- how the staff will be trained to use the new system.

The systems analyst is mainly responsible for the development of the feasibility report (the output from the investigation and analysis stage of the systems life cycle) including the requirements specification.

A major part of the role of the systems analyst is to liaise with the staff in the organisation. Those who work in the organisation will have expert knowledge of how the current system works and how it could be improved.

Systems designer

The systems designer will build on the findings of the systems analyst in order to design the new system. The designer's role is central to the process of designing, developing and implementing the defined requirements of the system. The roles and responsibilities of the systems analyst and designer are very similar and, if roles have to be combined in a project team, these roles can be given to the same person.

The role usually involves planning and designing the system so that hardware, software and communication technologies all integrate and interact. The systems designer will be involved with the development of the new system until it has been implemented.

The roles and responsibilities of a systems designer may include:

- completing the requirements analysis
- working with programmers and the end users
- planning and designing the system
- confirming the systems analyst's proposal (i.e. the choice of hardware, software and network requirements for the system)
- developing, documenting and revising system design procedures, test procedures and quality standards
- creating an architectural design with the necessary specifications for the hardware, software, data and staff resources.

Programmer

The programmer will create software that is required for the system being developed. A programmer can be a specialist in one area (e.g. a language) of computer programming or be a generalist who writes code for many kinds of software. Most systems, unless very specialised, such as for air traffic control, will be programmed by an applications programmer.

The programmer will be responsible, within the project team, for developing the applications system or modifying an existing software solution that will meet the defined needs of the system.

When the system has been developed, then one of the responsibilities of the programmer is to create the technical documentation.

Tester

The main role of the tester is to find any bugs in a system once it has been created, and to rectify them before the system goes live. All aspects of the system should be tested, including the associated manual procedures. The testers may not have been involved in the development of the system. The tester will often deliberately try to 'break' the system.

The tester's responsibilities include developing and using test plans to test the programs and modules that are included in the system. The tester must ensure that the system is free from bugs by using a variety of tests. These may include white box and black box tests. It is the responsibility of the tester to ensure that a range of test data is used, including normal, extreme and abnormal, to cover all aspects of the system.

The test plans will need to be created to enable a third party to carry out the testing without having to refer to the tester who created the plans. The tester will also need to record the results of the tests, usually on a test log. The test plans and logs may form part of the technical documentation which is passed to the end user when the system has been implemented.

QUESTIONS

1 Describe the role and responsibilities of a systems designer.
2 Describe the role and responsibilities of a programmer.

Describe, interpret and create critical path analysis (CPA) and Gantt charts as tools for project planning

A project manager can use several project planning tools when planning a project. Among these are critical path analysis and Gantt charts.

Critical path analysis

Critical path analysis (CPA) shows the relationship between the different parts of the project. A large project is usually made up of many of interrelated smaller ones. CPA can be defined as 'The process of identifying how the tasks within a project fit together so that all tasks occur in a logical order with minimal delay and resourcing issues'. The analysis is based on the assumption that some tasks will be dependent on others ands have to be completed prior to moving on.

It is important that enough time is allocated to each project task to enable them to be completed before moving to the next dependent task(s). If enough time has not been allocated to a task or if that task is delayed, and no slack time has been built in, then the delivery of the project may be delayed.

CPA lets the project manager identify the critical path through a project (i.e. the order in which the component tasks have to be completed and, usually, the path that takes the maximum time).

CPA assists the project manager to analyse and plan the order in which tasks in a project should take place and to define by when they should be completed. By doing this, resources can be provisionally allocated. The project manager is, essentially, charting the path that must be taken to ensure that the project is successful.

Any task that is dependent on another being completed is called a dependent or sequential activity (task). A task that can happen at any time is called a non-dependent or parallel activity (task).

When developing the CPA the project manager should ensure that tasks are not scheduled before the earliest start date, or, if they are dependent tasks, before the completion of the task(s) on which they are dependent. Most of the software-based project planning tools will have an automatic function that will check this.

Slack time, lead and lag, also needs to be built in so that any unforeseen issues do not lead to slippage of the completion date.

How to create a CPA diagram

1 List all the tasks that need to be completed. For each task, show the earliest start date/the estimated time it will take to complete the task and if the task is dependent or non-dependent.
2 Set up a chart, with the total timescale across the top.
3 Plot the tasks, one per line, on the chart. Start each task at the earliest start and draw a solid horizontal line to show how long the task is expected to last. End each task with a dot labelling the duration line with the name of the task.
4 Link the dependent tasks.

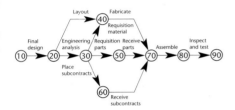

Figure 1.6 Example of a CPA diagram

<< Activity >>

To make a cup of tea:

■ The kettle must be filled with water (1 min).

■ The kettle must be boiled (2 mins) and while this is happening the tea must be put into the teapot (1 min).

■ When the kettle has boiled, the water must be poured into the teapot (2 min).

■ The tea must brew (2 mins) while the cups are got from the cupboard (1 min).

■ The tea is poured from the teapot into the cups (1 min).

Using the tasks shown above develop a CPA diagram for making a cup of tea.

Gantt chart

A Gantt chart is a diagram that shows each task as a block of time. Each block of time is labelled with the title/description of the task and the amount of time the block represents. A Gantt chart assists the project manager in planning as it will show how long each activity/task is expected to take and the order in which these will occur.

A Gantt chart will also model how long the overall project will take and where 'pressure' points can be expected. These points may occur when a number of tasks need to be completed prior to moving to the next part of the project or when all members of the project team are working at maximum levels and all resources are allocated.

A Gantt chart has four main features:

- Milestones: important checkpoints or interim goals for a project.
- Resources: it often helps project teams to have an additional column containing numbers or initials which identify who is responsible for a task.
- Status: the progress of a project can be seen by filling in task bars to a length proportional to the amount of work that has been finished and by 'ticking off' tasks that have been completed.
- Dependencies: an essential concept that some activities are dependent on other activities being completed first.

The critical path is shown on a Gantt chart as the longest sequence of dependent tasks.

Figure 1.7 shows a Gantt chart for building a house. The tasks are shown on the left side of the chart with the timescale shown along the top. Each task is shown as a blue rectangle with the dependent tasks being linked by a black arrow. Tasks that are completed at the same time are shown in the same time slot.

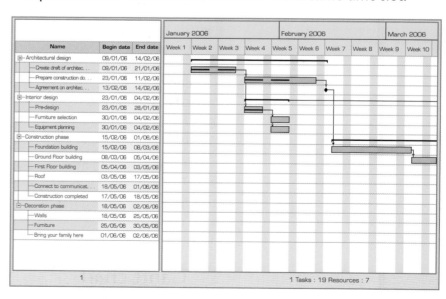

Figure 1.7 Example of a Gantt chart

Coursework chapter 9 covers more about Gantt charts.

< Activity >

Using the process shown in the previous activity, develop a Gantt chart for making a cup of tea.

QUESTIONS

1 Describe Gantt charts as a tool used in project planning.
2 How is the critical path defined?

Describe, interpret and create entity relationship diagrams, state transition diagrams, data flow diagrams and flowcharts, and for each explain its suitability for use in a given application

Data models will need to be completed during a system's life. If all the information collected previously exists, then all the information needed to complete the data modelling will be available.

Various techniques can be used during the design stage, all of which will enable a system to be developed that fully meets the needs of the organisation and the end users.

Among the tools and techniques that can be used are:

- entity-relationship diagrams (ERDs)
- state transition diagrams (STDs)
- data flow diagrams (DFDs)
- flowcharts.

The choice of tools and techniques used will depend on the type of system being developed. However, it is possible to combine more than one tool or technique when fully designing a new system.

Entity relationship diagram

An entity relationship diagram (ERD) is a diagram that represents the structure of data in a software system using entities and the relationships between those entities.

When the analyst is completing the analysis stage they will have sufficient knowledge and understanding of software development to be able to identify the entities, attributes and primary and foreign keys that will need to be used in the proposed system.

An entity is defined as a 'thing' that can be distinctly identified.

Entities are usually real-world things (e.g. books, students, products) that need to be represented in the software system.

An example of one entity in a system might be Products. This could be because information is held about products stocked by a company in the current system. This would be represented by:

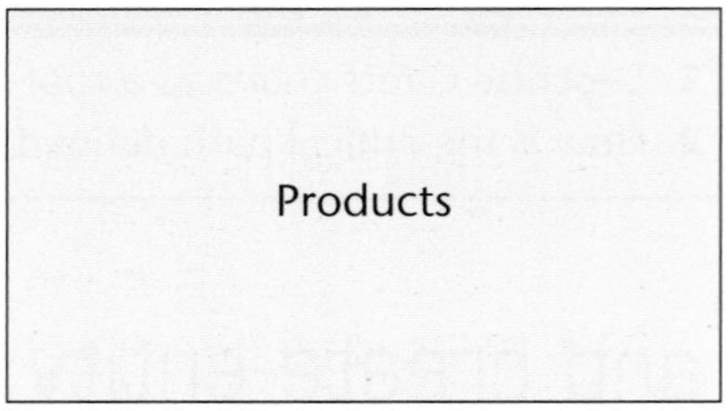

Products

Figure 1.8 Representation of an entity

Each entity has attributes. Attributes make up the information that is held on a system about the entity. The information held about the product could be:

Entity	Product
Attributes	Product Number
	Category
	Description
	Price
	Supplier

The entities and attributes are given in a specific format. There are many different formats that can be used. It is important that once a format has been selected it is used consistently throughout the ERD development. The following format is used in this chapter:

PRODUCT(Product Number, Category, Description, Price, Supplier)

The entity name is shown in capital letters with the attributes contained within brackets. However, when the ERD is developed the entity name is shown with an initial capital letter only (e.g. Product).

Each set of attributes for an entity should have a unique field that identifies each occurrence of an entity. This unique field is called the Primary key.

In the example of PRODUCT, the primary key would be Product_Number as no two products will have the same product number. It is the primary key that provides the links between the entities.

The entities are linked through relationships. Each relationship is given a degree. The degrees of relationships that may be used are:

- One-to-one (1:1) – shows that only one occurrence of each entity is used by the linked entity. For example one vet would use one treatment room, this is represented as:

Figure 1.9 Example one-to-one relationship

- Many-to-one (M:1) and one-to-many (1:M) – show that a single occurrence of one entity is linked to more than one occurrence of the linked entity. For example, one vet would have many appointments. This would be represented as:

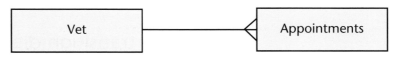

Figure 1.10 Example one-to-many relationship

- Many-to-many (M:M) – shows that many occurrences of one entity are linked to more than one occurrence of the linked entity. Although many-to-many occurrences are common in the real world, a linked entity must be used to break down or decompose the many-to-many relationship. For example, many vets will see many animals. This is represented as:

Figure 1.11 Example many-to-many relationship

This relationship can be decomposed to form two one-to-many relationships by using a link entity. This is represented as:

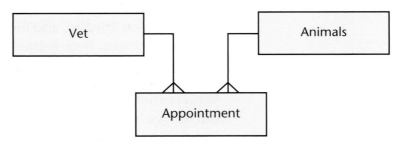

Figure 1.12 Example of using a link entity

A foreign key is used to link the tables together. A primary key is used to link one table to a field in another table. The data types must be the same. For example, the foreign key Product_Number is an attribute in the entity DELIVERY, but is the primary key in the entity PRODUCT.

Development of the ERD can start once the entities, attributes and primary and foreign keys have been identified.

In some cases the analyst must be aware that, at a later date, the system may be extended to incorporate different needs and requirements of the organisation.

Describe, interpret and create ERDs, STDs, DFDs and flowcharts, and for each explain its suitability for use in a given application

< Activity >

A small guesthouse registers its guests on a database. Three of the entities used in the database are CUSTOMER, ROOM and BOOKING.

Draw an entity relationship diagram to represent this part of the database.

QUESTIONS

1 Name the **three** types of relationships that are used in ERDs.
2 How is a many-to-many relationship decomposed?
3 Why might Staff Name not be used as a Primary key of a STAFF entity?

State transition diagram

State transition diagrams (STDs) define every state of a system diagrammatically. Some systems or objects can be in different states. A kettle may be full or empty, on or off, cold or hot, and the state will change under the influence of outside circumstances, or simply the passing of time.

A state transition diagram shows each state as a location, and the transitions between them as arrows. Each arrow is labelled with the reason for the state transition. The state of the system can be followed as different stimuli arrive because the same stimulus may have different effects according to the state the system is in at the time it arrives. One or more actions (outputs) may be associated with each transition.

State transition diagrams are ideal for describing the behaviour of a single object. They are also formal, so tools can be built which can execute them. Their biggest limitation is that they are not good at describing behaviour that involves several objects. For example, Figure 1.13 represents a machine in a bottling plant filling bottles. The bottle begins in an empty state. In that state it can receive 'squirt of liquid' events.

If the squirt event causes the bottle to become full, then it transitions to the full state, otherwise it stays in the empty state (indicated by the transition back to its own state). When in the full state the cap event will cause it to transition to the sealed state. The diagram indicates that a full bottle does not receive squirt events, and that an empty bottle does not receive cap events.

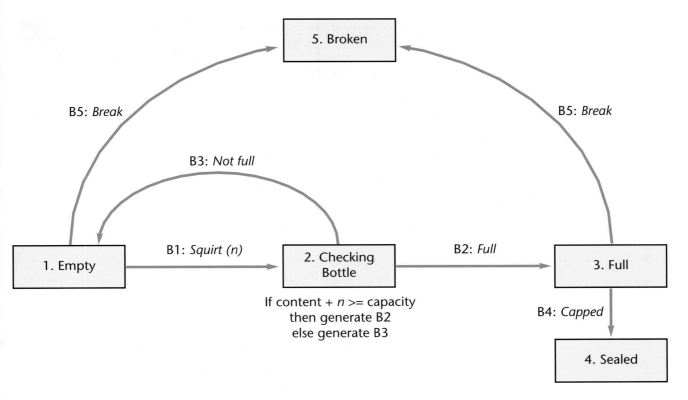

Figure 1.13 States of filling a bottle

Data flow diagram

Data flow diagrams (DFDs) show how data moves through a system. They focus on the processes that transform incoming data flows (inputs) into outgoing data flows (outputs). The processes that perform this transformation create and use data that is held in data stores.

A DFD will also show what and who the system interacts with in the form of external entities. Examples of external entities include people and other systems.

There are many different sets of symbols that can be used when constructing DFDs. It does not matter which set of symbols is used, but it is important that once the set of symbols has been selected that they are used consistently and are not changed part way through the analysis stage. One set of symbols that could be used are shown below in Figure 1.14.

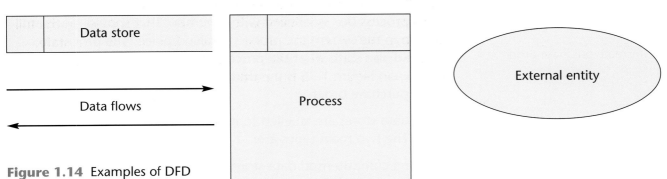

Figure 1.14 Examples of DFD symbols

33

- External entities are used to represent people, organisations or other systems that have a role in the system under development but are not necessarily part of it. They either put data into the system or receive data from it.
- A process represents an activity that takes place within, and is linked to, the system. All activities within a system have a process attached to them. A process models what happens to the data. It transforms incoming data flows into outgoing data flows. Usually a process will have one or more data inputs and produce one or more data outputs.
- A data store shows where data is stored. Examples of data stores include a database file, a paper form or a folder in a filing cabinet. A data store should be given a meaningful descriptive name (e.g. a customer file).
- Data flows indicate the direction or flow of data within the system. Data flows provide a link to other symbols within the DFD. Each flow should be given a simple meaningful descriptive name.

A DFD does not show the hardware or software required to operate the system. The analyst will use the DFD to show the:

- the external entities that the system interacts with
- the processes that happen
- the data stores that are used
- flow of the data and information.

There are certain rules about which DFD symbols can be linked. These are shown in the next table.

Data flow links	Data store	External entity	Process
Data store	✘	✘	✔
External entity	✘	✘	✔
Process	✔	✔	✔

The table shows that it is not possible to link an external entity with another external entity or a data store with an external entity.

Three of the symbols used in a DFD must also be labelled further.

The process box is labelled with a number that should represent when in the system the process is taking place. The process box should also state what the process is. For example, the process shown in Figure 1.15 is the third process and shows the creation of a purchase order.

The data stores are labelled to indicate the type of data store they are. The two main types are:

- D: a computerised data store (e.g. files on a database).
- M: a manual data store (e.g. a filing cabinet or paper form).

Figure 1.15 The DFD process symbol

Figure 1.16 The DFD data store symbol

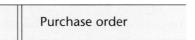

A data store can be used more than once in a system. This is called a repeating data store. If a data store is repeated, then the same numbering and description are used, but a second vertical line is inserted as shown in Figure 1.17.

Figure 1.17 The DFD repeating data store symbol

The external entities are labelled with the name of the person, organisation or system they represent. The external entity shown in Figure 1.18 shows the Customer as an external entity.

Figure 1.18 The DFD external entity symbol

It is possible to have repeating external entities. As with the data stores, the original name is kept and a line is used to show that it is repeated.

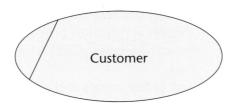

Figure 1.19 The DFD repeating external entity symbol

DFD levels

There are many different levels of DFD. The Level 0 (L0) or context diagram gives a summary of the system. It shows the main external entities and the information that flows in to and out of the system.

A Level 0 DFD does not show the processes that occur or the data stores that are used within the system – it simply provides an overview of the system under investigation.

Some systems will have more than one external entity, and the process of constructing the Level 0 DFD will be the same despite the number of external entities and flows involved.

The main aim of the L0 DFD construction is to identify the flows of data that occur between the system and the external entity(s). The flow of data has a source (where the data comes from) and a recipient (where the data goes to). It is convention that the initial flows in the system are shown as the top flows in the L0 DFD, while the flows that happen last are at the bottom.

Describe, interpret and create ERDs, STDs, DFDs and flowcharts, and for each explain its suitability for use in a given application

A Level 1 (L1) DFD provides an overview of what is happening within the system. The system is represented in the L0 DFD by the central process box. The overview includes types of data being passed within the system, documents and stores of data used (data stores), the activities (processes) and the people or organisations that the system interacts with (external entities).

This information may be put into a data flow table which will give the analyst a clearer understanding of the flows of information. It may also be easier for the client to check that all the flows are present. This table can also be used to construct the L0 DFD.

Ten-step plan for constructing a L1 DFD.

There is a wide range of methods that can be used to construct a L1 DFD. One method is given here.

1 Read through the information collected during the investigation and analysis stages.
2 Sort the information into clear sections identifying the people or organisations external to the system under investigation but who interact with it, the documents used in the system under investigation, the activities that take place within the system under investigation.
3 Produce a data flow table.
4 Convert external users to external entities.
5 Convert documentation to data stores.
6 Convert activities to processes identifying when in the system the activity takes place, who is involved, and any data stores used.
7 Look at the inputs and outputs for each process with the data stores that are used and use data flows to 'link' these.
8 Link each data store and external entity with the associated process.
9 Link the processes (remembering the rules about labelling processes).
10 Check for consistency (e.g. check the initial findings to ensure all documentation has been included, check the flows between external entities given on the context diagram are included, check with the end users of the current system to ensure nothing has been forgotten).

The analyst should perform some final checks before the DFD is shown to the organisation. These are detailed in the list below.

■ Does each process receive all the data it needs?
■ Does any data store have only data flows out and not in?
■ Does any data store appear to hold data that is never used?
■ Are all data flows consistent across the L0 and the L1 DFD?
■ Are all external entities shown on the L1 DFD also shown in the L0 diagram? Are all flows labelled? Are they documented in the data dictionary?

- Are there any data flows between two external entities, external entities to data stores and two data stores?
- Do any data flows cross other data flows on the diagram? If they do, use repeating external entities or data stores.

Flowcharts

Flowcharts are a diagrammatical representation of the operations/processes involved in a system. They are good at showing a general outline of the processing that is involved in the system under investigation but, generally, they do not relate very well to the actual software system which is eventually developed. Different shaped symbols are used to represent different actions.

There are many different sets of symbols that can be used. As with DFDs and ERDs it is important that once a set of symbols has been selected it is used consistently throughout the flowchart. One set of symbols is shown in Figure 1.20.

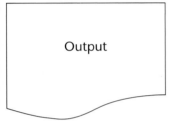

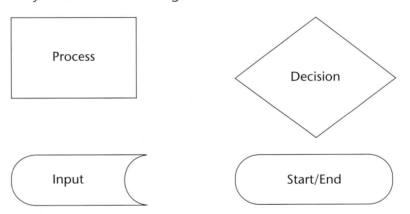

Figure 1.20 Some flowchart symbols

Flowcharts can be used to model all kinds of systems, not just computer systems. They can be used to break a process into small steps or to give an overview of a complete system.

People who are not involved in the IT industry can easily understand them. However, flowcharts do not translate easily into code and they can sometimes become so complex they can be hard to follow.

For these reasons flowcharts are used by the analyst to give a generalised overview of a system or the functions which make up a specific process.

There are some rules that must be followed when developing a flowchart:

- Every flowchart must begin with 'Start' and finish with 'End'.
- A decision must have two flows coming from it: 'Yes' and 'No'.

Before a flowchart is developed, it is important that the analyst gains a clear understanding of a system by clearly defining any input, output, decisions and processes that occur. Once this information has been clearly defined then the flowchart can be developed.

< Example >

A van hire company needs to take decisions about whether a van needs to be serviced, valeted or repaired after each hire period before it is hired out again. The information needed is taken from the van history log.

- A van needs to be serviced if it is more than six months or the mileage is more than 8,000 since the last service.
- A van needs to be valeted if it has been hired out five times since the last valeting.
- A van needs to be repaired if there are any dents or scratches on it.

The process of taking a decision of what action is required (if any) has to be identified by asking the following questions:

- Is it six or more months since the van was last serviced?
- Has the van done 8,000 or more miles since the last service?
- Has the van been hired out five times since the last valeting?
- Are there any scratches or dents on the van?

Based on the answers to these questions, a decision on a range of actions can be taken. It is possible that the answer to one or more of the questions is 'yes' and, therefore a number of actions may need to be completed on one van.

The actions that may be taken are:

- Service the van.
- Valet the van.
- Repair any dents or scratches.
- Do nothing.

The information needed to make the decisions and take the appropriate actions is found in the van history log.

< Activity >

Using the example, draw a flowchart to represent the process that occurs when deciding on what actions need to be taken with a van on its return to the company.

Summary

Stages of the system life cycle
Definition of the problem
Investigation and analysis
Design
Implementation
Testing
Documentation
Evaluation and maintenance

Different approaches to investigating a system
Questionnaires
Interviews
Meetings
Document analysis
Observation

Software development methodologies
Prototyping
Rapid approach development (RAD)

Testing
Purpose of test data
The importance of testing and test plans

Requirements specification

Design specification

System specification

Roles and responsibilities
Project manager
Systems analyst
Systems designer
Programmer
Tester

Project planning tools
Critical path analysis (CPA)
Gantt chart

Modelling tools
State transition diagram (STD)
Entity relationship diagram (ERD)
Data flow diagram (DFD)
Flowcharts

Test 1

1 Draw the ERD of the following entities:
DELIVERY, CUSTOMER, PRODUCT, STAFF, DELIVERY ROUND

You can use the following assumptions:
- One member of the delivery staff may do one or more delivery rounds.
- One customer may have one or more products delivered.
- One product category may have one or more products contained within it. [10]

2 Describe the investigation and analysis stage of the systems life cycle. [6]

3 Explain the importance of a test plan. [4]

Test 2

1 Describe the role and responsibility of the systems analyst. [6]

2 Discuss the use of questionnaires as an investigation method. [6]

3 Describe data flow diagrams (DFDs) and explain how they can be used in the systems life cycle. [8]

Designing computer-based information systems

Introduction

This chapter covers the different computer-based processing and operating systems that are available. The understanding of the different types of processing and operating systems that are available will assist you to understand the principles of design. You should also be able to apply your knowledge to a specified scenario.

You will learn about:

- **processing systems**
- **designing the user interface**

Discuss batch, interactive and real-time processing systems in terms of processing, response time and user interface requirements

Processing systems process data. There are many different types of processing systems but the most commonly used are batch, interactive and real-time. These are known as modes of operation (operational modes).

The decisions about which mode(s) should be used in a system are taken during the design phase of the life cycle. The operating system will then manage the functioning of the operational mode that is being used.

Batch

Batch processing systems process batches of data at regular intervals. The amount of data that is processed by a batch system is usually large with the data being of identical type. Batch processing could be used to produce utility bills, bank statements or payroll data.

The data in a batch system is collected together into batches, sent for processing, stored and processed at an appropriate time. No user interaction is needed in a batch processing system. The time when batch processing is carried out tends to be when there is less demand on the processor, such as at a weekend or at night.

This means that there is less disruption to daily work so peripherals remain accessible.

A major disadvantage of batch processing is the delay, hours or days, between collecting the data and receiving the output. The user interface requirements of a batch processing system tend to be code-based.

Payroll processing is one of the most common uses of a batch processing system. Each pay date, weekly or monthly, the payroll details for each employee are collected. The details that are collected could include hours worked, monthly salary, overtime completed and sick days to be deducted from payment. These details are then processed with reference to a master file which holds the details of employees' hourly pay rates, tax and national insurance details, and other regular deductions to be made such as pension contributions. The output from the system is the payslips for all employees.

Interactive

An interactive processing system is also known as a transactional processing system. This type of system handles transactions one at a time. Each transaction must be fully processed, the response given to the user and any associated files updated before the next transaction is processed.

The amount of data input for each transaction is generally small and is usually entered, interactively, by the user using a form on a screen. The input method is usually by means of a keyboard.

The user inputs responses to pre-defined questions on an input form which is displayed on a GUI. A database is then searched based on the responses. The results of the search are shown on the screen. The questions and responses are in a very structured, fixed format. The user effectively has a dialogue with the system, but without being able to deviate from responding to the questions asked on the input form or from the preferred options presented.

A typical use of an interactive or transactional processing system is for booking tickets. This type of system could be used to book any type of ticket without the risk of double-booking because each transaction is dealt with in turn.

For example, consider a customer who wants to buy a flight ticket. The details of the departure and destination airport along with the preferred dates of travel are input. When these details are submitted, the system checks the database for the seat availability. The flights that are available, based on the requirements given on the form, are shown on the screen. The flight is selected and a confirm action takes place. At this point the seat is confirmed as being booked – this means that no other customer can book the seat on the flight.

Real-time

A real-time processing system processes data at the time the data is input. The data must be handled within a specified maximum time limit. The time limit will depend on the user requirements and the processing the system has to carrying out.

It is usually accepted that the data will be processed as soon as it is received, thereby affecting the database records immediately.

This means that as soon as the user enters some data and the appropriate action is taken to confirm the data, then the processing will take place. The time taken to provide a response to the user must also be very quick. The response time of a real-time system is critical, but, depending on the user requirements, it should be less than four seconds.

A real-time system is generally accepted as being one that reacts fast enough to influence behaviour in the outside world. An example of a real-time system is an air-traffic control system. Real-time systems can also be found in embedded applications (systems within another system) such as mobile phones.

Summary

	Batch	Interactive	Real-time
Processing	Processed when the system is not busy and off-line.	Each transaction is completed before moving onto the next.	Data is processed as soon as it is received by the processor.
Response time	Delayed: there is a delay between the data being input and the results. This can be overnight or days.	Dependent on action from end-user.	Very quick, based on user requirements, but usually less than four seconds.
User interface requirements	Usually code-based.	Graphical User Interface (GUI)	Usually based on the user's requirements.

QUESTION

Describe a real-time processing system.

Describe the difference between types of operating systems (single-user, multi-user, multi-tasking, interactive, real time, batch processing and distributed processing systems) by identifying their major characteristics

An operating system (OS) is a program (or suite of programs) that controls the entire operation of the computer system. The operating system will also manage the functioning of the operational mode(s) being used.

An operating system is software that is responsible for allocating various system resources, such as memory, processor time and peripheral devices (e.g printers and monitor). All application programs will use the operating system to gain access to the system resources.

There are many different types of operating systems, including:

■ single-user
■ multi-user
■ multi-tasking
■ interactive
■ real-time
■ batch processing
■ distributed processing.

Single-user

A single-user OS provides access for one user at a time to use the computer. The OS can support more than one user account but only one account can be used at any one time. This means that if someone else is using the computer, then they must log off their account before someone else can use it.

When a single-user OS is used the processor is dedicated to the user, so multi-tasking can be performed.

Multi-user

A multi-user OS lets more than one user access the system at the same time. The access to a multi-user OS is usually provided by a network. A common setup is a network with a single-user OS connected by the network to a server that has a multi-user OS.

The multi-user system manages and runs all the user requests ensuring that they do not interfere with each other. Peripherals that can only be used by one user at a time, such as printers, must be shared among all users requesting them.

Multi-tasking

A multi-tasking OS involves the processor carrying out more than one task at a time, for example an author might use a word processor while using the internet. Most multi-tasking operating systems are not controlling two things at once; to do this would require multiple processors. The processor is completing part of one task, then changing to do part of another task, and then returning to the first task. This process continues until the two tasks are completed.

This process is completed so fast that it appears to the user that the computer is doing both tasks at the same time (concurrently). The latest processors can run multi-tasks, or threads, at the same time providing that the OS can manage the activities.

Interactive

An interactive OS is one in which there is direct user interaction while a program is running.

Real-time

A real-time OS is one that has been developed for real-time applications. Real-time operating systems are typically used for embedded applications, that is, for systems within another application. An example of this is the engine management system of a car.

Batch processing

A batch OS is given a set of tasks to run without any user intervention: the programs are collected, stored and run at an appropriate time which might be at night or at the weekend when there is less demand on the processor. Another time when a batch OS may complete the jobs is just before the results are required, for example, payroll calculations just before the end of the month.

Distributed processing

A distributed processing system comprises a number of computers connected together. Each computer completes part of the processing. When all the processing has been completed the results are combined to meet the requirements of the user.

QUESTIONS
1 What is the difference between a single-user and a multi-user OS?
2 How does a batch processing system differ from an interactive OS?

Discuss the use of colour, layout, quantity of information on screen, size of font, complexity of language and type of controls when designing a human–computer interface

A designer must consider the needs of the user at all times when a human–computer interface (HCI) is being designed.

A designer must consider:

■ use of colour
■ layout
■ quantity of the information on the screen
■ font size
■ complexity of language
■ type of controls.

Colour

During the design process a designer should always consider the current colours used. This will include consideration of the existing corporate style of the business. The colours used on the HCI should, as far as possible, follow the corporate colours. However, the suitability of these colours within the HCI should also be taken into account.

The colours selected for use in the HCI should not clash (e.g. bright pink and orange), and they should be easily read by the user. Care should be taken to ensure that a user with a sight impediment, such as colour blindness, can also use the HCI.

Colour can also be used to trigger a user's memory. For example, areas where mandatory information should be input could be in a different colour to optional information.

The number of colours used should be limited to four per screen and seven for the whole sequence of screens.

Colours can be used to code information (e.g. overdue accounts in red, non-overdue accounts in green). If this strategy is used, then the designer must make sure the user understands the code and that the colours used match the user's expectations (e.g. to a mapmaker blue means water, but to a scientist blue means cold).

Certain colours can be used to draw the user's attention. The most effective colours for this are white, yellow and red.

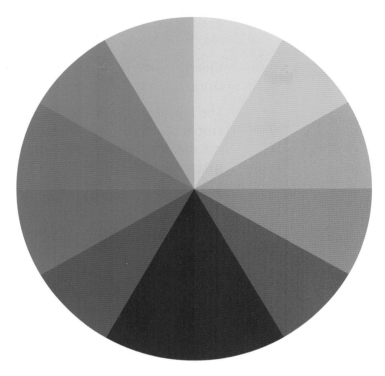

Figure 2.1 A colour wheel

If displayed information needs to be separated, then colours from different parts of the spectrum (red/green, blue/yellow, any colour/white) should be used. If similar information is shown, then colours which are close neighbours in the spectrum (orange/yellow, blue/violet) should be used.

It is important to remember that around 9% of the population is colour-blind, with red/green blindness being most common. Colour blind people can discriminate colours using black and white shades, but designers should check that the use of colour is not going to affect the performance of those users.

< Activity >

Investigate the colours that should be used if a user has:

■ colour blindness

■ dyslexia.

Layout

A designer must ensure that a consistent layout is used on all the screens of the HCI. The layout should follow the house style or corporate image of the business. The layout should follow, as far as possible, the layout of the original source documents used.

The layout of the information on the HCI should flow in a logical order. This should be applied to the information given to a user as well as to the information that has to be input by the user.

In addition, any buttons that are used (e.g. Back or Next) should also be in the same place on each screen of the HCI.

Clearly marked exits should be included in simple and helpful language and they should be in a consistent place on all screens.

The layout should include some white space. This is the amount of empty space (no text or images) on the HCI. Too little white space will mean that the HCI is difficult to read and use, too much white space will make the HCI look bare.

The layout of the HCI should, as far as possible, be consistent with the other applications that are used by the user. Labels and buttons should correspond with the user's idea of what will happen and their previous experience.

Information that needs attending to immediately should always be displayed in a prominent place to catch the user's eye (e.g. warning messages and alarms).

Information that is not needed very often (e.g. help facilities) should not be displayed, but should be available when requested. For example, a Help icon or menu option should appear on every screen.

Less urgent information should be placed in less prominent positions on the screen in a specific area where the user will know to look when this information is required.

Again, the consistency of the layout will enable users to become familiar with the layout quickly, so increasing confidence and learning.

Quantity of the information on the screen

The quantity of the information on the screen of the HCI is linked to the amount of white space that is used.

The amount of information available on the screens of the HCI should enable users to effectively use the screen and to complete their tasks. However, a designer must be aware that too much information on the screen can slow the user down because they have to read more information.

Too much information on the HCI can confuse a user when trying to locate the required information. If this happens then the user can begin to lose confidence, the rate of learning will decrease and so the rate at which tasks are completed will diminish.

Font size and style

The text used on the HCI must be in a font style that is clear and in a font size that is easy to read.

Font styles such as Verdana, Arial and Times New Roman are clearly legible. Other fonts are very difficult to read (e.g Brush Script MT or Edwardian Script IT).

The size of the font used on the HCI is also important and needs to be appropriate to the HCI, to the text in question and to the users. It would be very difficult to use the HCI if the entire font were size 8.

The font style and size of instructions must be clear and consistently used on the HCI and associated screens. Any error messages should also use the same font size and style.

< Activity >

Investigate other font styles and sizes that are available on the word-processing software available at your centre.

Ask a sample of 10 or more people to rank the font styles and sizes in order of usability for an HCI.

Complexity of language

The complexity of the language should be kept as low as possible. Any error messages and instructions used should be given in simple language.

If a user is faced with the error message 'Runtime error at line 89670', then they will probably not know what it means and so they will not know what they should do to rectify the error.

The language used should be helpful and simple, but should not be perceived as condescending by the user. The designer should also be aware of the readability of the language used. Technical language should be kept to a minimum, but should be fit for purpose.

< Activity >

Investigate the different readability tests that are available.

Type of controls

Controls can be included in the design of the HCI to ensure ease of use.

There are many different types of control that can be used. The designer should select the controls to be included in the HCI to ensure that the user can complete their tasks with ease.

Among the controls that could be used are buttons, forms and menus.

Discuss the use of colour, layout, quantity of information on screen, size of font, complexity of language and type of controls when designing a human-computer interface

Buttons

Buttons can be used to take the user to a specified page or to run a selected action/command. A macro can be run by the user clicking a button. For example a command button can be added to a database user interface to run a search, or to sort or edit data. A button can also display pictures or text.

In HCI terms, a macro is a set of stored commands that can be replayed by pressing a combination of keys or by clicking a button. A macro enables the user to automate tasks that are performed on a regular basis. This is done by recording a series of commands to be run whenever that task needs to be performed. The complexity of the macro is only limited by the task requirements and the ability of the user.

Once the macro has been recorded, then it can be run by pressing the keys assigned when it was recorded. A macro can also be activated by clicking an assigned button placed on the GUI. A macro will only run when the application program to which it is associated is being used. A macro will not run on its own or with a different application program.

Among the advantages of using a macro are:

- a repetitive task can be performed by using a simple action (e.g. pressing a key, clicking a button)
- errors may be reduced because the instructions included in the macro are run automatically and are the same every time
- inexperienced users can perform complex tasks by using a pre-recorded macro.

Among the disadvantages of using a macro are:

- error messages may occur if the conditions when the macro is run are different from those when it was recorded
- users must know and remember the key combination to run the macro (if one is required)
- a macro is pre-programmed so it may not do what the user wants
- if the macro is run from a different starting point than intended, then it may execute incorrectly
- a user can correct errors only if they have some knowledge of how the macro was recorded.

Forms

Forms can be used to assist data entry. A form can give the user help and guidance on what data should be input. Instructions to the user and error messages can be included on forms. It is also possible to include some validation when forms are being used in a system interface. A form may include drop-down boxes for data selection, option boxes and fill-in boxes, which can automatically help a user. Form controls can be used to increase the interactivity with the user and improve usability.

An common example of the use of an automatic fill-in box is when a postcode is entered and the street name and town automatically appear. The user has only to type in the house number.

Menus

Menus enable a user to select actions. There are several types of menu that can be used, including full-screen, pop-up and drop-down. Each type of menu gives the user available choices of actions.

> **< Activity >**
>
> Investigate different form controls that are available and describe how they could be used on a HCI.

In addition to the considerations mentioned above a designer must ensure that the HCI is easy to learn and use. This will minimise the training required and the number of instructions that will need to be learned and remembered by the user.

> **QUESTION**
>
> Explain how font size should be considered when designing an HCI.

Discuss different methods of dialogue that allow interaction between computer and person, person and computer and computer and computer

There are four main features of interaction between a computer and a person:

- prompts
- nature of input
- methods of input
- feedback.

The type of dialogue used will depend on the type of interface (e.g. a command line or a form) that is being used.

The designer is responsible for selecting the most appropriate method of dialogue to be used. The choice will depend on the investigations that have been completed, the tasks that the users need to complete and the requirements of the business.

Prompts

A prompt is most commonly used in a command line interface. It indicates that the user needs to input an appropriate command. When the command has been input the command line interface will then complete the required action. This type of dialogue can be difficult for 'every day' users to learn and so is best used for technical administration of a system.

Prompts can also be used in a graphical user interface (GUI). Unlike the command line interface, a GUI uses icons to prompt the user. The icons should be intuitive and simple to use and represent a concept that is familiar to a user, such as a dustbin image for deleting or an X to close a window.

A menu-driven interface will, by nature of its characteristics, use menus to offer the user a selection of possible inputs to choose from.

QUESTION

Describe how prompts could be used in a command line interface.

Nature of input

The nature of the input can also differ between interfaces. Interactive interfaces decide the nature of the next user input (e.g. by asking a question or by requiring a selection to be made) based on the response to the previous input. Forms might be used as the basis for the dialogue with those being displayed being decided by a pre-determined sequence of user inputs.

Method of input

If the dialogue is being completed using a command line interface, then the usual method of input is a keyboard. The user will have no need for other peripherals. Form-based interfaces can also be used with only a keyboard, however it is often simpler to also use a mouse. Touch screens have become a popular method of input (e.g. on cash machines).

< Activity >

Investigate other applications where the method of input is a touch screen.

Feedback

Any dialogue must provide feedback. This could be in the form of menus that provide options for the user to select. A menu option may be a sub-menu giving further options, for example a designer might provide a general menu with sub-menus that provide specific areas or tasks that need to be carried out.

The feedback given in a real-time or interactive interface is a further set of required responses or the completion of the task providing the user with the required results. This type of feedback will give the user very specific and limited choices because the responses given to each set of questions or choices will limit the response given.

Discuss the concept and implication of good methods of human–device communications, particularly human–computer interfaces (HCI) using command line interfaces, menus/submenus, graphical user interfaces (GUIs) natural language (including speech input–output) and forms dialogue

Figure 2.2 The BlackBerry phone

Many devices use an embedded human–computer interface (HCI) to enable the user to complete tasks, for example mobile phones, satellite navigation systems and washing machines.

A group of devices will have a common purpose, for example the main purpose of a mobile phone is to make phone calls. Some mobile phones enable users to complete other tasks in addition to the primary purpose of making phone calls and so they will have different HCIs (e.g. compare a BlackBerry and an iPhone) to communicate with the user. The mobile phones have embedded systems that enable the user to perform selected tasks.

A BlackBerry phone lets the user select the task they need to complete using menus and sub-menus. These are not customisable by the user. The menus that are given are those that are embedded in the HCI.

In addition to making phone calls, a BlackBerry lets the user email, use the organiser, browse the internet and access instant messaging. All these options are available by selecting appropriate menus and sub-menus.

Figure 2.3 The Apple iPhone

Figure 2.4 The TomTom GO 530

An Apple iPhone uses a GUI as the main means of HCI. Users can customise the GUI. They can rearrange the icons they see and also add or delete their own icons to the GUI. The iPhone does use some menus. If a menu is being used, then the back button (to move up the menu structure) is always displayed at the top left of the screen.

Some satellite navigation (satnav) devices use a natural-language HCI which lets a user input the address or postcode that they need to travel to by speaking them.

The satnav uses speech, as an output, to direct the driver to their destination.

If the required destination is input through the use of a form, then the satnav will offer the user destinations based on each element of the postcode input. The user is able, based on a part input, to select the destination they need.

As technology advances, more devices will begin to use different HCI methods. The designers of these devices must ensure that the HCI is appropriate to the tasks that the users need to complete and that the advances in technology do not render the devices incapable of delivering their primary function.

QUESTION

Explain how a natural language input could assist users of a satnav system.

Explain how a potential user's perception, attention, memory and learning can be taken into account when designing an interface

When a user interface is being designed a designer will have to consider many issues that are related to the potential user. Among these are the user's perception, attention, memory and learning. The use of the interface must be made as intuitive as possible. This means that a designer will have to draw on their knowledge of the user's perception, attention and memory. Designers should ensure that a new interface matches, as far as possible, the current system being used.

Perception

A user will perceive input from the sights and sounds taken from the user interface. Most users will have preconceived ideas that they will draw on when using the interface. For example, most users when faced with a graphic or text in red will have the perceived idea that this will mean 'stop'. Conversely text or graphics in green will, based on the perception of the user, indicate 'go'.

These common perceptions should be considered by the designer. If a user feels comfortable with the interface then, theoretically, their confidence with the interface will increase.

In addition to a user's perception of the colours used in the user interface, the use of sounds is also important. Users can perceive sounds as being happy or sad. This could relate to a sound that indicates a positive response (happy) or a negative response (sad).

< Activity >

Investigate sounds that might be perceived as being happy or sad.

If a user hears a sad (negative) sound, then their perception will be that they have done something incorrectly or even that they cannot correctly use the system. Conversely, when a user hears a happy (positive) sound, then their perception will be that they have done something right and that they are using the system correctly.

Attention

The designer needs to consider the attention span of a user. Most users have a limited attention span, which is also linked to the amount of time they can look at a screen. One way that a designer can maximise the use of a user's limited attention span is to make the screens uncluttered with the layout in a logical order. (See also the section on Memory below.)

The most important information on the screen needs to be obvious with the screens clearly labelled. Any area where data/information has to be inserted by the user also needs to be clearly labelled. The use of pop-up messages could also help keep a user's attention.

A designer could also use flashing graphics, sounds or pop-up messages to draw a user's attention to an action on the screen. These features should, however, be used sparingly as too many features can detract from the use of the screen. A user's attention span can become shorter if there are many features on a screen. Similarly, if the screen is permanently filled with, for example, flashing graphics, a user could become confused and feel uncomfortable with the screen.

Most screens will include some menus and sub-menus to help the user complete tasks. These menus should remain, as far as possible, consistent. The menus should be in the same place on the screen, and the words used should mean the same on each screen. In addition, if sub-menus are used, then these should relate to the same words on each screen and again be consistent. If graphics are used to denote a task, for example a pair of scissors to denote the action 'cut', then the graphic for this action must always be the same.

The screens will also need to have a consistent layout (i.e. buttons or groups of buttons should be in the same place on all screens). If the user has to search for information on each screen, then the attention span will decrease.

Screens should also be designed with a consistent colour scheme (which might link to the corporate style of the organisation for which the interface is being designed).

Figure 2.5 shows how a company can ensure that screens are laid out consistently with good use of the corporate style. The figure also shows how the menus and sub-menus are consistent on all screens.

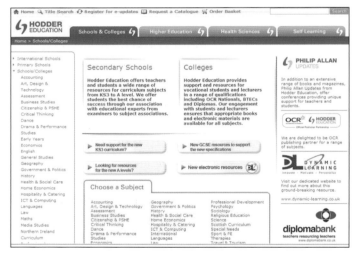

Figure 2.5 Screen consistency

Memory

Users will often use the same screen on a day-to-day basis, and as they do so they will memorise the actions required to use the interface. However, there will always be parts of a user interface that will be used infrequently and for which memory cannot be relied on. A designer must ensure that these screens are also easily used.

A designer must try to ensure that the actions required to use the interface are held in a user's short-term memory. This can be achieved through the use of a consistent and uncluttered page layout.

As far as possible a designer should consider the pre-existing knowledge of the user. It may be that user is already familiar with the interface and is simply using screens that they do not often use. If this is the case, then a designer must ensure that the user's existing knowledge will enable them to use the less familiar screens.

As the user moves through the interface from page to page they will be making use of their short-term memory. If the designer has considered, and used, consistency between screens, then this will help the recall of the skills and knowledge required to effectively use the interface. This in turn, will increase the speed at which the user learns to use the interface.

Learning

All users need to learn to use an interface. One of the considerations that a designer must take into account is how easy the interface is to learn. As far as possible the interface must draw on the previous experience of the user. Again, this is achieved by using consistent, but not distracting, screen layouts, colour and menus.

On-screen help, in the form of pop-up messages or an easy-to-use help feature, will help a user learn about the interface more quickly. These messages will need to be helpful and assist a user to easily correct their errors or to learn how to complete an unfamiliar task.

Figure 2.6 shows a helpful error message and an unhelpful one. The helpful message will help a user to correct the error they have made, so increasing the speed with which they learn to use the interface. If a user was given the unhelpful message, it would not help them continue with their task (although it might help the programmer who created the system).

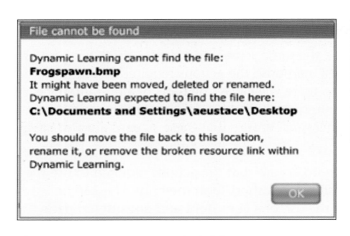

Figure 2.6 Error messages: helpful (left) and unhelpful (right)

Describe mental models and how they can be applied to the design of a user interface

Users of computer systems can be divided into two groups. Those who have some understanding of the operation of a computer and those who have little or no understanding.

Users in the first group are generally able to carry out and complete tasks more quickly and more effectively than those in the second group.

Users who have little understanding of the operation of a computer will generally read and follow a set of instructions with no clear comprehension of how the tasks are being processed by the computer. This may lead to an uncertainty, and possibly some panic, about how to deal with any messages that appear on the screen and which are not defined in the instructions being followed by the user.

When a 'new' user saves a file, it is often the case that they will be unable to locate the file again at a later date. This is because the user has a limited understanding of how the filing system of a computer works.

If a user has a mental model of the computer and has some knowledge of how it works, then they should be able to use the computer more effectively. The mental model a user has when working with a computer is based on the way people process tasks. The processing that is carried out will be based on various types of input. These inputs will be based on, for example, sound and visuals as well as experience.

The mental model of the user will not only cover such operational functions as the use of RAM, menus, sub-menus and file management, but should also cover the generic features of the software package being used. For example, if a user is creating a word-processed document, then the generic concepts of automatic word-wrapping at the end of a line of text and text formatting, will enable the user to produce an effective and appropriate document.

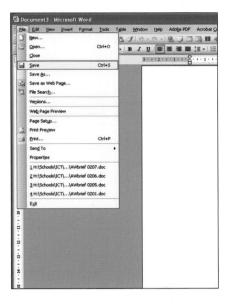 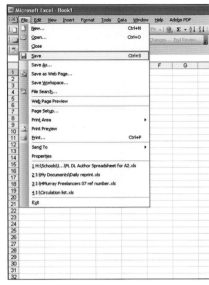

Figure 2.7 Menus

A user's mental model should let them envisage the results of an action. They will then use this experience again in the future to predict the actions that may be needed in another situation. This means that the mental model forms the basis of any further interactions with the computer and should enable the user to predict the performance of the computer based on past experiences. The action of the computer will then, hopefully, match the action that they intend to take or have taken. Figure 2.7 shows the file menus from a word-processing and a spreadsheet package. A user's mental model lets them base their actions to save a file in the spreadsheet package on those experienced in the word-processing package.

The development of an effective user interface will have to take into account the fact that different users will have different mental models. In general, this is related to the user's experience of using the interface. The designer must design the interface to ensure that the intention of the user is translated by the interface into the appropriate activity or action. Conversely, the action of the computer should match that anticipated by the user.

The actions of the computer can then be matched by using audio-visual indicators. For example, Figure 2.8 shows the print dialogue box from a word-processing package. The options that can be selected and set by the user can be highlighted (a visual indication) by stepping through the box areas by pressing the tab key.

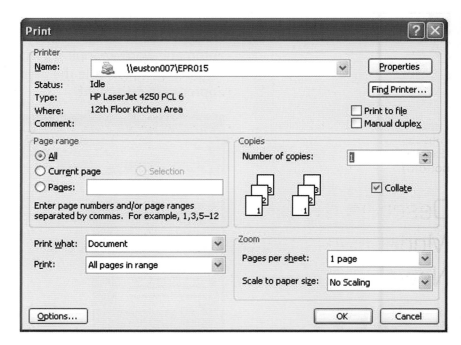

Figure 2.8 Visual indication on a dialogue box

The design of a user interface must take into account the perception of the majority of users. This means that a designer of the interface will have to maintain a natural method of completing an action by the user. When this action has been completed the interface display must reflect the current, and accurate, state of the system. This accuracy will then enable a user to carry out further actions.

Discuss the importance of designing a system model that matches closely the user's mental model

A designer must consider the mental model when designing a system model. This ensures that the final product matches the mental model as closely as possible. One of the most important reasons for this match is to ensure that the user does not 'get lost' while using the system. The system must, as far as possible, build on the experience of the user to ensure that previous experience can be used when the user is faced with any problems that might occur. This might mean the use of the same audio cue when an error occurs, or the display of a useful error message.

Users will bring their own preconceptions to any system. These will be based on their own mental model of a system. The designer must try to provide a convergence between the user mental model and the system model being created. For example, a user will expect the command 'open' to open a document or file. By ensuring that these expectations are met when the system is designed then the confidence of the users will increase as they use the system model.

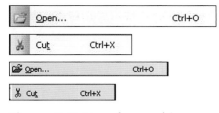

Figure 2.9 Use of a graphic consistently in different applications (Excel at the top and Word at the bottom)

Another reason for the system matching the mental model is that the speed with which the user will learn to confidently use the system will be increased.

Describe the user interface design tool known as the Model Human Processor, developed by Card, Moran and Newell, and its application

The Model Human Processor (MHP) attempts to portray the user of a computer system as a computer with memory areas and processors.

The MHP was developed by Card, Moran and Newell in their book titled *The Psychology of Human–Computer Interaction*, published in 1983. Figure 2.10 shows a very simplified version of the model.

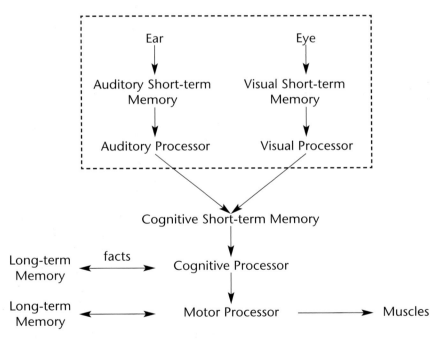

Figure 2.10 The MHP model

Information is received through the eyes and ears: this is the input. The information is then passed to the Working Memory by the Perceptual Processor. The Working Memory comprises two separate storage sections: one for visual images and one for auditory images. The Working Memory also includes those sections of the Long-term Memory that are currently of interest to the users and those sections that are required so the current task can be completed. This process can be related to the process of loading data from a disk into RAM.

The Recognise-act Cycle of the Cognitive Processor can be related to the fetch-execute cycle. On each cycle the current contents of the Working Memory are used to trigger actions to be carried out by the Motor Processor.

The MHP draws on the appropriate information held in the Long-term Memory to enable a task or action to be completed. For example, the Working Memory could hold the information that 'a left click of the mouse is needed' but the information required to complete this process will be held in the Long-term Memory.

The Working Memory demonstrates the importance of a user's short-term memory for the successful completion of tasks. If the memory becomes full of information before a task or action can be completed then the user will have to pause or re-read supporting documentation. As a result of this the user may start to make mistakes. To avoid these mistakes the user will often breakdown a task into manageable sections. The software interface that is being used must enable this to happen. For example, menus should be hierarchically divided to ensure the user can select exactly what they are looking for.

In summary, the MHP draws an analogy between the processing and storage of a computer with the perceptual, cognitive, motor and memory activities of the computer user.

This is done by a visual or audible stimulus being captured by the user with the physical attributes of the stimulus being decoded. For example, a user's attention is drawn to a box on the screen. The response that is needed will then be interpreted by the user. A motor response is then initiated to satisfy the response needed, for example, the click of a mouse button.

◾ The application of the MHP

The model can be applied to many situations related to the use of computers. However, the application the model was developed for is that of the design of a user interface.

Examples of how the model can be applied to the design of a user interface include:

- logically ordering inputs, possibly those required from the user
- using an on-screen flashing cursor to show where data is to be input
- using an audible stimulus (e.g. a beep sound) to indicate when an error has been made by the user.

QUESTION

Describe the user interface design tool known as the Model Human
Processor.

Summary

Processing systems
Batch
Interactive
Real-time
    in terms of processing, response time and user interface requirements.

Types of operating system
Single-user
Multi-user
Multi-tasking
Interactive
Real-time
Batch processing
Distributed processing

Designing and using a human–computer interface
Colour
Layout
Quantity of on-screen information
Size of font
Complexity of language
Type of controls

Different methods of dialogue
Computer and person
Person and computer
Computer and computer

Methods of human–device communications, particularly HCI
Command line interfaces
Menus/sub-menus
Graphical User Interfaces (GUIs)
Natural language (including speech input–output)
Forms dialogue

Designing an interface
A potential user's
    perception
    attention
    memory
    learning
should be taken into account

Mental models

How they can be applied to the design of a user interface.

The importance of designing a system model that matches closely the user's mental model.

The user interface design tool known as the Model Human Processor, developed by Card, Moran and Newell, and its application.

Test 1

A company wants to introduce a stock ordering system. A user interface will need to be designed.

1 Describe the user interface tool known as the Model Human Processor (MHP).	[6]
2 Identify and explain two examples of how the MHP could be applied to the interface.	[4]
3 The system will be a real-time system. Describe a real-time system.	[6]

Test 2

A publishing company is updating the accounts system that is currently in use.

1 Explain how a user's perception and memory should be considered when the accounts system interface is being designed.	[6]
2 The new system will use a multi-user operating system. Describe a multi-user operating system.	[4]
3 Explain how colour should be considered when designing the HCI.	[4]

Networks and communications

Introduction

This chapter is about how people, computers and devices communicate. In order to communicate, networks are required and so a significant part of this chapter is about understanding how networks work.

Throughout the chapter, the emphasis is on describing and comparing different methods, including looking at advantages and disadvantages of each.

You will learn about:

- types of network
- methods of connecting computers and devices together
- components of networks
- communication applications
- how data is accessed on networks.

Compare the characteristics of a local area network (LAN), a wide area network (WAN) and a virtual network

A computer can either be standalone or connected to a network. If it is standalone, then it can not communicate with any other computers. A computer connected to a network can communicate with one or more other computers. This communication may include, for example:

- messages or emails
- file transfers
- application sharing
- print sharing.

Local area network

A local area network (LAN) is usually confined within a local geographic area such as a building or campus. LANs are often found in schools, colleges, businesses and libraries. You will also find small LANs in private homes. A LAN has the following characteristics:

- computers are within a local geographic area
- the workstations have network cards or wireless connectivity

- workstations and peripherals are connected via dedicated cables (or wireless devices) owned by the company
- it often has shared peripherals (e.g. printers)
- software and data can be shared.

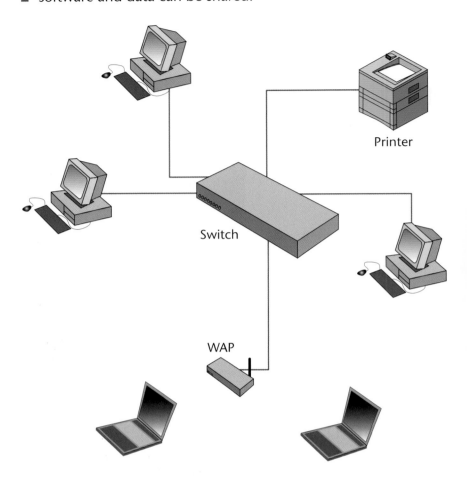

Printer

Switch

WAP

Figure 3.1 A LAN configuration

Wide area network

A wide area network (WAN) consists of computers that are geographically remote from each other. The characteristics of a WAN are:

- computers are not close together
- external communications equipment, such as a telephone line, leased line or mobile phone are used to connect computers
- a modem, router or other physical device is needed to connect to the WAN.

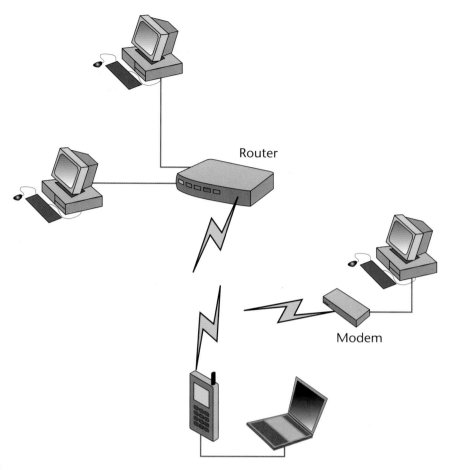

Figure 3.2 A WAN configuration

The internet is the largest example of a WAN. Many computers are connected together through external communication links and information is shared via the World Wide Web and messages can be sent via email and internet relay chat.

In order to connect to the internet, an Internet Service Provider (ISP) is needed to provide the connection to the internet. An ISP offers services such as email, web hosting and file transfer.

WANs are also used in large organisations. Some examples include:

- universities which have multiple campuses a long way from each other
- local education authorities which connect together many schools
- airline booking systems
- National Lottery terminals
- automated teller machines (ATMs)
- train timetable systems
- large businesses with many offices or shops.

Connecting a LAN and a WAN

Most LANs are connected to a WAN. This means that if you are using a computer on a LAN, you will also be able to connect to other computers on a WAN. This is usually done using a router which is a device that connects the LAN to an external communication device that allows communication with a WAN (e.g. the internet).

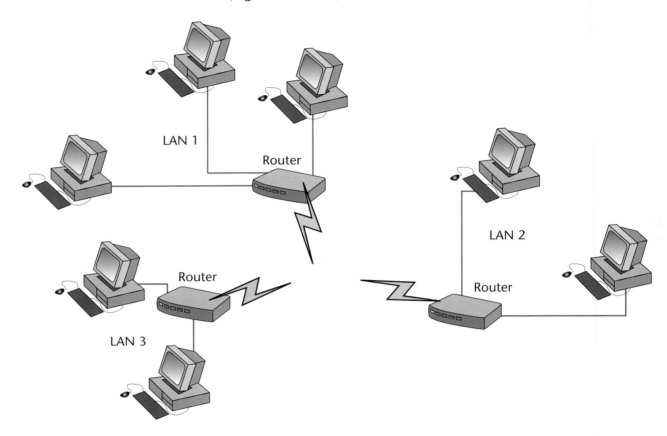

Figure 3.3 Connect LANs via a WAN

< Activity >

Ask your school or college network manager to explain how your school LAN is built and how it connects to a local authority or other WAN. Draw a diagram showing the connections that are involved.

Virtual network

A virtual network allows computers to communicate with each other as if they were within a single LAN, but without knowing that they may be part of a bigger network.

A virtual network could exist within a single LAN so that a set of computers could communicate only with each other, even though there are other physical connections. In Figure 3.4, the green computers are part of a virtual network. They do not know that any of the grey computers exist on the network because the

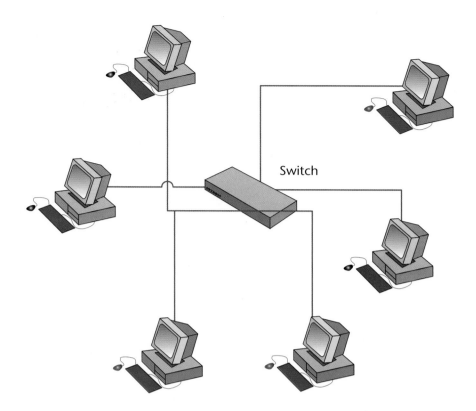

Figure 3.4 A virtual network within a LAN

switching device that connects them all together is 'hiding' the other computers.

A virtual network could also exist across more than one LAN through a WAN or the internet. In Figure 3.5, the green computers are part of a virtual network. They operate as if they were part of a single LAN. Other computers and devices cannot communicate directly with the green computers on the virtual network. Data for a virtual network travelling through cables on a LAN does not affect data from the LAN or other virtual networks.

In a virtual network, users will have access to the same services they would on a single LAN, such as print sharing, file sharing and application sharing.

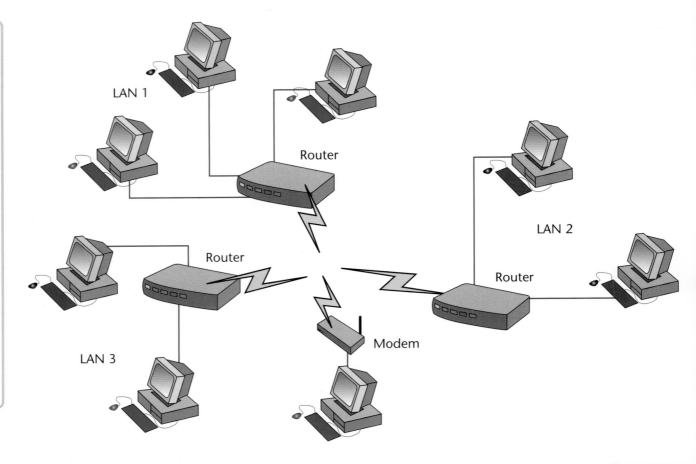

Figure 3.5 A virtual network within a WAN

QUESTIONS

1 Identify **three** characteristics of a LAN.
2 Identify **two** characteristics of a WAN.
3 Describe the purpose of a virtual LAN.
4 Identify **four** services offered by an ISP.

Discuss the characteristics and purpose of intranets, the internet and extranets

Internet

Characteristics

The internet is not the same as the World Wide Web and it is important not to get the two terms mixed up. The internet is the infrastructure provided to connect computers together across the globe using telecommunications systems such as telephone lines, leased lines, mobile phones and satellites. It uses the TCP/IP protocol for communication between devices. Any computer with an external communication link can connect to the internet, meaning that the internet can be referred to as an OPEN network.

Purpose

Once connected to the internet, users can gain access to a number of services, for example:

- Email
- World Wide Web
- internet relay chat (IRC – instant messaging)
- File transfer

Software is required to access these services. While most services can be accessed using a web browser, there are dedicated software packages available for email (e.g. Qualcomm Eudora), file transfer (e.g. Ipswitch WS_FTP) and IRC (e.g. Microsoft Messenger). Remember in an examination that you should refer to the types of software and not the brand names. These services are available for communicating all over the world. For example, you might want to send an email to somebody in Japan, chat to a friend in the next street using IRC, visit the BBC website or transfer files to update your anti-virus software.

Intranet

Characteristics

The intranet provides the same services as the internet, but only within one organisation. It is secure as it can only be used by authorised people within that organisation and will almost certainly require the use of a username and password to gain access. The intranet may be provided through a LAN or in a larger organisation it will be available through a virtual network within a WAN. Only computers that are part of the LAN or virtual network will be able to gain access to the intranet, meaning that it can be referred to as a closed network. The intranet uses the same TCP/IP protocol as the internet.

Purpose

Users of an intranet have access to the same services as they do on the internet, but they can only communicate within their own organisation. Services include:

- internal email
- internal web pages
- internal chat
- file transfer.

As with the internet, software is required to access these services. These services are available for communication only within the organisation. For example, an employee might want to send an email to a colleague at the head office, chat to a colleague in the Birmingham office, find out about the Health & Safety policy from the internal web pages or download a piece of software that is licensed for use within the organisation.

Using an intranet means that users can provide information and communicate with others knowing that nobody outside of the organisation can gain access to that information. This means that sensitive documents, such as business plans, remain confidential.

< Activity >

With a partner, list the facilities available on your school intranet.

Extranet

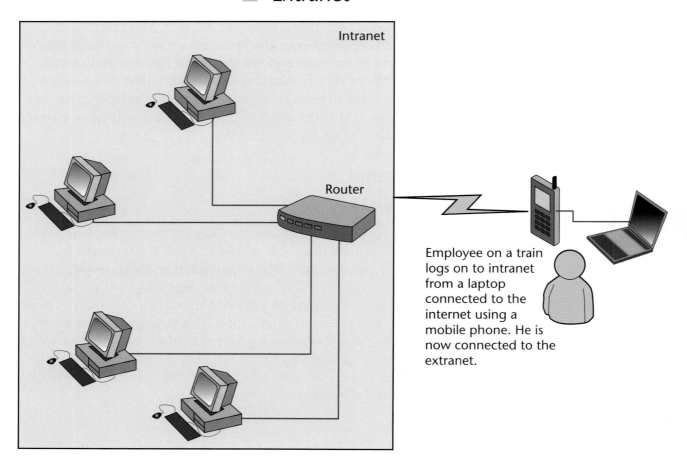

Figure 3.6 A extranet

Characteristics

Users of an extranet have access to an intranet using a username and password from an internet-connected computer. Once connected to the extranet, the user has access to all the intranet services of the organisation. Access is usually provided by logging on to a secure server from a web page, although some organisations will provide secure software that has to be installed before access can be provided to the extranet.

Purpose

These services are still only available for communication within the organisation, but employees and registered users can access the services from any internet-connected computer. For example, an employee working from home may want to send an email or chat to a colleague who is away working on business in a foreign country, find out the direct telephone number for a colleague or download files needed to prepare a report.

Using an intranet means that users can provide information and communicate with others knowing that nobody outside of the organisation can gain access to that information. Confidentiality is maintained, but there is added risk that somebody could hack into the extranet because it is available from any internet-connected computer.

< Activity >

List the facilities of your school network that you can access from home.

QUESTIONS

1 Describe **three** facilities available on the internet, intranet and extranet.
2 Explain how an intranet differs from the internet.
3 Describe the purpose of an extranet.

Discussing the characteristics and purpose

In an examination, it is likely that you will be asked to discuss the characteristics and purpose of intranets, the internet and extranets. You will therefore need to be able to write a balanced argument that compares the advantages and disadvantages of each. The table below gives a summary of the characteristics and purposes.

	Intranet	Internet	Extranet
Characteristics	■ Enables communication within an organisation. ■ Uses LANs or virtual networks across a WAN. ■ Requires a username and password to gain access. ■ Uses the TCP/IP protocol. ■ Only available within the physical network infrastructure of an organisation.	■ Infrastructure provided to connect computers together across the globe. ■ Uses telecommunications systems such as telephone lines, leased lines, mobile phones and satellites. ■ Web pages are available to anybody – other resources may require usernames and passwords. ■ Uses the TCP/IP protocol. ■ Available to the whole world.	■ Enables communication within an organisation from any internet-connected computer. ■ Uses the internet to provide access to an intranet. ■ Requires a username and password to gain access. ■ Uses the TCP/IP protocol. ■ Available from the internet, but only to employees within an organisation.

73

	Intranet	Internet	Extranet
Purpose	■ Provides email communication only to other members of the organisation. ■ Web pages within the organisation can be visited to find internal information about the organisation. ■ Chat conversations can take place with other employees within the organisation. ■ Files that belong to the organisation can be downloaded for use within the organisation. ■ Information that is shared is securely retained within the organisation so that external users cannot gain access to it.	■ Provides email communication to any other internet-connected user. ■ Web pages can be visited anywhere on the World Wide Web to find out publicly available information. ■ Chat conversations can take place with any other internet-connected user. ■ Files can be transferred to/from any file transfer site.	■ Employees working away from the office can send and receive internal emails. ■ Employees working away from the office can find internal information about the organisation. ■ Employees working away from the office can chat with their colleagues. ■ Employees working away from the office can download files needed to carry out their duties. ■ Employees do not have to be physically within the organisation's premises but providing access from the internet means there is a security risk if a hacker can find out a username and password.

Describe client–server and peer-to-peer networks giving advantages and disadvantages of each

A client–server network is often found in medium- to large-sized organisations whereas a peer-to-peer network is often found in small organisations (e.g. local churches, a family run shop, a solicitor's practice) and homes.

Client–server network

A client–server network requires at least one computer that performs the role of a server. A server performs roles such as:

■ file storage
■ back-up
■ application sharing
■ printer management.

The client computers are all connected to the server via a switch or other network communication device. In order to access resources such as files or printers on the network, users are required to log on at the client computers using a username and password. Some client computers use swipe cards instead of usernames or finger print recognition instead of usernames and

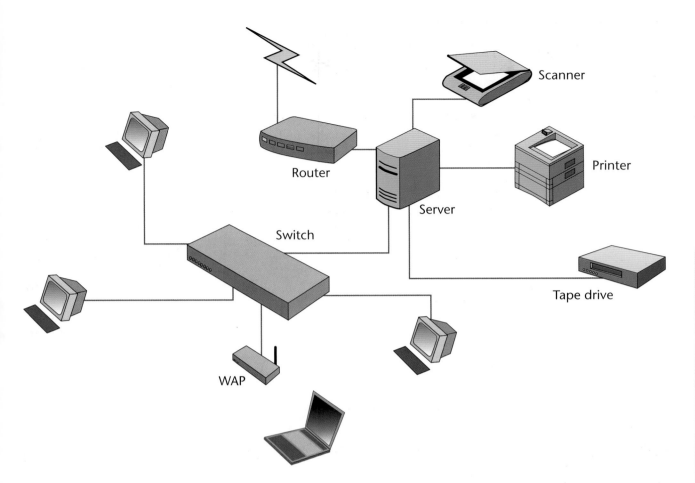

Figure 3.7 Client–server network topology

passwords. Once connected to the server, a user will have access to:

- a dedicated amount of storage space that is private to the user
- printers
- files, if permission has been granted
- software used within the organisation.

A user can log on to the server from any client and the resources available will be the same.

In large organisations, there is likely to be more than one server, with each server carrying out specific roles. Software can be automatically deployed to all clients on a client–server network, anti-virus software can be managed centrally and back-ups can be taken of all the data on the server. However, servers require specialist technical staff and if a server fails then clients will lose access to data. See page 87 to find out about the different types of server that might be used in a client–server network.

Peer-to-peer network

A peer-to-peer network has no central server. Each computer performs its own functions and may share some resources with other computers on the network.

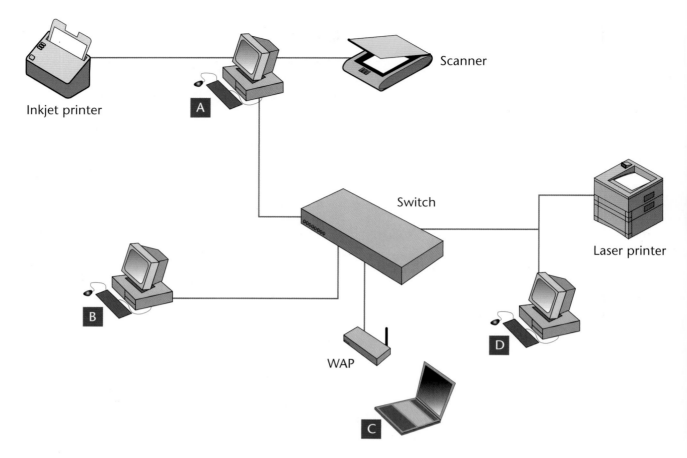

Figure 3.8 Peer-to-peer network topology. Computer A has a colour printer and scanner connected to it. If computer B wishes to print in colour, it has to use the services of computer A. If computer A wants to print a high quality document on a laser printer, then it relies on the services of computer D. If computer C needs to access some files that are stored on computer B, then it needs to have been given permission to access them.

All of the computers in the network are equivalent 'peers' – none of them acts as the 'leader' as none of them have a server role to play. Each computer may have resources such as files and printers that other computers may need to access.

This type of network is much easier to set up and that is why it is often found in homes and small businesses. However, each computer has to be maintained individually which can lead to unreliability within the network.

Advantages and disadvantages

Client–server	Peer-to-peer
■ Back-ups are managed centrally so users do not have to become involved with them.	■ Each user is responsible for backing up their own data.
■ Anti-virus solutions are managed centrally taking the onus away from users.	■ Anti-virus software has to be installed by the user of each computer and regularly kept up to date.
■ All network processing is done centrally at the server, meaning that the clients have more processing power available.	■ All processing is done by each computer (e.g. including printing) meaning that some tasks may take longer to complete – especially if other computers are using files or printers on that particular computer.
■ Data and applications are available from any client.	
■ Security is managed centrally in a structured manner.	
■ Software can be deployed quickly to client machines by the network manager using the server, meaning the user does not have to install any software.	■ The user has to use the same computer each time in order to access data and software.
	■ Security is 'ad-hoc' meaning that some users may be able to access some printers, but others might not. Some confidential files might be available to all users on the network as it is more difficult to set up data structures.
■ Servers require a lot of processing power, large hard disks and lots of memory meaning they can be very expensive.	
■ If the server fails, then users lose access to network resources.	■ Software has to be installed on each computer on the network individually which takes up a lot of human resource time.
■ A network manager is required to maintain the complicated structure of a server.	■ Each computer works independently, only providing some shared resources, meaning an ordinary computer will suffice.
■ If applications are run directly from the server then there can be a lot of network traffic, which slows down other tasks.	■ There is no reliance on a single server, so if a computer fails, only its shared resources are lost.
	■ In a small office or within the home, a peer-to-peer network can be set up by a reasonably competent person.
	■ Network traffic is minimal as most resources are provided by each computer.

QUESTIONS

1 Describe **three** advantages of networking computers.
2 What is the main difference between a client–server network and a peer-to-peer network?
3 Describe **three** advantages of a client–server network compared with a peer-to peer network.
4 Describe **two** disadvantages of a client–server network.
5 Describe **two** advantages of a peer-to-peer network.

Describe client-server and peer-to-peer networks giving advantages and disadvantages of each

Explain the importance of bandwidth when transmitting data and how different types of communication media (cables, wireless, optical) govern the bandwidth available (knowledge of examples of different communication media is expected)

▦ Bandwidth

Bandwidth measures how much data can be transferred along a communications channel. The more frequencies available to the communications channel, the more data that can be transferred at once. While bandwidth is officially measured as a frequency (Hz), it is more generally reported in bits per second (bps). For example, a bandwidth of 8 Mbps means that 8 megabits of data can be transferred at once every second. Megabits are often confused with megabytes. A byte consists of eight bits. Therefore, a bandwidth of 8 Mbps is equivalent to one megabyte per second.

A higher bandwidth means that more data can flow per second which has a positive effect on the speed of data transfer as data is likely to arrive more quickly.

Figure 3.9 A bandwidth analogy

A way of understanding bandwidth is to consider a busy motorway. In Figure 3.9, you can see how four lanes of traffic are stuck in a traffic jam. The motorway has a 'bandwidth' of four cars. In other words, four cars can travel at once along the motorway. If the number of lanes was increased to six, then six cars could travel at once along the motorway. The same applies with bandwidth. The more frequencies (lanes) available on a channel (motorway), then the more data (cars) that can travel at once.

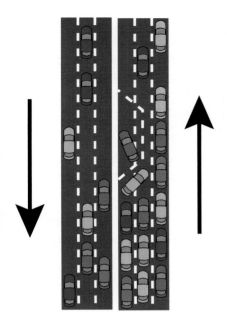

Figure 3.10 The bottleneck analogy

Figure 3.11 The original bottleneck

Figure 3.12 An internet 'bottleneck'

Bottlenecks

You may have found using the activity above that your bandwidth is higher than your download speed. This is caused by 'bottlenecks' somewhere within the internet. A bottleneck is the smallest bandwidth that exists between the user and the place that data is being downloaded from.

Imagine some road works on a motorway. There are normally three lanes of traffic but for half a mile, there are only two lanes due to a lane closure. Before the closure, three cars were able to travel at once, now only two cars can. This causes a 'bottleneck'.

The term 'bottleneck' comes from the idea that water can only pour out through the neck (the narrowest part) of the bottle. This effectively slows down the flow rate.

Similarly, with communication channels, bottlenecks are caused by the narrowest bandwidth.

In Figure 3.12, the user is connected to their own ISP by an 8 Mbps bandwidth. The user is downloading a file from a website that is connected using a 2 Mbps bandwidth. Therefore, the bottleneck is 2 Mbps, meaning that the user can only download the data from the website at a maximum rate of 2 Mbps. If lots of people are downloading at once from the same website, then the 2 Mbps is shared among those users and so the effective download rate will be much lower.

Importance of bandwidth

The importance of bandwidth depends on the application that the user is running and how much data needs to be downloaded in a short space of time. If a user only sends an occasional email with no attachments, then a small bandwidth (e.g. 56 kbps through a modem) is perfectly acceptable.

Explain the importance of bandwidth when transmitting data and how different types of communication media govern the bandwidth available

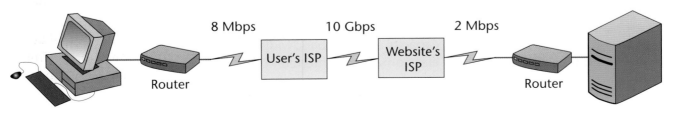

8 Mbps   10 Gbps   2 Mbps

Router   User's ISP   Website's ISP   Router

However, if a user is participating in a video conference, then lots of data needs to be transferred every second, meaning that a high bandwidth is required. The video and sound associated with video conferences consist of large packets of data. If these are not delivered on time, then the video conference will have time lags resulting in broken or missing pictures and sound.

If the user is listening to live radio (streamed), then a high bandwidth is required in order that the sound is delivered on time and so that breaks are not experienced within the broadcast.

However, if the user is downloading a pre-recorded radio programme, then it does not matter as much how long it takes to download as it can be listened to once the whole programme has been downloaded. This may be inconvenient to the user in terms of having to wait, but it does not affect the final user experience of listening to the programme.

The importance of bandwidth is therefore important when accessing content that is being delivered in real time (i.e. it is live). Without a high bandwidth, images and sound are broken up, become out of sync and freeze, making the conversation, viewing or listing very difficult. However, if the content is not live, then it can be downloaded for later listening or viewing and, even though it may take a long time to download, once it is downloaded it will be able to be listened to or watched without distortion. If a user wants to download something quickly, so they can turn their computer off, then bandwidth is important.

QUESTIONS

1 How many megabytes can be downloaded each second at a bandwidth of 16 Mbps?
2 Describe the term bandwidth.
3 If a user has an 8 Mpbs connection to the internet, why might it take 30 seconds to download 1 MB of data?
4 Give **two** examples of when it is important to have a high bandwidth
5 Why is bandwidth unimportant if downloading a television programme from the internet to watch at a later time?

■ Cable

Copper cable is one option for transmitting data. Older networks used co-axial (coax) cables which consisted of two wires. Coax cables are still used within the television industry due to its capacity for high bandwidths. The outer cable acts as a shield to electromagnetic interference which reduces signal loss.

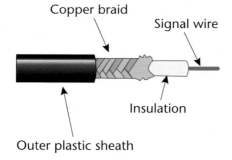

Copper braid

Signal wire

Insulation

Outer plastic sheath

Figure 3.13 Co-axial cable

Figure 3.14 Twisted pair cable

Figure 3.15 An Ethernet cable and connector (with twisted pair wires visible)

Copper cables in modern networks are usually in the form of twisted pairs of wire. These are narrow strands of wire, insulated with plastic, then twisted together. Most of these cables are unshielded which means there is no earth wire – this is known as unshielded twisted pair (UTP) or more commonly as Ethernet cables. This can result in data packets being lost, particularly data being transmitted at higher frequencies.

There are also Shielded Twisted Pair cables (STP) where each pair of wires has a metal shield which reduces electromagnetic interference. These cables are sometimes used in high-speed networks where higher bandwidths are required.

Copper cable is used within local area networks and can support data transmission of up to 1 Gbps using standard CAT 5e cables (four twisted pairs). CAT 6 and CAT 7 cables can transmit up to 10 Gbps.

While copper cables are cheaper than optical cables, they are limited to a maximum of 100 metres. Beyond this the data signal becomes too weak. The bandwidth is limited by the frequencies that the copper cable is able to cope with. Copper cables are also prone to electrical interference which results in lost data packets that will reduce the overall transmission rate.

< Activity >

Fill in the table to compare the different types of cables available.

	Co-axial	UTP	STP
Main use			
Shielding			
Number of cable cores			

Optical

Fibre-optic cables are minute glass tubes that reflect light along the length of the tube. They are used where more than 100 metres of cable is required and in modern cable TV networks. Fibre optics are not susceptible to electrical interference and suffer very little loss of data, meaning that the bandwidths available are much higher than copper. The bandwidth available is increasing all the time as technology develops. In 2000, Siemens carried out a successful test of transmitting 7.04 Tbps (terrabits per second) along a single fibre-optic cable. In 2008, Virgin Media were offering 20 Gbps broadband connections to home users using fibre-optic cable.

Figure 3.16 Bundled optical cable

Figure 3.17 Light showing at the end of optical fibres

Wireless

Wireless communication can consist of many methods, such as radio, satellite and infrared. These are explained in more depth later in this chapter. There is a smaller range of frequencies available for wireless transmission than for copper cable or fibre optics, which means that the bandwidth available is less with wireless communication methods. Further to this, obstacles such as walls and steel can interrupt wireless signals causing lost packets and wireless is susceptible to other interference which reduces the transmission rate.

QUESTIONS

1 Why can't copper cable be used over long distances?
2 What is the difference between UTP and STP?
3 In what circumstances might STP be used instead of UTP?
4 Why are fibre-optic bandwidths higher than copper bandwidths?
5 Why are wireless bandwidths lower than cable bandwidths?
6 Why might wireless signals be weakened?

Compare the role of the following network components: switches, hubs, wireless access points, network interface cards, wireless network interface cards, routers, repeaters, bridges and servers (file, applications, mail, proxy, print, back-up) and identify where their use would be appropriate

■ Switch

Figure 3.18 A typical switch

A switch is a device that connects several devices (e.g. computer, printer) together to enable communication to take place between those devices. It consists of a number of ports into which cables can be connected. Data packets that are received by the switch are examined for their destination and then sent to the port which is connected to the recipient device. In a large organisation, several switches will be used together and connect to a core switch. The core switch (sometimes known as a backbone switch) will manage all the data being received by other switches and then route it to other switches connected to it.

Managed switches can be configured so that data through each port can be controlled in different ways. Bandwidths can be limited to each port or priority can be given to data on a particular port. For example, some ports may be set to run at 1 Gbps, whereas others may be set to 100 Mbps. Switches can also be configured for QoS (Quality of Service) whereby priority can be given to particular applications which require a guaranteed bandwidth, such as video conferencing or voice over IP (VoIP).

Patch panels

Fibre patch panel

Switch

Core switch

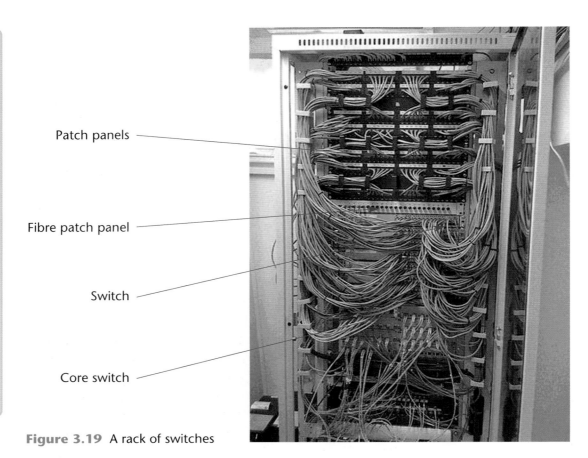

Figure 3.19 A rack of switches

Other configurations include being able to set up a virtual LAN and being able to monitor traffic for potential problems.

For example, if two devices are connected to ports 1 and 2 and they need to communicate, then this can happen at the same time as two devices on ports 3 and 4 because the ports operate independently of each other and thus collisions do not occur.

< Activity >

This is a whole class activity. One person should be the switch. Another can be a printer. Other people should be the computers connected to the switch. Each printer and computer should have an address (their name). Each person acting as a computer can send a message to another computer or the printer. The switch must accept each message and deliver it to the correct location. Each message must include the address and the content of the message. The printer should only respond with appropriate messages such as 'out of paper'. Before carrying out this activity, decide as a whole class what responses the printer can give. During the activity, one of the computers can turn off. Think about what the switch should do if a message is delivered in this circumstance.

Hub

A hub looks physically the same as a switch and has the same purpose of enabling communication to take place between devices that are connected to it. However, it does not examine the data packets, but instead sends them out to every port that is connected to it. This means that data then has to be filtered by recipient devices to see whether it is intended for that device. It also means that data is more susceptible to interception. Another problem caused by sending data out through all ports is that more collisions can occur. Considering the activity (page 84) used for a switch, the two devices connected to ports 1 and 2 are communicating at the same time as ports 3 and 4, but because there is no independence between the ports, collisions will occur.

Wireless access point

A wireless access point (WAP) is a hub that communicates wirelessly instead of having physical connections through ports. The WAP is usually connected to the main network infrastructure through a single cable connected to a switch. Any wireless enabled devices such as laptops, PDAs and mobile phones can connect to a WAP. Radio signals are sent from the devices and received by the WAP and then sent to the network or another wireless device. When a WAP receives a signal intended to be received by a wireless device, it broadcasts it and the receiving device collects the data packets.

A major problem with WAPs is the potential for hackers to intercept data. Therefore, WAPs provide encryption methods. WAPs are used in homes, small organisations and large organisations where wireless devices need to be connected to the network.

Figure 3.20 A wireless access point

Network interface card

A network interface card (NIC) enables a computer to be connected to a network using a cable. More modern computers include the network interface as part of the circuitry on the motherboard of the computer, but it is also possible to add network interface cards to computers.

Each NIC has a media access control (MAC) address that is unique to that card. Other devices that are connected to networks also have MAC addresses so they can be identified uniquely.

Wireless network interface card

In order to communicate with a WAP, a device needs to have a wireless NIC. These can take the form of:

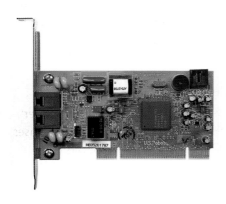

Figure 3.21 A network interface card

Compare the role of network components and identify where their use would be appropriate

Figure 3.22 A wireless NIC dongle

Figure 3.23 A router

Figure 3.24 Using a router

- part of the internal circuitry of a laptop computer or printer
- a USB wireless dongle that can be connected to any USB port (Figure 3.22)
- an adapter card that fits in to a PCMCIA slot on a laptop or an expansion slot on a desktop computer.

The wireless NIC must support the same communication standard (e.g. 802.11g) as the WAP. It will have a MAC address like a NIC.

Router

A router is an advanced version of a switch. It stores the addresses of devices connected to it and sends data to recipient devices using an efficient route. It is mainly used to connect a LAN to a WAN. Routers were once used exclusively by large organisations, but smaller versions of routers are now available to connect home computers to the internet.

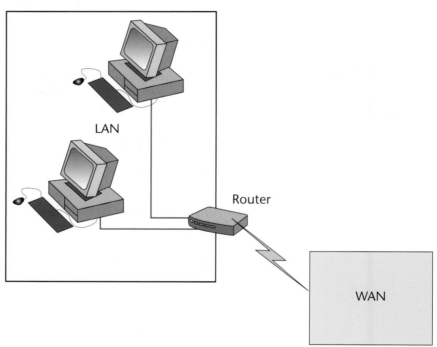

Repeater

Signals deteriorate along long cables, so a device is required to extend the range of cables. A repeater will sit between two segments of cable. It receives the signal from one cable and then re-sends the signal along the next cable. It is used when copper cable needs to be used over distances longer than 100 metres.

Bridge

A bridge is used to connect two LANs together. It is different to a router in that it does not store the addresses of devices connected to it.

Servers

A server is a powerful computer that performs functions on behalf of clients connected to it. There are many different types of server and the size and functionality of a network will dictate how many are needed. The most common types are described below.

File server

A file server stores files available on the network. It will normally have storage areas set aside for each user on the network that are only accessible to those users. It is also likely to have 'shared' files that are available to some or all users. Examples of shared areas in a school could be:

- Student – all users on the network can read any files stored in this area.
- ICT – only the ICT staff can make changes to the files.
- Geography – only the Geography staff can make changes to the files.
- History – only the History staff can make changes to the files.
- Staff – staff can read any files, but students can not access the files at all.
- Secure – only staff who have been given permission can read or change files stored in this area.
- Finance – only finance staff can read or change files.
- Admin – only administrative staff can read or change files.

Users can access their files from any client connected to the network.

Application server

An application server stores software for use across the network. It performs two main functions:

- Storing software so that it can be run from the application server by a client computer.
- Storing software installation files so that software can be deployed to client computers.

Compare the role of network components and identify where their use would be appropriate

87

When software is stored so it can be run from the application server, this saves storage space, memory and processing power on client computers, but does increase the amount of network traffic. When software is deployed to client computers, reliance on the network is reduced, but more processing power, storage space and memory are required by the clients.

Mail server

A mail server manages all email for an organisation. It will receive all incoming emails and allocate them to the appropriate inbox. It will only allow authorised users to access their own mail boxes. Any emails sent by users will be sent by the mail server either to another user on the LAN or via a router to a WAN or the internet. The mail server will perform additional functions such as:

■ checking all incoming emails for viruses
■ filtering out any SPAM (unsolicited) emails
■ providing a central address book for the organisation
■ setting limits to the size of mailboxes
■ calendars.

Proxy server

A proxy server manages access to the internet within an organisation. It can carry out the following functions:

■ Store web pages that have been visited in a cache so that the next user to visit web pages stored in the cache will have faster access to them.
■ A firewall that examines all data coming in to (and sometimes going out of) the network and blocks access to unacceptable internet traffic.
■ Filter access to web pages so that undesirable web pages are blocked.

Print server

A print server manages access to printers within a LAN. Print jobs are sent by client computers to the print server where the print job is processed, reducing the processing burden on the client computers. The print server will put all the print jobs for each printer into a queue and deal with them in turn. It may also provide some of the following functions:

■ Prioritise print jobs so that urgent ones can 'jump' the queue.
■ Charge users for each print job.
■ Restrict the number of pages that can be printed at once to a printer.
■ Restrict access to certain printers so they can only be used by specific users.
■ Provide reports of who has printed what.

Back-up server

The role of a back-up server is to back-up all data on a network so that individual users do not have to back-up their own data. While many users rely on back-up servers as their sole form of back-up, it is good practice for users to back-up their own personal files. A back-up server will usually have tape drives connected to it and back-up jobs will be scheduled so that they run automatically each day – usually overnight.

< Activity >

Ask your teacher or network manager to explain the system for backing up the network servers at your school or college. Find out how many tape drives are used, how many tapes are used in total and what the 'cycle' of tapes is.

QUESTIONS

1 Describe the purpose of a file server.
2 Describe the purpose of an application server.
3 List **three** functions of a mail server.
4 Describe the purpose of a proxy server.
5 List **three** functions of a print server.
6 Describe how a back-up server might make centralised back-ups.

Describe optical communication methods (infrared, fibre optic, laser), their advantages and disadvantages and typical applications

Infrared

Infrared communications have been available for many years within remote controls used for televisions, video recorders, CD players etc. Infrared was used in early laptop computers to enable them to communicate with printers and other laptops. It is also used by mobile phones, enabling them to communicate with each other to share files and play games. Infrared was the main method for wireless communication between a laptop and mobile phone before technologies such as Bluetooth®.

Infrared requires direct line of sight and can only work at short distances of no more than 10 metres, usually much less. Infrared bandwidth is restricted to 115.2 kbps.

Fibre optic

Fibre optics were introduced on page 81. Data travels at the speed of light and bandwidths available are the highest among optical communications methods. Fibre optics are used in LANs where distances of more than 100 metres need to be covered and in WANs. Virgin Media use fibre optics to broadcast cable television signals and provide broadband throughout towns and cities to homes across the UK.

Laser

Laser communications work by having two laser devices in direct line of sight to each other. Each device sends a laser beam to the other device and is able to receive a laser beam from another device. Data travels at the speed of light, like with fibre optics, but does not require a physical connection. However, laser communication only works in line of sight. Laser communications can be set up relatively quickly and are portable so they could be used at live sporting events or for transmitting live video from an aircraft. They are also used for connecting LANs between two buildings where line of sight is available. A problem with laser communications is that atmospheric conditions can cause interference.

Laser communications are used in laser tag games in which laser guns are used to aim a laser beam at other contenders. If the laser hits another contender's laser receiver (usually a special jacket) then the contender scores points.

Laser communications are not commonplace but there have been several experiments to use lasers for communication between satellites in space. Bandwidth for laser devices is changing all the time, but in 2008 a company called TS4B was offering bandwidths up to 1.5 Gbps at distances of up to four kilometres.

< Activity >

Fill in the table below to summarise the advantages and disadvantages of each optical communication method.

Optical communication method	Advantages	Disadvantages
Infrared		
Fibre optic		
Laser		

QUESTIONS

1 Give **three** situations when infrared might be used.
2 Give **two** situations when fibre-optic cables might be used.
3 Give **three** situations when laser might be used for communication.

Describe wireless communication methods (Bluetooth®, radio), their advantages, disadvantages and typical applications

▨ Bluetooth®

Bluetooth® is a protocol for wireless communication. It has a range of about 10 metres and does not require line of sight. It was created to enable widespread communication between portable devices. The first Bluetooth® protocol (version 1.2) enabled data transfer rates of 1 Mbps which was suitable for data transfer between laptops and mobile phones. A later version enabled data transfer rates of 2 Mbps which was more suitable for laptops connecting to 3G mobile phones capable of connecting at higher bandwidths to the internet. In 2009, there are plans to produce a third version capable of transfer rates up to 480 Mbps.

Typical applications include:

■ Bluetooth® headset working with a mobile phone
■ transferring files between two mobile phones
■ connecting a mobile phone to a laptop to enable:
   – file transfers
   – using the mobile phone as a modem for the laptop
   – connecting a mobile phone to a GPS receiver for satellite navigation.

Figure 3.25 Bluetooth® earpiece for mobile phone

Advantages	Limitations
■ It is widely available on many portable devices. ■ A radio frequency licence is not required. ■ It does not require line of sight. ■ A pass key can be used to prevent non-authorised devices from connecting.	■ Current data transfer rates. ■ Maximum range of 10 metres. ■ Can connect only one device to one other device at a time (e.g. a Bluetooth® headset can not be used at the same time as a laptop connected to the same mobile phone).

▨ Radio

Wireless communication using radio frequencies was first introduced on page 82. It is more commonly known as wi-fi. Wireless communication supports three main standards – 802.11a, 802.11b and 802.11g. 801.11b supports bandwidth up to 11 Mbps, whereas 802.11g supports bandwidth up to

54 Mbps. There is also a draft 802.11n standard that supports a higher bandwidth, but at the time of writing, this standard has not been universally accepted.

> **< Activity >**
>
> Research what the requirements are for each wireless communication standard.

Typical applications include:

- wireless-enabled laptops being able to connect to an organisation's network
- laptops connecting to the internet using wireless 'hotspots' in places such as hotels, internet cafés, pubs, airports and train stations
- laptops connecting to home networks
- PCs with wireless NICs being able to connect to a network where cabling would be expensive or difficult to install
- mobile phones and PDAs being able to access the internet using wireless networks instead of being charged per minute or per megabyte
- games consoles can be connected to the internet within the home without the need for cables
- printers can be connected to a wireless network.

Advantages	Limitations
■ No need to connect devices using cables. ■ Portable devices are not restricted to a particular location for network access. ■ Users can save money by using mobile phones and PDAs on wireless networks at home and at work. ■ No line of sight is required. ■ Transfer rates are sufficient for internet communication. ■ Standard wi-fi standards mean that any laptop can connect to any compatible wireless network across the world.	■ Transfer rates are restricted for network communication. ■ The range is about 30 metres indoors and further restricted by walls and steel construction. ■ If too many laptops or other devices are connected to a single WAP, then bandwidth is shared and transfer rates reduced. ■ If encryption is not set up properly, then wireless networks are susceptible to hacking.

QUESTIONS

1 Describe **two** applications of Bluetooth®.
2 Discuss the advantages and limitations of Bluetooth®.
3 Describe **three** applications of wireless communication.
4 Why are standards necessary for wireless networks?
5 Why is encryption necessary on a wireless network?

Describe the facilities of the following communication applications: fax, email, bulletin (discussion) boards, tele/video conferencing and internet relay chat (IRC) and compare their use for a given application

Figure 3.26 A typical fax machine

Fax

A fax (facsimile) machine is a device which looks a bit like a printer with a number pad for dialling telephone numbers. It includes a scanner within it. A two-dimensional document can be fed through the fax machine and sent electronically via a telephone line to another fax machine which will print the document. The quality of the document received will be considerably less than the quality of the original document. The cost of sending a fax is the same as the cost of a phone call for the same duration.

The main advantage of fax machines is that documents can be sent almost instantaneously to a recipient. However, confidentiality can not be assured as the document is likely to be received at a fax machine in a shared office area. There is much debate as to whether a faxed document is legally binding. Some court cases have deemed faxed contracts to have been effectively delivered in writing and are thus legally binding, but there is no specific law that confirms that faxed documents form a legally binding contract.

Typical uses include sending:

- advertising material to potential customers
- draft copies of contracts
- directions including pre-drawn or hand-drawn maps
- printed diagrams.

Facilities of a fax machine include the ability to:

- send and receive two-dimensional documents
- send to multiple recipients using auto-dial (although this is done in a serial nature – one recipient after another)
- receive faxed documents automatically
- block unrecognised callers
- produce a delivery receipt
- produce a summary of all faxes sent and received over a period of time.

< Activity >

Look for some different fax machines on the internet and compare their facilities.

▪ Email

Email is by far the most popular method of communication in the developed world. Messages and attached files can be sent to one or multiple recipients and are received almost instantaneously if the recipient is logged on. Confidentiality can be maintained as the recipient must log on to read the email. Unlike faxed documents, quality is not lost as documents are sent as digital attachments which are received in exactly the same electronic format as they were sent. The cost of sending emails is almost zero on the assumption that a broadband connection is used.

A similar debate exists about legally binding contracts as with faxed documents. UK law allows for electronic signatures (or digital signatures) to be used, but they must be recognised in law. The requirements of electronic signatures under the Electronic Communications Act (ECA) are very complex and so while it is possible to use emails as contractual documents, they should not be relied on for this purpose. See http://www.opsi.gov.uk/acts/acts2000/ukpga_20000007_en_2 for an insight into the complexity of electronic signatures.

Emails are no longer confined to being sent and received from computers. Mobile phones and email-enabled landline telephones are able to send and receive emails. Cable television providers offer email services through the television using a digi-box.

Typical uses include sending:

- advertising material to potential customers
- newsletters to members of an organisation
- messages to friends and family
- documents to suppliers and clients.

Facilities of email include the ability to:
- send and receive messages
- send messages to multiple recipients at once
- use an address book
- include an electronic signature (with your name, business address and business telephone number)
- send attachments
- reply directly to received emails
- forward received emails to other recipients
- request a read receipt
- filter out junk email
- encryption.

Many email systems include a personal calendar and task management facilities.

< Activity >

Use your school or college email system to try out some of the facilities listed above.

■ Bulletin boards

Bulletin (discussion) boards enable people to discuss topics with other people who are interested in the same topic. This may be for leisure purposes or business reasons. Users post messages on the discussion board, usually asking a question, and other users can respond. A discussion board has the following structure:

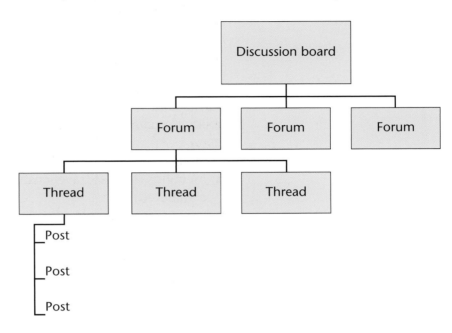

Figure 3.27 A discussion board structure

The discussion board is the whole discussion website (e.g. Microsoft Office). Forums are the subjects of discussion (e.g. Microsoft Word, Microsoft Excel). Threads are the topics of discussion (e.g. 'Using mail merge with word'). Posts are the individual posts (e.g. 'I am trying to perform a mail merge using Microsoft Word. How do I view the mail merge toolbar?').

Typical uses include discussing:

- computer games
- software applications
- political issues
- educational issues.

Facilities of discussion boards include the ability to:

- post new messages
- create new threads
- read messages that have been posted
- search discussion boards for specific information
- subscribe to threads and forums so that new posts are sent by email
- find out about other users' public profiles.

< Activity >

Look at a discussion forum, such as http://idomus.co.uk/forum/, and find examples of:

- forums
- threads
- posts.

▪ Tele/video conferencing

Teleconferencing and video conferencing enable communication between groups of people to take place. Teleconferencing enables participants to talk to each other. Video conferencing includes the ability for participants to see each other while they talk.

Typical uses include:

- meetings (so that travel costs and travel time can be eliminated)
- lessons (for example a Russian language lesson that could be shared among four schools who each only have one or two students opting for that subject)
- virtual museum visits for schools
- social chat in lieu of a phone call.

Facilities of tele and video conferencing include:

- multiple participation by two or more locations
- ability to hear all participants
- shared whiteboard where ideas can be brain stormed and discussed
- shared applications, such as presentations software or word-processing software, so that documents can be shared
- being able to dial a number to make a call
- being able to receive a call manually or automatically.

Facilities of video conferencing only:

- ability to see all participants
- ability to control your own camera (pan and zoom) and sometimes to control the remote camera.

< Activity >

With a partner, discuss what equipment is needed by each participant in order for a video conference to take place.

< Activity >

Have a look at some of the video conferences for education that can be booked through
http://www.cleo.net.uk/index.php?category_id=52 and
http://www.ja.net/communities/schools/videoconferencing/content.html

Internet Relay Chat (IRC)

Typical uses include:

- sharing ideas with colleagues
- social communication.

Facilities of IRC include:

- two or more people can communicate using text
- seeing what other participants have written
- keeping logs of conversations
- sending files within a conversation
- the use of emoticons (e.g. ☺)
- being able to invite somebody else to an existing conversation
- blocking users that you do not want to communicate with
- setting a status such as 'online', 'away' and 'busy'.

Some IRC software includes basic tele and video conferencing facilities. A typical example is MSN Messenger. (Remember, in an examination, you must refer to IRC or messaging software and not the commercial name of any software like MSN Messenger.)

< Activity >

Compare the facilities available in each of these communication applications.

Fax	Email	Bulletin board	Tele/video conferencing	Internet relay chat

---

< Activity >

For each of the following, list the facilities that are similar for each communications application.

Fax and email

IRC and bulletin board

Teleconferencing and IRC

Email and bulletin board

Compare different types of broadband connection and give suitable situations where the use of each would be appropriate: asymmetric digital subscriber line (ADSL), cable, wireless, leased line, satellite

Asymmetric digital subscriber line

Asymmetric digital subscriber line (ADSL) is when a range of frequencies are used on an existing copper telephone line to provide a broadband connection to the internet. Asymmetric means that the downstream bandwidth is different to the upstream bandwidth. As the vast majority of ADSL connections are used for downloading data from the internet, more frequencies are allocated to downstream bandwidth than to upstream bandwidth. A typical ADSL line with 8 Mbps downstream bandwidth, may only have 512 kbps or 1 Mbps upstream bandwidth. This is why it takes longer to upload a file to a web page than to download a file and why it takes longer to send an email than receive an email. A much smaller range of frequencies is left available for the public switched telephone network (PSTN).

ADSL provides 'always on' internet access and does not prevent the telephone from being used at the same time. In 2009, ADSL was available at up to 24 Mbps. In order to be able to use ADSL, a subscriber needs to be connected to a compatible telephone exchange within a workable distance. A number of factors can affect the available bandwidth:

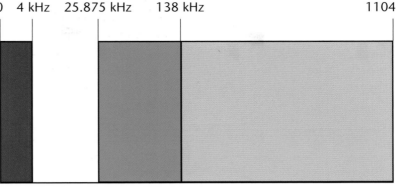

0   4 kHz   25.875 kHz   138 kHz   1104 kHz

PSTN   Upstream   Downstream

Figure 3.28 ADSL frequency plan

- Distance from the telephone exchange.
- Local AM radio stations causing interference (this may reduce the number of usable frequencies and thus reduces the bandwidth).
- Other devices, such as fax machines, connected to the telephone line.
- Electrical interference on the copper cable.

ADSL is mainly used in homes as no extra installation of cable is required. While it is used in businesses, it is not favoured in large businesses where more upstream bandwidth is required. A common problem with ADSL is the contention ratio, which refers to the number of subscribers that are sharing a bandwidth. A larger contention ratio means that there is more chance of not being able to download data using the full bandwidth – see the section on bottlenecks on page 79.

< Activity >

Look at http://www.uswitch.com/broadband/ and compare the different ADSL broadband packages.

Cable

Broadband internet access can be provided by cable television companies. The main infrastructure uses fibre-optic links meaning that higher bandwidths are available. In 2009, in the UK, downstream bandwidths of 50 Mbps were available for business users and 20 Mbps were available for home users. Cable, like ADSL, is asymmetric because it has different upstream and downstream bandwidths. While some cable television providers claim that there are no contention ratios with cable broadband, this is not actually true because there may still be a bottleneck when a number of households share the same fibre-optic link from the street to the cable company.

Compare different types of broadband connection and give suitable situations where the use of each would be appropriate

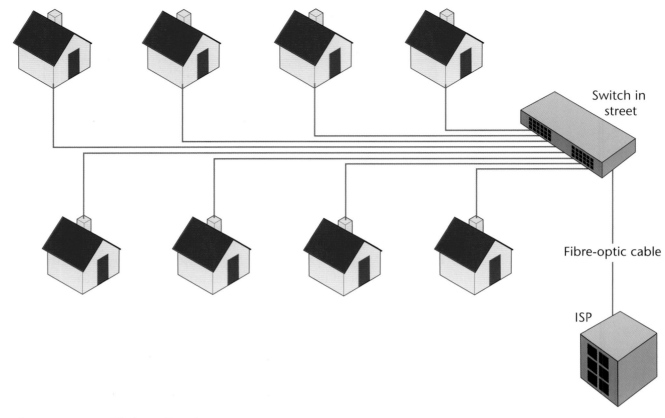

Figure 3.29 Cable broadband

▇ Wireless

Since the introduction of 3G on mobile telephone networks, wireless broadband access has become far more popular. 3G was introduced to enable video calls and high bandwidth internet connections. In 2009, mobile telephone networks were offering bandwidths of up to 7.2 Mbps, although 3G is capable of providing up to 14.4 Mbps downstream and 5.8 Mbps upstream, meaning that it is asymmetric.

Wireless broadband enables users to use the internet while not at home and also while travelling. However, it does require a good 3G signal to be available. A computer can connect to a wireless broadband connection by either connecting through a mobile phone using Bluetooth®, a USB cable or by using a USB modem stick.

< Activity >

Compare the deals available for mobile broadband at http://www.broadbandwatchdog .co.uk/mobile-broadband-providers.php

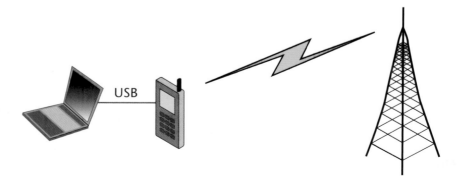

Figure 3.30 Wireless broadband

Leased line

A leased line exists between two locations only. There are no contention ratios as the line is a direct connection between one router and another router. This means the bandwidth is guaranteed. The line must be installed especially for an organisation and so this makes leased lines very expensive. Leased lines are symmetric, meaning that there is the same amount of upstream bandwidth available as downstream bandwidth. Therefore leased lines are preferred by large businesses and organisations providing access into their own networks using an extranet.

Many local education authorities have a 'Grid for Learning', which provides each school with a leased fibre-optic line that connects to the local authority. In 2009, the Birmingham Grid for Learning was providing 10 Mbps leased lines to all of its schools. Secondary schools have hundreds of computers that could be accessing the internet at the same time, including multimedia applications that use up a lot of bandwidth. Some local authorities are now looking at the possibility of upgrading the 10 Mbps connections to 100 Mbps. A bottleneck can still exist between a local authority and the internet though, particularly if lots of schools are downloading lots of data at once.

Satellite

Satellite broadband is used in remote areas where physical and wireless connections are not available. These areas could include some locations in the countryside or ships at sea. There are two types of satellite broadband:

- One-way satellite broadband uses a satellite connection for downloading data from the internet, but uses a modem and telephone line for uploading data.

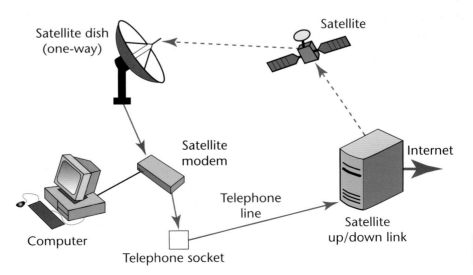

Figure 3.31 One-way satellite broadband

- Two-way satellite broadband allows both downloading and uploading of data through the satellite connection. It is asymmetric meaning downstream has a higher bandwidth than upstream (like ADSL).

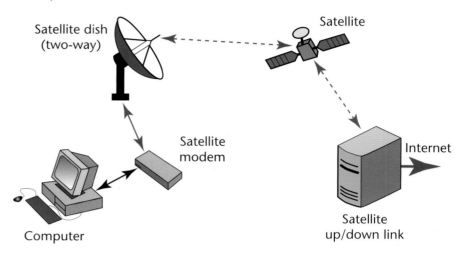

Figure 3.32 Two-way satellite broadband

Satellite broadband uses geosynchronous satellites which are approximately 37,000 km above the Earth. This means that there is a latency (delay) between data being sent and data being received of about 0.7 seconds. This is not too much of a problem for downloading data and sending/receiving emails, but it means interactive applications, such as internet gaming, are not practically possible. Using this method for video conferencing can also be very frustrating due to the delay.

Line of sight is required, so low Earth orbit satellites cannot be used as they do not remain in a fixed point above the Earth.

This table compares the different types of broadband connection using 2009 data.

	ADSL	Cable	Wireless	Leased line	Satellite
Bandwidth	24 Mbps	50 Mbps	14.4 Mbps	100 Mbps	20 kbps
Cost	Cheap	Cheap	Medium	Highest	High
Asymmetric/symmetric	Asymmetric	Asymmetric	Asymmetric	Symmetric	Asymmetric
Connection type	Copper cable	Fibre-optic backbone	Mobile phone radio waves	Fibre optic	Microwaves
Contention	Yes	Yes	Yes	No	Yes (very high ratio)

Describe how a mobile phone network operates (cellular and satellite) and the advantages and disadvantages of cellular and satellite mobile phone systems and their use

Cellular phone network

How it works

Cellular telephone networks are named as such because the area covered by the network is divided into 'cells'. A cellular telephone network consists of a number of components that enable mobile communication to take place:

- Mobile stations (MS) (e.g. a mobile phone).
- Cells that have base station transceivers (BST) – often known as a mobile phone mast that gives signal coverage to a cell.
- Mobile switching centre (MSC) – this controls all the calls taking place on the mobile telephone network.
- Base station controller (BSC) – this manages the communication between a set of BSTs and the MSC.
- Public switched telephone network (PSTN) – when a call is being made from one mobile phone company to another mobile phone company or to a landline, then the call needs to go through the PSTN.

When a phone call is placed from a mobile phone to a landline phone, a number of actions take place, which include the following:

1 The caller dials the landline number from the mobile phone.
2 A call request is sent by microwaves to the BST for the cell that the mobile phone is currently connected to.
3 This request is passed to the MSC.
4 The MSC checks the caller's status, including whether:
   ■ there is enough credit to make the call
   ■ the dialled number is allowed (e.g. international calls or premium rate calls might be blocked).
5 The MSC then connects the call through the PSTN and allocates a frequency to the MS.

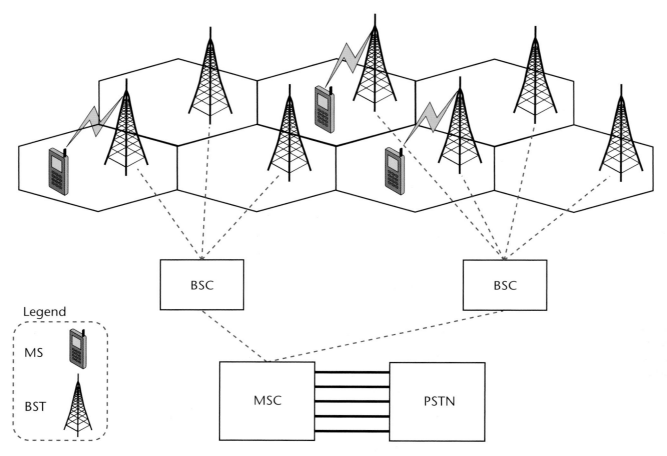

Figure 3.33 Cellular phone network

Legend

MS

BST

When a phone call is made to a mobile phone, the following actions take place:

1 The MSC receives a request for a call to a mobile phone number.
2 The MSC identifies within its active database which BSC the mobile phone is connected to.
3 The request is passed to that BSC.
4 The request to dial the mobile phone number is then broadcast through all the BSTs under the control of the BSC.
5 The mobile phone being called receives the request and acknowledges this to the BST.
6 The call is then connected by the MSC using a frequency allocated to voice calls.

If a mobile phone user is moving, then the mobile phone system needs to keep track of where the mobile phone is. This is done by:

- A database stores all the current cell locations (BSCs) of mobile phones.
- When a mobile phone moves into another cell, it registers with the cell and the database is updated.
- As the mobile phone moves from one cell to another, the user does not notice this change unless the signal is weak at the borders of the cells.
- If a mobile phone is in an area that is covered by more than one cell (i.e. where the cell borders overlap), then it will seek the strongest signal and register with that cell.

Applications

Mobile phones are so common now that most people in the UK possess one. They can be used in business for travelling employees to keep in touch with colleagues or socially for friends to communicate with each other. They are useful in case of emergencies (e.g. a child might carry one in order to be able to call its parents or dial the emergency services). The main services available on a mobile phone include:

- making and receiving phone calls, including video calls
- sending and receiving SMS (text messages) and MMS (video, sound and picture messages)
- browsing the World Wide Web
- sending and receiving emails.

Some mobile phones, known as 'smart' phones, can be used for other applications. Some of these include:

- contact list, task list and calendar
- music player
- FM radio
- navigation software with built-in GPS (global positioning system)
- currency converter
- camera.

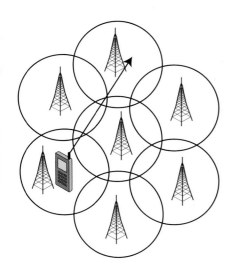

Figure 3.34 This mobile phone is moving through four different cells. Where the cells overlap, the strongest signal will be used

Advantages	Disadvantages
■ Convenience – can be used anywhere there is a signal (public phone need not be found) – users are not restricted to sitting in an office or at home to make and receive calls. ■ Can be used anywhere there is a signal to summon help in emergency. ■ The extra applications available mean that they can be used for other activities as well as just making and receiving calls. ■ Text messages can be used by people with hearing and speech impairments. ■ Access to information on the World Wide Web is available anywhere there is a signal.	■ The battery may run out meaning that calls cannot be made or received. ■ If a signal is weak or non-existent then calls cannot be made or it can be difficult to hold a conversation because the call 'breaks up'. ■ Users have no place to hide, they are always contactable (if the phone is on). ■ Text message bullying has become a problem for some children. ■ The convenience of being able to use them anywhere means that it is easy to call or be called at inappropriate times, the distraction of which could be dangerous (e.g. when driving or operating machinery). ■ There may not be enough credit to make a call from a 'pay as you go' phone. ■ Calls can disturb people in the vicinity, such as in a meeting or public place. ■ Built-up areas can restrict the range of a BST to less than half a mile.

▊ Satellite phone

How it works

A satellite phone looks similar to a mobile phone, but instead it connects directly to satellites orbiting the Earth instead of land-based base station transceivers. Satellites are capable of covering the whole globe, so coverage can be obtained in remote areas. There are two types of satellites used by satellite phones:

■ Low Earth orbit (LEO) satellites such as Iridium. Iridium has 66 satellites that orbit the Earth at altitudes averaging 900 km. These satellites orbit the Earth approximately twice every hour and so global coverage is always available. Obstacles, such as mountains, can be overcome as the next satellite moves into the line of sight.

■ Geosynchronous Earth orbit (GEO) satellites such as Thuraya. Thuraya has three satellites that orbit the Earth at altitudes of 35,000 km. This means that there is a latency (delay) experienced in calls. The satellites remain in a fixed position above the Earth, so obstacles, such as mountains, can prevent calls from being made at certain locations. The Thuraya satellite system covers Europe, Africa, the Middle East and Australia.

The actions that take place when a satellite phone call is made include:

1 A number is dialled from a satellite phone.
2 The request is transmitted by microwaves to the satellite in space.
3 The request is either passed to another satellite or sent to a satellite receiver on the Earth using a different frequency.
4 The call is connected through the PSTN.
5 If the call is to another satellite phone, then the signal is sent back to a satellite in space and then down to the receiving satellite phone.

Applications

Satellite phones have a number of uses including:

- communicating in remote areas (e.g. expeditions in the Antarctic or by the military in desert regions) or at sea (e.g. for cruise passengers or sailing expeditions) where there is no mobile phone signal
- after natural disasters (e.g. following a hurricane) where the mobile phone network may be unavailable
- communication by people (e.g. terrorists) who want to avoid their calls being 'tapped' – satellite-to-satellite communications do not go through the PSTN.

Advantages	Disadvantages
<ul><li>Global coverage available anywhere in the world.</li><li>Size is comparable with that of mobile phones.</li><li>Users can avoid their conversations being monitored.</li><li>Can be used in emergencies when the mobile phone system is not available.</li></ul>	<ul><li>Cost is very high compared with mobile phones.</li><li>Battery life is limited (which can be a problem on a long expedition or journey).</li><li>Line of sight to the satellite is required so will not work if buildings or if a mountain is in the way.</li><li>Data transfer rates are very limited with many satellites offering less than 10 kbps.</li><li>Latency can be experienced if using GEO satellites.</li></ul>

QUESTIONS

1 Describe each of the five components of a cellular network.
2 Identify the limitations of using a mobile phone to make an emergency call.
3 Identify **three** ways in which a child might use a mobile phone.
4 Why would a user use a satellite phone instead of a mobile phone?
5 Give **two** reasons why a user would prefer to use a mobile phone rather than a satellite phone.

Describe how satellite communications systems are used and work in global positioning, weather, data transfer systems and television, explaining the advantages and disadvantages of using satellites for these applications

Satellites are objects in orbit in space. A common misconception is that a dish with a transceiver in it is a satellite, it is not. A satellite actually looks like the one in Figure 3.35. A satellite dish is what is used on Earth to send and receive signals to satellites.

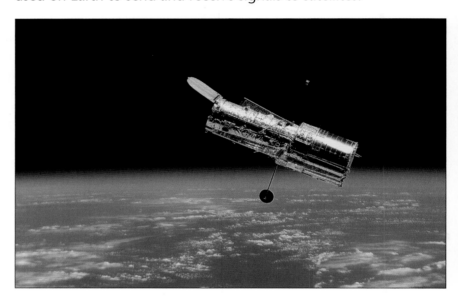

Figure 3.35 A typical satellite

Global positioning

How a global positioning system is used

Global position systems (GPS) were first used by the US military to help locate troops and vehicles on the ground. In 1983, the US GPS system was made available for civilian use. There is now another GPS system operated by Russia (GLONASS) and India plan to have their IRNSS system operating by 2012 with the European Galileo project due to be operational by 2013.

GPS uses include map making, land surveying, navigation for ships and aircraft, and use by the military. The system has become very popular with car satellite navigation systems (satnav), which use GPS satellites to identify their location. This is then shown on an interactive map. The navigation software includes instructions telling the driver where to go at each junction. As the navigation software uses the GPS to identify exactly where the vehicle is, if a wrong turn is made then the software will recognise this and identify a new route. To start a new journey, a driver needs to input the destination – this is usually selected from a list of favourites, or entered using a postcode or street address and name of town. It's also possible to enter points of interest such as railway stations, airports and city centres. The navigation software calculates the route to the destination taking account of the current position given by the GPS. The software is also able to tell the driver how long it will take to reach the destination, the distance left to the destination and what the driver's current speed is. All of this is achieved by the software constantly being told the vehicle's current location by the GPS receiver.

Figure 3.36 A satnav display

GPS can be used for many social activities, including orienteering and a game called geocaching. The latter is a worldwide game in which participants have to find a hidden 'cache'. Participants look at the geocaching website to find caches that are hidden in a particular area. They are then given the latitude and longitude co-ordinates of the cache and use a GPS device to find it.

< Activity >

Visit the website http://www.geocaching.com/ and see if you can find a geocache in your local area. If you have a GPS capable of displaying real-time latitude and longitude co-ordinates, see if you can find the geocache.

How GPS works

The GPS consists of 24 satellites in orbit as part of the NAVSTAR constellation. Each satellite orbits the Earth twice a day and there are always at least four satellites in line of site from any point on the Earth at any time. A GPS receiver will look for communication to at least three satellites (preferably four) and then use a method called trilateration to calculate the distance to each satellite and determine its location.

Advantages	Disadvantages
GPS ■ The accuracy of GPS can be as good as 30 cm. ■ If lost, a person can be found by giving the latitude and longitude or their position. **Satnav** ■ There is no need for a driver to use a map, meaning that they can concentrate on driving. ■ Time can be saved by not having to plan journeys because the software does it automatically. ■ A new route is calculated if the driver makes an error following the instructions or takes a detour. ■ Maps in the navigation software can be updated from the internet. ■ Journeys can be planned in advance with some navigation software by entering destinations into a website.	**GPS** ■ Blindspots mean that satellites may not be in line of sight (e.g. in a building or tunnel). ■ Atmospheric conditions can affect accuracy. **Satnav** ■ Navigation systems may not have up-to-date maps meaning the driver is given incorrect instructions. ■ Over reliance on satnav might mean people lose map-reading skills, and they might get lost if the system fails. ■ Setting a destination while driving is dangerous. ■ Destinations may not be recognised in the navigation software.

Weather

How weather satellites are used

Satellites can be used to monitor weather patterns across the globe. The most common use of the satellites is to view photographs taken of cloud formations which can then be used to predict the direction of weather fronts. Satellites are also able to collect other information such as snow and ice cover, the effects of pollution, fires, smog, dust, haze and movements of hot and cold water in oceans (known as ocean currents).

How weather satellites work

Weather satellites are either in geostationary orbit (fixed position above the equator) or polar orbiting. Geostationary orbit is similar to geosynchronous orbit in that the satellite is in a fixed position above the Earth, but instead it follows the line of the equator. In Europe, the Meteosat series of satellites are used over the Atlantic and Indian oceans. These geostationary satellites are used by television companies to provide pictures of cloud formations. Polar-orbiting satellites follow an orbit between the two poles of the Earth, from north to south and south to north. They are only 850 km above the Earth compared with 35,000 km for geostationary satellites. Therefore, the photographs provided by polar-orbiting satellites are of a much higher quality. The polar-orbiting satellites use thermal and infrared images that can be used to calculate land and water temperatures by seeing the cloud types and heights.

Advantages	Disadvantages
■ Fires can be monitored in areas such as Australia so that their movement can be determined. ■ Hurricanes can be monitored so that residents are warned in advance. ■ Energy usage can be monitored in terms of lighting used in built-up areas. ■ Sand clouds in the Middle East can be tracked so that people are warned before their arrival.	■ Satellites are expensive to build and to launch. ■ Although most weather forecasting is calculated using scientific methods, these are not always accurate and mistakes are made. ■ Some people are concerned that meteorological satellites that take photographs can be used to monitor the movements of people.

Data transfer

Satellite broadband was first discussed on page 101. However, this is not the only method of data transfer used by satellites. All the satellite applications discussed in this section of the book are transferring data. For example, television signals are data and meteorological photographs are data. All satellites transfer data.

Television

How satellite television is used

Satellite television lets viewers watch more channels than would normally be available using an ordinary aerial. A satellite can broadcast using high bandwidths, so there are hundreds of channels available through satellite.

In the UK, there are two satellite television providers. Sky Digital uses the Astra satellite system to provide both free–to-air television channels and subscription channels. Freesat also uses the Astra satellite system but is only a free-to-air unencrypted service managed by the BBC and ITV.

> **< Activity >**
>
> Look at http://science.nasa.gov/Realtime/jtrack/3d/JTrack3D.html and find the Astra satellites.

Free-to-air channels do not require a subscription and so can be viewed by anybody who has a satellite dish and set-top box. Subscription channels are available to viewers who pay extra to view those channels. These channels include sports, movies, entertainment, music, children's programmes and foreign TV. Viewers can also buy programmes on a pay-per-view basis. This means that the viewer pays to watch a single programme, such as a football game, a concert or a movie.

Set-top boxes let the viewer to see an electronic programme guide so that they can see what is currently being broadcast and what will be broadcast in the near future. Some set-top boxes include a hard disk so that programmes can be recorded simply by selecting them from the electronic programme guide.

How satellite television works

Traditionally, television has been broadcast using powerful aerials that transmit radio waves. The signals are picked up using aerials. There are a number of problems with this system, including the limited number of frequencies available to transmit channels and the need to be in near line of sight with the transmitter on the Earth.

It would probably surprise you to know that satellite television first started broadcasting in the former Soviet Union in 1967. Satellite television companies send television signals from the Earth to a satellite in geosynchronous orbit about 35,000 km above the Earth. The satellites then broadcast the television signal using a method called direct broadcast satellite (DBS). Most DBS systems encrypt the signal that is being sent to the home, so that specialist equipment is required to receive the signal and homes will only receive the channels they have paid for. This signal is also compressed so that more channels can be broadcast using one satellite frequency. A satellite dish is a specialised aerial that receives the microwave signals from the satellite in space. A receiver, more commonly known as a set-top box, is then required to decode and decrypt the signals. The correct decryption key is required to decrypt the signal meaning that viewers can only receive the channels they have subscribed to. The receiver will also decompress the signal and extract the individual channels.

A common misconception is that emailing, shopping and games can be played using satellite communication signals. While these features may be available on some set-top boxes, it is actually a telephone line that is used to send data from the user's home

Figure 3.37 Satellite television system

back to the television company as television satellite dishes are only capable of receiving data.

Advantages	Disadvantages
■ Hundreds of channels are available due to the high bandwidth of satellite communication. ■ Television signals can be received in remote areas where a traditional aerial signal is too weak. ■ Viewers can choose to purchase one-off programmes. ■ Signals are encrypted which enables television companies to charge for specialist channels.	■ Equipment is initially expensive to purchase or a subscription contract has to be purchased. ■ Satellite television channels cannot be fed to multiple rooms unless extra set-top boxes are purchased. ■ Severe weather conditions can affect a satellite signal. ■ A satellite dish is required which can be unsightly on a home.

QUESTIONS

1 Describe **three** features of navigation software.
2 Why will the location on the map be lost when travelling through a tunnel.
3 How can driving be made safer using GPS and navigation software?
4 List **four** types of information about weather that can be collected by satellites.
5 Why are photographs provided by polar-orbiting satellites a much higher quality than those taken from satellites in geostationary orbit?
6 Why are more channels available through satellite television than terrestrial television?
7 List the equipment required to receive satellite television in the home.
8 How are signals broadcast using DBS?

Discuss the implications of being able to communicate from anywhere in the world using mobile technology

For this section, you will need to be able to combine a number of sections from this part of the specification in order to answer questions that may be based on a particular theme. You will need to be able to discuss the following technologies:

■ wireless networks
■ cellular networks
■ satellite communication systems.

You will need to answer a question based on this topic in the context in which the question is asked. For example, the question may be about how a child on holiday can use a mobile phone abroad. Implications can be both positive and negative. When you discuss implications, it is important to look at what the real benefits and real costs are. The example below shows how a question might be answered.

< Example >

Discuss the implications for a child of using a laptop and mobile telephone while on a school trip abroad.

Point to make	Description	Real implication
Children often receive many text messages. These will be received while abroad.	The child can continue to keep in touch with his/her family and friends. It will cost money to receive each text message.	The child may not feel as homesick and therefore enjoy the trip more. The credit available on the phone will soon run out meaning that no more text messages can be sent or received which may leave the child feeling lonely.
Phone calls can be made to parents at home.	The child can talk to his/her parents about his/her feelings. Phone calls using a mobile phone cost a lot of money from foreign countries.	The child may be upset by missing his/her parents and can now share his/her feelings, making him/her happier. The child won't have the real experience of being away from home and may spend too much time talking to his/her parents rather than benefitting from the trip. The child will run up a large phone bill meaning that it will have to be paid for and the child may not have the funds to pay for it on his/her return home.
The child can link its laptop to the mobile phone.	The child can check emails, browse the World Wide Web and chat to friends on instant messaging software.	The child can see what the weather is going to be like the next day to ensure he/she is wearing the appropriate clothing. Data downloads cost a lot of money, particularly abroad and so the child will have to sacrifice something else, such as not being able to buy a memento of the trip.

QUESTIONS

1 Discuss the implications for a manager of a large company being able to communicate with the company while on a business trip to Japan using mobile technology.
2 Discuss the implications of a person sailing around the world being able to communicate using mobile technology with family, friends and their support team.
3 Discuss the implications for army troops in the desert being able to communicate using mobile technology with their commanding officer based at the barracks.

Explain the importance of standards for communicating between devices and explain how protocols are used to enable this communication

Importance of standards

Imagine you are on holiday in Japan and you want to purchase some bread. You ask for the bread in English but the shopkeeper does not understand you. The shopkeeper asks you in Japanese what you would like to buy and you don't understand the shopkeeper. There is no 'standard' method of communication between you. However, if you knew that the shopkeeper spoke French and you could also speak in French, then you could hold a conversation together using French as the 'standard' language.

Physical devices in a network need a method of communicating together. They can't all use their own language as they wouldn't be able to understand each other. Therefore they use a third language known as a protocol. If you purchase a wireless access point from one manufacturer then you would expect it to work with a wireless network interface card from a different manufacturer. This is because a standard is used, such as 802.11g.

Standards also ensure that products meet a minimum specification and set of criteria. Knowing that a product meets that standard gives the consumer confidence in the product. Having universal standards that are not specific to one manufacturer gives consumers the opportunity to purchase from different suppliers and this increases competition within the market.

De jure standards are set by an organisation such as the British Standards Institute (BSI), International Standards Organisation (ISO) or the Institute of Electrical and Electronics Engineers (IEEE). These are formal and deliberately created. *De facto* standards are developed naturally because common practice has become established. Microsoft have developed many *de facto* standards due to their market place dominance. One of these is the use of Windows Live ID as an emerging *de facto* standard for user authentication on the Web.

Protocols

A protocol is a standard method. For example, it is standard protocol to shake somebody's hand when you meet them. Communication protocols are standard methods for communicating electronically. There are too many protocols to describe in any detail but a few common protocols are listed on the next page:

- Transmission control protocol/internet protocol (TCP/IP) – This defines how signals are sent across the internet and enable internet users to communicate with each other.
- Simple mail transfer protocol (SMTP) – This governs the sending of emails so that a device will be able to send successfully an email to another device.
- Point-to-point protocol (PPP) – This sets standards for how two computers that are connected directly to each other should communicate. It is most often used in ADSL connections where a computer needs to connect to an ISP.

< Activity >

Carry out some research to find out about **three** other protocols including what their purpose is.

QUESTIONS

1 Give **two** reasons why standards required within a network?
2 Describe the difference between a *de jure* standard and a *de facto* standard.
3 Define the term protocol in a network context.

Summary

Characteristics of Local Area Networks
- Local geographical area
- Network cards / wireless connectivity
- Dedicated cables owned by company
- Shared peripherals
- Shared software

Characteristics of Wide Area Networks
- Computers are not close together
- External telecommunications
- Physical device needed to connect to WAN

Connecting a LAN and WAN
- Router
- ISP

Virtual Network
- Can be across a LAN or WAN
- Behaves like a single network
- Will have physical connections to computers outside the virtual network
- Cannot see computers outside the virtual network

Internet
- Communication links, e.g. leased lines
- Open Network
- Email
- World Wide Web
- Internet relay chat
- File transfer

Intranet
- Same services as internet
- Only exists on a LAN or company WAN

Extranet
- Secure access to an intranet from outside the LAN or company WAN
- User name and password required

Client-Server Network
- Servers needed to manage
  - File storage
  - Back-up
  - Application sharing
  - Print management
- Clients can access services provided by servers
- Clients log on to server

Peer-to-peer network
- No central server
- Each computer (peer) may offer shared services

Importance of Bandwidth
- Bandwidth measured in bits per second, often megabits per second
- Amount of data that can travel at any one time along a communication link
- Bottlenecks reduce bandwidth available
- Higher bandwidth required for live applications, e.g. video conferencing

Cable
- Co-axial
- UTP
- STP

Fibre-optics
- Reflects light along tiny tubes of flexible glass
- Very high bandwidths

Wireless
- Smaller bandwidths than cable and fibre-optics
- Obstacles reduce bandwidth available

Network components
- Switch
- Hub
- Wireless access point
- Network interface cards
- Wireless network interface cards
- Routers
- Repeaters
- Bridges
- Servers
  - File
  - Applications
  - Mail
  - Proxy
  - Print
  - Back-up

Optical communications
- Infrared
- Fibre optic
- Laser

Wireless communications
- Radio
- Bluetooth ®

Communication applications
    Fax
    Email
    Bulletin (discussion) boards
        Forum
        Thread
        Post
    Tele/video conferencing
    Internet relay chat
Broadband connections
    Asymmetric digital subscriber line
    Cable
    Wireless
    Leased line
    Satellite
    One Way
    Two Way
Cellular Phone Network
    Mobile stations
    Base station receivers
    Mobile switching centre
    Base station controller
    Public switched telephone network

Satellite Phone
    Low earth orbit
    Geosynchronous earth orbit
Satellite communication systems
    Global positioning
    Weather
    Data transfer systems
    Television
Implications of communicating anywhere in the world
    Consider different user groups using:
        Wireless networks
        Cellular networks
        Satellite communication systems
Importance of standards
    Devices need common language to communicate
    De jure standards
    De facto standards
    Protocols

Test 1

St John's Clinic in Walmley uses many forms of communication in their practice. They have had a LAN for a few years now. They have merged with a group of other practices in the Walmley area.

1 Describe **two** items of hardware needed to connect their LAN to a wide area network (WAN) that will be used for all the practices. [4]

2 a) Describe **two** facilities of video conferencing that would be useful for the practices. [4]
   b) Explain the importance of bandwidth when running a video conference. [4]

3 St John's Clinic has used fax for a long time. Explain how the facilities of a fax machine can be used to send a fax from St John's Clinic to another practice. [4]

4 St John's Clinic is quite a large building and it wants to introduce a wireless network to the practice.
   a) Describe the equipment that will be required to create a wireless network. [4]
   b) Describe **two** advantages to the doctors at St John's of using a wireless network. [4]
   c) Describe **two** disadvantages to St John's Clinic of using a wireless network. [4]

The doctors have to visit patients at home. While they are away from the practice, they use a mobile phone.

5 a) Describe the stages involved when Dr O'Brien uses his mobile phone on mobile network *ABC* to call Dr Pinder who has a mobile phone on mobile network *123*. [6]
   b) Describe how the phone call is kept connected as Dr O'Brien drives in his car that has a hands-free kit. [4]
   c) Describe **two** ways in which Dr Pinder might use Bluetooth® on her mobile phone, giving an advantage of each. [4]

St John's Surgery is going to create an internet relay chat (IRC) area for patients to contact the on-call doctor out of hours.

6 Describe **three** facilities available in internet relay chat applications. [3]

Test 2

A school has just received a large amount of money to expand its ICT facilities. It would like to have satellite television installed.

1 Describe how the television signals will be sent by the television company and received by the school.   [6]

The school is considering whether to upgrade its existing ADSL connection to the internet to a leased-line connection.

2 Explain why a leased line would be better for the school.   [6]

Some students regularly go on sailing trips from Portsmouth to Ryde and some students go mountain climbing in Snowdonia.

3 a) Describe how the staff and students could use GPS devices while on these trips?   [4]
   b) Describe **one** advantages to the staff running the trips of using a satellite telephone while on the trips.   [2]

The school is going to develop an intranet.

4 a) Describe the facilities the school could make available on its intranet.   [4]
   b) Describe the purpose of an extranet for the school.   [2]

The school is going to expand its LAN which will include purchasing new network components.

5 a) Compare the roles of a switch and a hub.   [4]
   b) Explain the importance of ensuring the new network components comply with standards.   [4]
   c) Explain how protocols can be used to enable the new network components and applications to communicate with each other.   [4]
   d) Explain why fibre-optic cables will be used between different areas of the school.   [4]
   e) Describe unshielded twisted pair cables which will be used to connect network points in the classrooms.   [4]

The school will be using a client–server network.

6 a) Describe why a peer-to-peer network would be inappropriate.   [6]
   b) Identify how each of the following servers could be used: [3]
      i)   file server
      ii) print server
      iii) proxy server

The school will be installing a bulletin board to its website.

7 a) Describe **three** facilities of bulletin boards.   [3]
   b) Compare the use of a bulletin board with internet relay chat (IRC) for the students to share information about a topic.   [4]

Introduction

Applications of ICT are ways in which ICT can be used. You will learn about many ways in which ICT is used to assist users with tasks and how ICT can be used to train users to complete certain tasks. This chapter covers:

- the limitations of ICT and how networks are used at work and home
- distributed databases (how data can be stored in more than one physical location)
- how expert systems and management information systems can be used to make decisions
- how ICT is used with interactive television
- how ICT is used within businesses and organisations and the ways in which organisations and their systems work.

Describe the use of telecommunication and information technology in telephone systems, banking, production control, global positioning systems, navigation and weather forecasting

Telephone systems

Voice mail

Before voice mail systems, some telephone users had answer machines. These often included a small audio tape that would play a message to the caller if the call went unanswered. The caller would then leave a message and the recipient could play it back when they became available.

Voice mail is much more sophisticated in that it includes a number of different features. These include the ability to:

- delete or store multiple messages
- forward the message to another voice mail inbox, including being able to add an extra message to explain why it has been forwarded
- have different messages depending on whether the phone is engaged, not answered or the user is on holiday

- retrieve the message from another phone by dialling into the voice mail system and using a PIN (personal identification number)
- use voice recognition to have the voice mail forwarded to the user by email either as an attachment or as text.

Voice mail systems can be on a single phone or it could be part of a mobile phone system, or part of a digital phone system within an organisation.

Menus

Menus are set up on digital phone systems within an organisation to provide the caller with a choice of services available. Some people find these frustrating because the menus do not always cover the service the caller wants and they then cannot very easily get to speak to the person they want. Others find the menu system useful because they can quickly select the options required to get through to the service they require. Organisations sometimes use menus so they don't need a receptionist to answer all calls.

An example of a menu system is that used by a school. A caller is offered a number of options, for example, 'Welcome to The Hodder School of Education. If you know the extension number you require, please dial it now. If you wish to report a student absence, please press 1. If you need to speak to the Key Stage 3 office, please press 3. If you need to speak to the Key Stage 4 office, please press 4. To speak to the site manager, please press 5. To speak to ICT services, please press 6. For all other services, please press 0 or hold to speak to the operator.'

Other organisations might have lower levels of menus as well. Figure 4.1 shows an example of how a menu structure might be set up for a delivery company.

Ringback

When a caller makes a telephone call and the recipient is engaged on another call, they may have the option to press a number to request a 'ring back'. When the recipient has finished their telephone call, the telephone of the caller who requested the ring back will ring. When the caller picks up the phone, it will call the recipient who was originally engaged.

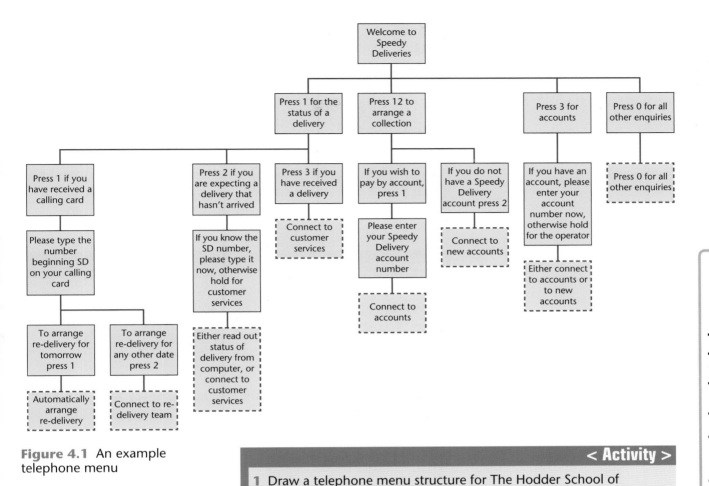

Figure 4.1 An example telephone menu

< Activity >

1 Draw a telephone menu structure for The Hodder School of Education.

2 Design your own menu system with prompts for calling a doctor's surgery.

Videophone

Many mobile phones now include the facility to make videophone calls. This facility also exists on some landline handsets. When making a video call, the caller and recipient can see each other as well as hear each other.

Caller display

When receiving a telephone call, the recipient can look at a display screen to see the number of the person calling. The recipient can then decide whether or not to accept the call. If a set of contact names and numbers has been set up and the caller's number is in the address book, then the recipient will be able to see the name of the caller. Some mobile phones will even give different ring tones based on the person who is calling.

However, some callers withhold their number which means that the recipient will not know who is calling. Many organisations also withhold their number. The recipient then has to decide whether to take the call or not without the knowledge of who is calling. Some phone companies will automatically answer withheld numbers and tell the caller that the recipient will only accept calls from numbers that are not withheld.

Conference call

The vast majority of telephone calls are between two people. However, it is possible to hold conference calls. One person, who is part of the ordinary telephone call, will hold the conversation and dial another number to invite another person to join the conversation.

QUESTIONS

1 Describe **three** facilities of voice mail.
2 Why do organisations use menus to answer the telephone?
3 Give an example of when a conference call might be used.

Banking

ICT is used extensively throughout banking. This book will focus on three uses of ICT in the banking sector: ATMs (automated teller machines), credit/debit cards and cheques.

Automated teller machines

Figure 4.2 A typical ATM

A 'teller' is an alternative term used for bank cashiers (widely used in the USA). Therefore, an ATM (more commonly known as a cash machine) can carry out some of the tasks of bank cashiers. Customers have to insert their cash card into the ATM. Before money can be withdrawn or another service requested, the ATM reads the customer's sort code and account number from the magnetic stripe on the back of the card. The card will be checked to ensure that it has not been reported lost or stolen. The customer is then asked to input their PIN (personal identification number). The ATM will request the customer's bank record from the main database across communication links, and check that the PIN recorded in the database matches the PIN entered by the customer.

Part of the database table may look like this:

< Example >

Sort code	Account number	PIN	Balance	Overdraft agreement
40-12-24	0544781	3290	£250	£0
30-15-23	0234928	4899	– £125	– £500

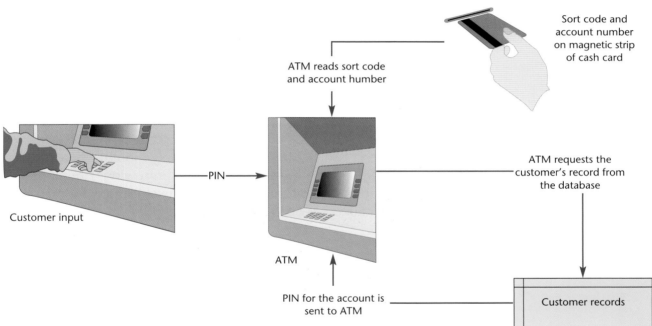

ATM reads sort code and account humber

Sort code and account number on magnetic strip of cash card

PIN

Customer input

ATM requests the customer's record from the database

ATM

PIN for the account is sent to ATM

Customer records

Figure 4.3 Authenticating a cash card at an ATM

If the PIN matches, then the ATM gives the customer access to their account where they can carry out a number of transactions, including:

- withdrawing cash (with or without a receipt)
- requesting a mini-statement
- requesting a balance
- requesting a new cheque book
- changing their PIN
- depositing cheques and cash (in some machines only).

The customer's cash card can be used at any ATM in the world to withdraw money in the currency of that country.

Describe the use of telecommunication and information technology in telephone systems, banking, production control, global positioning systems, navigation and weather forecasting

< Activity >

Design a main menu screen and one other screen for an ATM. You could do this as part of practising requirements analysis and design interviews.

Figure 4.4 A cash card

Credit/debit card

Credit and debit cards are used as part of Electronic Funds Transfer at the Point of Sale (EFTPOS). This means that goods and services can be purchased using credit and debit cards, and funds are transferred from the buyer's account to the vendor's account electronically.

There is a difference between credit and debit cards. When a debit card is used to pay for the goods or services, the money is transferred directly from the buyer's bank account to the vendor's account. If there is not enough money in the buyer's bank account, then the transaction will be refused. With credit cards, the buyer is given a temporary loan by the credit card company to pay for the goods or services. The amount charged is added to the list of other charges the buyer has accrued over time and this contributes to the total amount that the buyer owes to the credit card company. Some credit card holders pay their bill every month, whereas others will pay interest on the money they are borrowing. Figure 4.5 shows part of a credit card statement. The credit from Homebase is where a refund has been made by the vendor.

Transactions

Period ending 11 Dec 2008			
Transaction date	**Transaction description**	**Debits**	**Credits**
09 Dec 2008	TESCO STORE 2933	£20.47	
08 Dec 2008	LAITHWAITES	£56.98	
08 Dec 2008	MY WORD	£11.98	
07 Dec 2008	HOMEBASE LTD 306		£33.93
07 Dec 2008	HOMEBASE LTD 306	£9.78	
05 Dec 2008	TESCO UPT 3953	£57.38	
04 Dec 2008	NORWICH UNION HEAL	£66.12	
03 Dec 2008	ACTIONAID	£60.00	
03 Dec 2008	ACTIONAID	£40.00	
01 Dec 2008	NHS PRESCRIPTION	£27.85	
01 Dec 2008	FOCUS DIY	£19.48	

Figure 4.5 Example of a credit card statement

Customers have a limit on how much they can borrow from the credit card company (e.g. £5,000). If the limit is exceeded, then any further transactions will be denied.

When a credit or debit card is used to pay for goods or services, the computer will also check that the card is not reported as lost or stolen. If it is lost or stolen, then the transaction will be denied. The chip and pin card reader will then read the account number and expiry date from the chip on the credit card (and extra information from the debit card) and the customer will then be asked to enter their PIN to confirm the card belongs to them. If the transaction is taking place over the telephone or online, then a three digit security code is required from the reverse of the card. Below is the card information asked for by Amazon when buying a product.

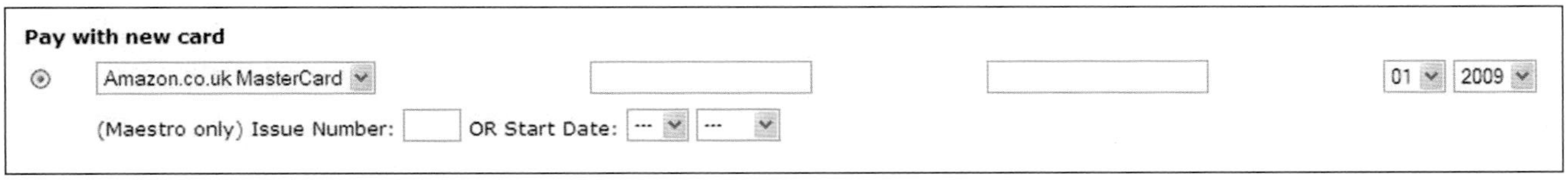

Pay with new card

○ Amazon.co.uk MasterCard ▾ [   ] [   ] 01 ▾ 2009 ▾

(Maestro only) Issue Number: [   ] OR Start Date: ▾ ▾

Figure 4.6 Details required during an Amazon online transaction

> **< Activity >**
>
> 1 Compare the use of a PIN to a signature. Which do you think is more secure and why?
>
> 2 Find out what the extra information required for a debit card is.

Cheques

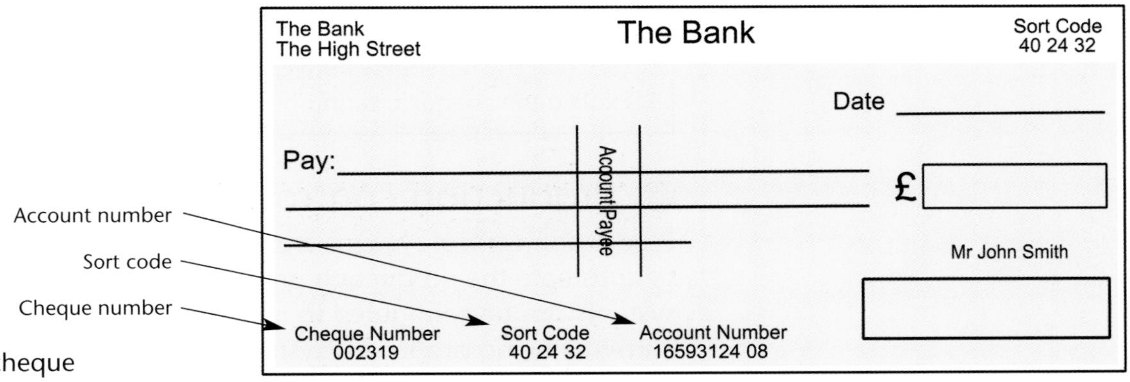

Figure 4.7 A cheque

Cheques may seem quite old fashioned, but they are still used by many retailers who do not want to pay credit and debit card fees. They are also used for sending money in the post. The magnetic ink character recognition (MICR) characters used at the bottom of a cheque are produced using a special magnetic ink and include the following information:

- Cheque number
- Sort code
- Account number.

The sort code identifies the bank and branch. The account number identifies the account within that branch. Together, they unique identify the account. When the cheque number is added to this information, each cheque can be uniquely identified.

When cheques are received by a 'clearing house' they go through an automated clearing process which includes:

- using optical character recognition (OCR) to read the amount of the cheque
- using MICR to read the cheque number, sort code and account number
- sorting the cheques so they are grouped by the originating bank – this is done by knowing the sort code
- recording the transaction (i.e. the amount of money to be taken from the bank account).

< Activity >

1 Find out about the Mondex card from http://www.mondex.org/ and make some notes about what its purpose was and how it was used in the UK.

2 Log on to your own Internet banking service, ask a friend to show you theirs or have a look at the Lloyds TSB demo at http://www.lloydstsb.com/ib_demo/flash/index.html Make a list of all the online banking tasks that can be completed using the Internet.

QUESTIONS

1 Describe **two** transactions that can take place at an ATM.
2 Describe the difference between a credit card and a debit card.
3 Explain the cheque clearing process.

Production control

Production control systems are used in the manufacturing industry to automate the production process. The production control systems can be configured to change their role based on what is currently being produced. Systems vary based on the type of manufacturing and each individual company. Robots are usually used to carry out the actual production.

< Activity >

In small groups, use the World Wide Web to research other production control systems. Present your findings in three to four minutes to your class.

< Example >

One example is Cadbury Trebor Bassett. All of their production lines are fully automated and operate 24 hours a day, seven days a week. Unlike humans, the robots don't get tired working continuously without breaks. Computer Aided Design (CAD) is used to design the chocolate bars and can analyse and predict stress points, including how liquids will behave. Computer Aided Manufacture (CAM) is then used to produce the chocolate bars. An operator will use the production control system to select which chocolate bar is to be made and how many. The production control system will ensure that the correct ingredients are put into each chocolate bar and by the correct amount. A system called *Flow Wrap* is used to wrap about 800 chocolate bars every minute and this is managed by the production control system.

Figure 4.8 *A Flow Wrap* machine

■ Global positioning systems

Global positioning systems (GPS) have become very popular with car satellite navigation systems. These use GPS satellites to identify their location and this is then shown on an interactive map. The navigation software includes instructions that are given to the driver to tell them where they should be going at each junction. The navigation software uses the GPS to identify exactly where the vehicle is, so if a wrong turn is made then the software will recognise this and identify a new route. To start a new journey, a driver needs to input the destination – this is usually selected from a list of favourites, or entered using a postcode or street address and name of town. It's also possible to enter points of interest such as railway stations, airports and city centres. The navigation software then calculates the route by using GPS to determine the current position of the vehicle and then plans a route to the destination. The software is also able to tell the driver how long it will take to reach the destination, the distance left to the destination and what the driver's current speed is. All of this is achieved by the software constantly being told the vehicle's current location by the GPS receiver.

■ Navigation

Navigation can also be achieved using web-based software such as Multimap or Google Maps. The user is asked to enter a starting position and a destination which could be a street name, point of interest or postcode. The user can also include 'via' points, which are places that should be passed as part of the route. The navigation software will then calculate a route and produce a set of directions. Options can be set, such as avoiding motorways, avoiding toll roads, directions for travel by car or directions for walking.

< Example >

The example in Figure 4.9 shows the directions from the Hodder offices to Buckingham Palace. These were obtained by entering the Hodder postcode as the starting point and 'Buckingham Palace' as the destination.

Driving directions to Buckingham Palace
3.3 mi – about 14 mins

(A) Camden, London NW1 3BH
UK

1.	Head **east** on **Diana Pl** toward **Triton Square**	92 ft
2.	Turn **left** at **Triton Square**	292 ft
3.	Turn **left** at **Longford St**	253 ft
4.	Turn **left** at **Osnaburgh St**	0.2 mi
5.	Turn **left** at **A501/Marylebone Rd**	0.9 mi
6.	Slight **left** at **Old Marylebone Rd**	0.2 mi
7.	Turn **left** at **A5/Edgware Rd**	0.5 mi
8.	Turn **left** at **A40/Marble Arch**	299 ft
9.	Turn **right** at **Park Ln**	0.8 mi
10.	At the roundabout, take the **2nd** exit onto **Duke of Wellington Pl**	0.1 mi
11.	Slight **left** at **Constitution Hill** Entering toll zone	0.4 mi
12.	Turn **right**	210 ft
13.	Turn **right**	180 ft

(B) Buckingham Palace
London, SW1A 1

Figure 4.9 Directions using Google Maps

Some navigation software systems allow the users to see what the terrain looks like or even see a bird's-eye view of the route including buildings, traffic lights, fences and paths. Some systems allow the user to see what the traffic is currently like on the route and an alternative route can be chosen to avoid the traffic.

< Activity >

1 Use online navigation software to find the route from your home to school.

2 Look at the options available when requesting a route. List the options that are available, such as 'avoid tolls'.

Weather forecasting

Weather forecasting consists of three main elements: measuring and recording data, modelling a forecast and producing the forecast information.

Measuring and recording data

In order to provide an accurate forecast, it is necessary to record what has recently happened and what is currently happening with the weather. These measurements include:

Figure 4.10 Some weather forecast icons

- satellite images
- temperatures
- moisture in the atmosphere
- humidity
- rainfall
- wind speed
- wind direction
- cloud cover
- atmospheric pressure
- sunshine.

These measurements are taken at hundreds of remote locations around the world at regular time intervals in order to gather as much information about what the weather is and has been doing. Some observation points are based on satellites, others on the ground, others on buoys at sea and some from balloons.

Modelling a forecast

Once meteorologists know what the weather has been doing, they can use complex computer models to predict what the weather will do in the future. The global telecommunication system (GTS) enables weather observations to be passed around the world using high-speed communication links.

Extremely powerful super-computers are required to carry out the modelling process because of the vast amount of data that is needed for forecasting. The computer model will look at all the data and the changes in the atmosphere that have recently been taking place in order to model the likely changes that will happen next. Once a short-term forecast (about 15 minutes) has been made, that data can then be used to produce a new forecast for the next 15 minutes and this process continues to give a longer forecast. In the UK, a six-day forecast can be produced in about an hour. The computer model cannot be relied on completely and so meteorologists are needed to correct any errors that may occur.

Producing a forecast

This is what most people are interested in. They don't want to see what has happened or what is happening now, they want to know what is going to happen with the weather in the future. A weather forecast can be selected by typing in a postcode or town, or by selecting regions from a map. The sorts of information that can be made available include predicted:

- temperatures
- wind speeds
- wind directions
- visibility
- cloud cover
- rain (or snow) fall.

Different types of forecasts can be shown including hour-by-hour, a single day, five-day or ten-day forecasts. The accuracy of the information provided reduces when longer future forecasts are required. Some weather forecasting websites include webcams which show what the current weather conditions are like – these are particularly popular in ski resorts.

< Example >

Figure 4.11 shows an example of an online weather forecast:

Five-day forecast: Sutton Coldfield

Date	Time	Weather	Temp	Wind Dir	Wind Speed	Wind Gust	Visibility
Mon 16 Feb	1500		9°C	WNW	9 mph	20 mph	Moderate
	1800		7°C	NW	7 mph		Moderate
	2100		6°C	NW	9 mph		Moderate
Tue 17 Feb	0000		6°C	WNW	7 mph		Moderate
	0300		6°C	WNW	7 mph	19 mph	Moderate
	0600		6°C	NW	9 mph	22 mph	Moderate
	0900		6°C	NW	12 mph	24 mph	Very Good
	1200		9°C	NW	12 mph	24 mph	Very Good
	1500		9°C	NW	12 mph	25 mph	Very Good
	1800		8°C	NW	10 mph	20 mph	Very Good
	Night		4°C	WNW	9 mph		Poor
Wed 18 Feb	Day		9°C	W	7 mph		Very Good
	Night		2°C	SW	6 mph		Very Good
Thu 19 Feb	Day		8°C	NW	15 mph		Good
	Night		0°C	NW	6 mph		Very Good
Fri 20 Feb	Day		7°C	W	7 mph		Very Good
	Night		5°C	WSW	14 mph		Poor

Last updated: 1301 on Mon 16 Feb 2009

Figure 4.11 Example of an online weather forecast

QUESTIONS

1 Describe the difference between CAD and CAM.
2 Explain how an in-car GPS navigation system differs from a web-based navigation system.
3 Give **three** items of data that might be recorded about the weather.
4 Give **three** different items of data that people may like to know about the weather tomorrow.

Discuss the use of software-based training methods

Figure 4.12 Using software-based training

Computer-based training (CBT) is using the computer to assist with training. This training might be for students, employees or members of an organisation. CBT can range from something as simple as a presentation or set of web pages that the trainee reads through to a complex piece of software that monitors the way in which the student learns and gives feedback to both the trainee and tutor.

A basic training package could be a website whereby the trainee selects options (hyperlinks) to the tasks they wish to learn. However, the website could be made more complex by including videos which show the trainee how something actually works. Sound can be used to read out instructions or give guidance. Pictures can be incorporated to show an item. Imagine how much easier it is to show somebody how to change gear in a car using a video than explaining by just using text. The use of multimedia therefore brings training software alive.

If the training package is to show how to use a piece of software, then video screen captures can be used to explain how to use that software. Words and shapes can be added to the video screen captures to highlight certain parts of the interface.

< Activity >

Have a look at some of the video tutorials at http://www.teach-ict.com/videohome.htm

Quizzes can be built that enable the user to interact. This means that instead of simply being presented with information, the trainee becomes involved, for example by having to answer questions, match words to pictures or match phrases. If your school has the network edition of the Dynamic Learning CD for

133

this text book, then you can see many examples of quizzes being used as Interactive Activities.

Some CBT software includes more advanced features including:

- Log on, whereby each trainee has a user ID and password so that their progress can be recorded. When the trainee returns to the software it will remember where the trainee had got to last time. The trainee can also see which modules they have completed so far.
- Feedback to the trainee so that the trainee knows whether they have answered questions correctly or not. Some systems will make the trainee repeat a training module if not enough questions are answered correctly. The trainee can also see an overview of how they have done for each topic so they can see where their strengths and weaknesses are.
- Pre-assessment, by which some systems ask a number of questions in advance to work out what the trainee already knows so that the trainee only has to learn things they don't know already.
- Feedback to the tutor so that the tutor can monitor the progress that each trainee is making. The tutor can monitor how long each trainee is spending on the CBT software, how many marks each trainee gets for each section and which trainees have or have not completed particular training modules. The tutor can also identify questions which all trainees are finding difficult so that extra teaching can be given on that topic area.
- Target setting that means the trainee sets themselves targets to achieve and the software will determine how long it will take to achieve each of those targets and can therefore create a learning plan for the trainee to follow.
- Assignment setting, where a tutor can set an assignment to a group of trainees. The trainees will then be notified they have been set this assignment and the deadline. When they have completed the assignment they return it to the tutor. Some systems will automatically mark the assignment. The tutor will also be given a summary of who has and has not completed the assignments.

There are a number of advantages and disadvantages to using software-based training methods. Some of these include:

Advantages to the trainee	Disadvantages to the trainee
■ Multimedia methods such as pictures, animations, sounds and videos can be used to give more detailed explanations. ■ Interactive quizzes allow interaction with the software. ■ Can easily return to place reached in course saving them time trying to work out where they had left off. ■ Can monitor their own progress to see how much work they still need to do or where their strengths/weaknesses lie. ■ Can receive feedback on how well they are doing. ■ Can complete pre-assessments so that they can save time by only having to complete the modules they need to. ■ Targets can be set so that the trainee can plan their learning pathway. ■ Assignments can be set so the trainee knows what work has got to be done and when it has to be completed by. ■ Can work at their own pace meaning that they are not held up by slower members of a class or are not left behind when they find tasks more difficult.	■ Self-motivation is needed because there is not always a tutor to monitor their progress. ■ Access to a tutor to ask questions may not be available if they get stuck. ■ If all learning is delivered through CBT, the trainee may find the delivery style monotonous, particularly if they are auditory learners. ■ Possible frustration having to work through modules that they already know about, even if it is to learn just one small thing. ■ May read through the training materials too quickly and not learn the material deeply enough. ■ May leave learning to the last minute if they are not being monitored closely and therefore may miss deadlines.

Advantages to the tutor	Disadvantages to the tutor
■ Does not need to plan or prepare learning materials which saves a lot of time. ■ If assignments are marked automatically then this saves a lot of time, enabling analysis of the results in more detail. ■ Can easily identify students who are not progressing quickly enough or who are struggling, and intervene appropriately. ■ Can identify common areas of weakness so that extra teaching can be given on those topics. ■ Can easily see which students have completed modules and are ready to progress to the next stage or take formal tests. ■ Can easily set assignments for students to complete and will know when they have been completed or not.	■ Has to rely on training materials that somebody else has prepared and has to trust those materials are adequate. ■ Some work cannot be marked by CBT software which means on-screen marking will be necessary and this is quite difficult to do. ■ Has to support trainees who are all learning at different stages and so has to have a lot of topics fresh in their mind at the same time. ■ Needs to be available at all times to support the trainees if they have difficulties because they will be working online at all times of the day. ■ Where the tutor has to assess the work themselves, this can take longer as they will not be assessing the same piece of work for a whole class but will be assessing lots of different pieces of work at the same time.

In an examination, you may be asked to give advantages and disadvantages for a particular group of people, for example the trainers. If this is the case, then do not give advantages such as 'the trainee can receive feedback about their marks' because this is not an advantage to the trainer.

QUESTIONS

1 Explain how multimedia can enhance online training.
2 Explain the advantages to the tutor of feedback within software-based training.
3 Explain the disadvantages to students of not having a tutor available when using software-based training.

Explain the limitations of using ICT in society today and how advances in technology may overcome some of those limitations

This section is asking you to look at two elements of ICT in society. Firstly, you need to consider the limitations of current uses of ICT. This means that a piece of technology exists, but it may not complete the task fully or to the best of its ability. Secondly, you need to look at how new technologies may overcome those limitations. It is impossible to identify all possible limitations of ICT in society and so only some examples are given below.

Limitations of ICT	Potential advances in technology
A laptop can be used for only about three hours when not connected to the mains power supply, meaning that it is not very suitable for camping holidays.	The development of larger solid state storage rather than hard disks will mean less battery power is required in the future. Solar powered cells may be produced that can be integrated into the lid of the laptop to charge the battery. Longer life batteries could be developed in the future.
Watching live television across the Internet is not a very good quality and high definition is not possible due to current bandwidths.	Future developments giving larger bandwidths (e.g. 100 Mbps) to the home may provide the potential for higher quality, and maybe high definition, video to be streamed live across the Internet, although contention ratios may still be an issue as well as the bandwidth available from the broadcaster.
Mobile phone screen size is currently too small to look at web pages effectively because the whole page cannot be seen at once without the font size being too small.	Fold-up screens may be developed in the future meaning that a mobile phone's screen could be folded away and then opened up when needed.
Wireless network signals have difficulty penetrating walls and other structures meaning that some areas of buildings may suffer from poor connectivity.	Developments may take place with wireless networks with frequencies that are easily able to penetrate walls meaning that wireless networks can be extended to cover much larger areas.
Some people find the track pad on a laptop very difficult to use, and many of them do not include the use of a scroll wheel.	Laptops may be developed to include a scroll wheel or similar device. A mini-wireless or Bluetooth® mouse that could be slotted into the side of a laptop might be developed.

Limitations of ICT	Potential advances in technology
Credit cards require the owner to remember a PIN (personal identification number) – this can be problematic if the owner has several PINs and passwords to remember.	Biometric identification may be used in the future which may mean that people need not even carry a credit card because they could simply present their finger or eye and this would uniquely identify them, meaning that authentication and authorisation are completed both at the same time. The person could then choose a method of payment from the virtual cards that they have available.

In an examination, you may be given a scenario where you may have to explain what the limitations of the current technology are and then go on to explain what advances in technology might become available in the future to overcome the limitiations.

QUESTION

Explain the limitations of entertainment systems within cars and how developments in technology may overcome these limitations.

Discuss the use of networks of computers at work and at home

Network technology is explained in Chapter 3. This learning objective is expecting you to be able to discuss the use of networks. Therefore, you need to be able to consider situations in which networks could be used, both at work and at home, and then look at the advantages and disadvantages of using those networks. In an examination, you may be given a scenario that is new to you, but these general principles are likely to be the same. Therefore, the scenarios below are only possible situations in which networks might be used at work or at home.

< Example >

Family with children

Consider a family with three computers. One is used by the father, another is a laptop used by the mother, and the third computer is shared between the two children. The family has a single ADSL connection connected to a wireless router. The father's computer is near the router and so is plugged into the switch part of the router. The laptop is connected wirelessly. A wired connection is needed for the children's computer.

Advantages	Disadvantages
• Only one printer is required because it can be shared by the family. • The family can share an Internet connection so they can communicate with friends and colleagues, and research information for homework. • All the computers can receive security and virus updates via the Internet, increasing the protection from security threats. • The laptop can be used anywhere within the house using a WAP. • The parents can remotely monitor what the children are doing using their own computers.	• Access to the World Wide Web means that the children may access undesirable material or spend too much time playing games rather than working. • The children may spend too much time using instant messaging software through the Internet meaning that there is less family social interaction. • Unless security is set up correctly, the wireless network could be used by other people in the street. • A wired connection for the children's connection could be difficult to install between rooms and the cable could be unsightly.

< Example >

House rented by students

Consider five music students renting a house. Two of them have laptop computers and three have desktop computers. They share a 2 Mbps ADSL connection.

Advantages	Disadvantages
• The students can share the cost of one Internet broadband connection. • The students can work together and collaborate, sharing files that they have produced, such as compositions, across the network. • The students with the laptop computers will be able to move to any part of the house which could be useful if they need to collaborate with another student using both of their computers.	• The students might not be allowed to run network cables through the house because they rent it. • The house might be too large for a single WAP. • If they share a printer, they might not know who has printed which documents. This might cause arguments about who pays for replacement cartridges. • If they connect all the computers through a cabled connection (e.g. in a single room), then there may not be enough ports on the switch/router. • Music students are likely to use a lot of bandwidth to download music, and 2 Mbps shared between five people means they will suffer slow access to files on the Internet.

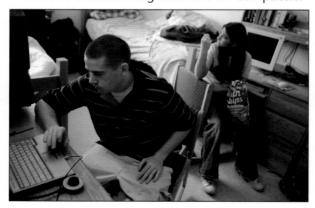

Figure 4.13 Networking scenario 2: student house

< Example >

Small business

Consider a small business that has four desktop computers used by its staff. They have a LAN with an 8 Mbps ADSL router with four switched ports.

Figure 4.14 Networking scenario 3: small business

Advantages	Disadvantages
• The Internet connection can be shared so that all employees can use email to communicate with other organisations.	• The employees may use email and the World Wide Web for social reasons meaning that they are not as productive as they should be.
• A peer-to-peer network can be set up so that files can be shared between employees meaning that they can work collaboratively.	• Confidential files may be viewed by some employees who are not supposed to have access to them.
• A colour printer and laser printer can be shared across the network meaning that each computer will not need its own, saving the business money.	• The computers that the printers are connected to must be always turned on in order for the printers to receive print jobs from other computers. This uses up electricity which adds to running costs.
• All the computers can receive security and virus updates via the Internet, increasing the protection from security threats.	

Discuss the use of networks of computers at work and at home

Large enterprise

Consider a large organisation with over 400 computers using a network with both wireless connectivity for laptops and UTP cabling for desktops. It has a 20 Mbps SDSL leased-line connection to the Internet.

Figure 4.15 Networking scenario 4: large enterprise

Advantages	Disadvantages
• Back-ups can be made centrally meaning that employees are not responsible for their own back-ups, saving the employees time and reducing the risk of lost work. • Software can be deployed automatically to each of the computers saving lots of technician time and thus saving money in terms of salaries. • The computers can be set up to receive security updates and anti-virus updates from a central location on the network meaning that each user is not responsible for ensuring the updates take place. This reduces the risk of attack from hackers and viruses. • Printers can be shared and accounting software installed to manage how much printing each employee is allowed to do or to charge print jobs directly to departments. This will reduce the overhead costs of the company.	• The amount of cabling needed for the organisation will be extensive with several kilometres of UTP cabling used – this will be expensive to install. • A large number of WAPs will be required to cover the whole building as walls will get in the way. This has to be planned carefully to avoid interference from one WAP to another. • Specialist technical staff are required to manage the network which has additional salary costs to the company. • Reliance on the network means that a failure could leave all employees not being able to work productively.

< Activity >

Describe the advantages and disadvantages to a school of networking its computers.

Advantages	Disadvantages

QUESTIONS

1 Identify **two** disadvantages of networking computers in a home.
2 Describe **three** advantages of networking computers in a large organisation.

Explain how databases may be stored in more than one physical location and how distribution may be carried out using different approaches: partitioned between sites (vertical and horizontal), entire databases duplicated at each site, central database with remote local indexes

Data stored in a database is usually stored in one location on one central computer – this is the sort of database you are most likely to be familiar with at school. Distributed databases store the data in more than one location across a LAN or WAN. However, the user is usually unaware of how a database is configured.

Partitioned databases

A partitioned database has different parts of the data stored at different sites. No single site stores all the data: each site only stores part of the data. A 'site' can be a server at a particular location or a single computer.

Horizontal partitioning

Horizontal partitioning means that data is separated across sites based on records.

Explain how databases may be stored in more than one physical location and how distribution may be carried out using different approaches

141

< Example >

The table below represents a distributed database for an estate agency which has three branches in the Midlands:

House ID	House Number	Postcode	Branch
ABC123	12	B73 5PW	Boldmere
DEF456	29	B73 6TW	Boldmere
GHI789	139	B73 4AP	Boldmere
JKL123	22	B76 2LK	Walmley
MNO456	4a	B76 3BA	Walmley
PQR789	10	B76 9BZ	Walmley
STU123	12	B23 3WP	Erdington
VWX456	18	B23 4SD	Erdington
YZA789	79	B23 6PW	Erdington

In this example, the estate agency distributes its database horizontally by storing all the records about houses on sale in Boldmere on the server in the Boldmere branch. Similarly, it stores all the records about houses on sale in Walmley on the server in the Walmley branch, and all the records about houses on sale in Erdington on the server in the Erdington Branch. The database has a structure that looks like this:

HOUSE (Boldmere)	HOUSE (Walmley)	HOUSE (Erdington)
House ID House Number Postcode	**House ID** House Number Postcode	**House ID** House Number Postcode

Figure 4.16 Horizontally partitioned database

If a member of staff in Walmley wants to search for information about a house in Boldmere, then the request for the data is sent from the server in Walmley to the server in Boldmere, and the resulting data is returned to the member of staff in Walmley.

The data is stored like this:

BOLDMERE

House ID	House Number	Postcode	Branch
ABC123	12	B73 5PW	Boldmere
DEF456	29	B73 6TW	Boldmere
GHI789	139	B73 4AP	Boldmere

WALMLEY

House ID	House Number	Postcode	Branch
JKL123	22	B76 2LK	Walmley
MNO456	4a	B76 3BA	Walmley
PQR789	10	B76 9BZ	Walmley

ERDINGTON

House ID	House Number	Postcode	Branch
STU123	12	B23 3WP	Erdington
VWX456	18	B23 4SD	Erdington
YZA789	79	B23 6PW	Erdington

< Activity >

Design a horizontally partitioned database for a college where students studying Social Sciences and Sciences are based at Campus A, students studying English and Humanities are based at Campus B, students studying art subjects are based at Campus C and students studying maths and technology subjects are based at Campus D.

Vertical partitioning

Vertically partitioned data is separated across sites based on fields.

< Example >

The table below represents a distributed database for an estate agency that has three departments. The three departments are concerned with houses, conveyancing and customers.

House ID	House Number	Postcode	Branch	Price	Vendor ID	Surname
ABC123	12	B73 5PW	Boldmere	£285,000	9123	Smith
DEF456	29	B73 6TW	Boldmere	£315,450	2837	Jones
GHI789	139	B73 4AP	Boldmere	£295,000	2891	Brown
JKL123	22	B76 2LK	Walmley	£295,000	3472	Adams
MNO456	4a	B76 3BA	Walmley	£289,999	2987	Burns
PQR789	10	B76 9BZ	Walmley	£304,950	2372	Lloyd
STU123	12	B23 3WP	Erdington	£189,950	3092	Braid
VWX456	18	B23 4SD	Erdington	£210,990	3097	Cooper
YZA789	79	B23 6PW	Erdington	£165,450	2891	Brown

In this example, the estate agency distributes its data vertically by storing all the fields to do with houses (House ID, House Number, Postcode, Branch) at the head office in Sutton Coldfield, all the fields to do with conveyancing (House ID, Price) at the conveyancing office in Boldmere and all the fields to do with vendors (House ID, Vendor ID, Surname) at the customer services office in Walmley. The database has a structure that looks like this:

HOUSE (Sutton Coldfield)	CONVEYANCE (Boldmere)	VENDOR (Walmley)
House ID House Number Postcode Branch	House ID Price	House ID Vendor ID Surname

Figure 4.17 Vertically partitioned database

Explain how databases may be stored in more than one physical location and how distribution may be carried out using different approaches

143

The customer services department is based in Walmley, so each time they want to find information about a vendor, they only have to search the database stored on their own server. If a customer goes to the Walmley branch and wants to find out information about a particular house, then the request for the data is sent from the server in Walmley to the server in Sutton Coldfield and the resulting data is sent back to Walmley.

The data is stored like this:

SUTTON COLDFIELD

House ID	House Number	Postcode	Branch
ABC123	12	B73 5PW	Boldmere
DEF456	29	B73 6TW	Boldmere
GHI789	139	B73 4AP	Boldmere
JKL123	22	B76 2LK	Walmley
MNO456	4a	B76 3BA	Walmley
PQR789	10	B76 9BZ	Walmley
STU123	12	B23 3WP	Erdington
VWX456	18	B23 4SD	Erdington
YZA789	79	B23 6PW	Erdington

BOLDMERE

House ID	Price
ABC123	£285,000
DEF456	£315,450
GHI789	£295,000
JKL123	£295,000
MNO456	£289,999
PQR789	£304,950
STU123	£189,950
VWX456	£210,990
YZA789	£165,450

WALMLEY

House ID	Vendor ID	Surname
ABC123	9123	Smith
DEF456	2837	Jones
GHI789	2891	Brown
JKL123	3472	Adams
MNO456	2987	Burns
PQR789	2372	Lloyd
STU123	3092	Braid
VWX456	3097	Cooper
YZA789	2891	Brown

< Activity >

Replicated databases

Replicated databases are copied in their entirety at each site within the network.

< Example >

In the example below, records about bank accounts are all stored at every branch across the country.

Account number	Surname	Forename	Balance (£)
JKL123	Adams	Frank	– 25
STU123	Braid	David	300
GHI789	Brown	Jonathan	50
YZA789	Brown	Jonathan	10298
MNO456	Burns	Joanne	39
VWX456	Cooper	Martin	250
DEF456	Jones	Michael	2039
PQR789	Lloyd	Susan	258
ABC123	Smith	Wendy	5827

This means that if a customer asks for their balance at a branch in Sunderland, then the information can be found at the server in Sunderland because it has an entire replica of the database. If the same customer asks for their balance at a branch in Newcastle, the information can still be found at the server in Newcastle because another replica is stored in Newcastle.

Central database with remote local indexes

A central database is only stored in one single location.

Explain how databases may be stored in more than one physical location and how distribution may be carried out using different approaches

< Example >

For example, the data for the bank might only be stored at the head office in Durham. However, indexes exist at each site so that the search for data can be speeded up. Instead of sending a request to the head office to search the database, the local site can search its own index which will give the result of the address of the data being searched for. Then the request is sent to head office for the record directly from that address.

LOCAL INDEX IN NEWCASTLE

Account Number	Record Address
ABC123	9
DEF456	7
GHI789	3
JKL123	1
MNO456	5
PQR789	8
STU123	2
VWX456	6
YZA789	4

DATA STORED AT HEAD OFFICE IN DURHAM

Record Address	Account Number	Surname	Forename	Balance (£)
1	JKL123	Adams	Frank	– 25
2	STU123	Braid	David	300
3	GHI789	Brown	Jonathan	50
4	YZA789	Brown	Jonathan	10298
5	MNO456	Burns	Joanne	39
6	VWX456	Cooper	Martin	250
7	DEF456	Jones	Michael	2039
8	PQR789	Lloyd	Susan	258
9	ABC123	Smith	Wendy	5827

A bank clerk in Newcastle requests data for account number PQR789. The index stored in Newcastle is searched and the software is told the record can be found at address position 8. The server in Newcastle sends a request to Durham for the record at address position 8 and that record is sent to Newcastle.

Other indexes may exist at each site too, such as those sorted by surname or postcode.

QUESTIONS

1 Identify **three** methods of distributing databases.
2 Describe how data can be distributed using horizontal partitioning.
3 Describe the difference between horizontal and vertical partitioning.
4 How can local indexes be used with a centralised database?

Discuss the use of different types of distributed database systems

You may be asked in an examination to discuss the use of distributed database systems. This may refer to one particular type (e.g. partitioned) or to distributed databases in general. You will need to consider both the advantages and the disadvantages of each type of distributed database system. Security and updates with regard to data integrity are discussed in the next section of this chapter.

	Partitioned databases	Replicated databases	Centralised databases with local indexes
Storage	Less storage space is required at a central location because the database is partitioned across multiple sites meaning that storage can be utilised from other servers. This increases the overall capacity for storage. However, this does mean that storage must be available at the local servers.	Far more storage space is required because the whole database is stored at each site. This can be very expensive because each server at each site will need to have large capacity hard disks as well as complex setups such as RAID configurations.	Storage is required only in the central location for the centralised database. However, this will need to be high quality storage that is capable of allowing multi-user access to data and therefore will not be cheap. Similarly, very powerful processors will be required for the central server. The local indexes stored at each site will be small because they will only contain the secondary keys and record addresses.
Queries	Local queries for data that are stored at the local site are much quicker than if the query had to be sent to a central server. In the estate agency example used earlier, this means that information about houses in the local area can be found very quickly. However, if information about houses in a different area is needed, then the global query will be slower than the local query because data will need to be sent across various communication links.	All data is stored at the local site so all queries are much quicker than sending requests to a central server. There is no fragmentation because the whole database is replicated at each site, so there is no difference between local and global queries because global queries are performed locally on the replica of the database.	Where a local index exists for data that is searched for, then the query should be quite fast because the processing will be performed on the index at the local site and then the data retrieved directly from its record location at the central site. However, if an index does not exist for the data being searched for, then the query will be performed at the central location which means that processing will be slower because it will have to take its turn with all the other tasks being performed on the central server. The time taken to send the request for data across the external communication link and for the data to be sent back using the external communication link will be slower than local queries.

Partitioned databases	Replicated databases	Centralised databases with local indexes

Data availability

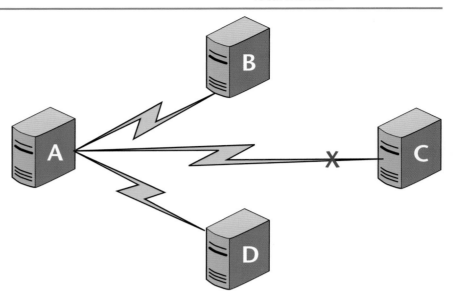

Figure 4.18 Data availability

Imagine data being stored at each of the locations B, C and D in Figure 4.18. If the link between A and C breaks, then C may seem to be isolated. However, C can continue to work locally with its local data whether it be horizontally or vertically fragmented. While it can not get data from B or D, it can still perform local queries which means that the network break down is not a complete disaster. Similarly, sites A, B and D can still access data from all the other sites except site C so the disruption to these sites is lessened.

Each site stores a complete replica of the database, so it can continue to work independently of the rest of the organisation because it can still find data from its own replica. However, it does mean that any updates to the database can be problematic because the updates cannot be distributed to the other replicas while a link is broken. Even when the communication links are available, the data may not be up to date. Updates to data may be carried out every few hours or every few minutes. A balance has to be found between the importance of having up-to-date data and reducing the amount of traffic across communication links. Therefore, a replicated database is not suitable for real-time systems such as for flight bookings where data must always be up to date. However, it is very suitable to a system where immediate updates are not crucial (e.g. in supermarket stock control systems). Each site has its own replica of the database, so more than one user can view the data at the same time.

In a centralised database, all the data is stored at a single site – in this example all the data is stored on server A. If the communication link between C and A breaks down, then site C becomes isolated from the rest of the network and no data can be retrieved at site C. If the server at site A breaks down, then none of the sites in the whole network will be able to access any data.
The data is stored only in one location, so data will always be up to date and there are no potential conflicts which may compromise integrity. This makes this type of database suitable where real-time data is required such as ticket reservation systems.

	Partitioned databases	Replicated databases	Centralised databases with local indexes
Local control	Each site has local control of its data meaning that it can customise the database to its own requirements. However, unless this is done in a controlled manner, it could result in data becoming unavailable or not provided in its correct format to other sites.	Each site has local control of its data as with fragmented systems. Each replica is stored at each site, so it is possible for the replica of the database to be customised, including adding extra fields or tables that are useful to the local site.	The database is stored centrally and managed centrally, so no other sites have any control over the configuration of the database. This can be an advantage because it means that the database configuration is maintained and therefore its integrity is maintained, but it also means that local sites cannot customise the database to their own needs.
Database design	The design of the partitioned database is very complex and requires highly trained specialists to create and maintain the database structure.	Similar to partitioned databases, although the design issues are different in nature.	The design of a centralised database is quite straightforward because it follows normal relational database design. The only complex parts are the local indexes that need to be stored at the local sites, but these are no more complex than local indexes for a relational database.
Back-ups	The data is partitioned to several sites, so back-ups cannot be taken centrally. Therefore a back-up system needs to be in place at all sites and this must be managed at each site too, including detail such as swapping tapes, storing tapes off-site and testing that back-ups have worked by attempting test restores.	Each replica acts as a natural back-up to the database because there are various copies replicated throughout the system. Therefore, back-ups are not necessary at each site. However, back-ups do still need to be taken at least at one of the sites in case data becomes corrupted across the whole system and the database might need restoring to a previous time.	The data is stored only in one central location, so it is essential that a fail-safe back-up system is created that includes: ■ changing tapes daily ■ tape rotations so that data can be recalled from several weeks ago ■ off-site storage of back-up tapes ■ daily testing that back-ups can be restored.

< Activity >

Fill in the table below:

Distributed database	Advantages	Disadvantages
Fragmented		
Replicated		
Central with local indexes		

Discuss the use of different types of distributed database systems

Explain security issues of distributed databases: interception of data, physical access to data, consistency and integrity of data and describe methods of overcoming these issues

As with databases stored at a single location, it is important to ensure that data within a distributed database system is kept secure from hackers.

Interception of data

With fragmented and central databases with local indexes, there is a lot of data moving around communication links between sites which increases the risk of interception of data. Therefore, high quality encryption techniques are required.

Replicated databases do not involve as much data movement between sites, although there are still updates that are required.

Physical access to data

With fragmented and replicated databases, each site stores data and therefore security to prevent unauthorised access must be in place at every single site, resulting in an increase in security costs that include:

- physical security
- user-level security
- anti-virus software
- firewall
- anti-spyware software
- encryption.

With central databases with local indexes, the index does not store information of any value and therefore the security listed above only needs to be at the central site.

Consistency and integrity of data

Centralised with local indexes

With a centralised database with local indexes, all the data is stored in one single place and updated in one single place. The only changes that occur at the local sites are the updates of the indexes which are fairly straightforward to perform and can be done at regular intervals.

Vertically partitioned databases

With vertically partitioned databases, sets of fields are kept in their entirety at a site. The data is linked to other fields through a common primary key. If the primary key is changed at one site, then it is essential to ensure that the primary key is also changed at other sites. Imagine the scenario below:

< Example >

The House ID PQR789 needs to be changed to PQP789. It is changed at Sutton Coldfield:

SUTTON COLDFIELD

House ID	House Number	Postcode	Branch
ABC123	12	B73 5PW	Boldmere
DEF456	29	B73 6TW	Boldmere
GHI789	139	B73 4AP	Boldmere
JKL123	22	B76 2LK	Walmley
MNO456	4a	B76 3BA	Walmley
PQP789	10	B76 9BZ	Walmley
STU123	12	B23 3WP	Erdington
VWX456	18	B23 4SD	Erdington
YZA789	79	B23 6PW	Erdington

The vendor has agreed to drop the price of the same house to £299,950. This change is made in Boldmere and there is no problem.

BOLDMERE

House ID	Price
ABC123	£285,000
DEF456	£315,450
GHI789	£295,000
JKL123	£295,000
MNO456	£289,999
PQR789	£299,950
STU123	£189,950
VWX456	£210,990
YZA789	£165,450

Explain security issues of distributed databases: interception of data, physical access to data, consistency and integrity of data and describe methods of overcoming these issues

WALMLEY

House ID	Vendor ID	Surname
ABC123	9123	Smith
DEF456	2837	Jones
GHI789	2891	Brown
JKL123	3472	Adams
MNO456	2987	Burns
PQR789	2372	Lloyd
STU123	3092	Braid
VWX456	3097	Cooper
YZA789	2891	Brown

A customer goes to the Boldmere branch and asks for the price of property PQR789. They are told it is £299,950. They then ask for the address so they can go and see it. The Boldmere branch server sends a request to the Sutton Coldfield branch for the details of house PQR789. The Sutton Coldfield branch returns an error stating that the house could not be found.

This error has occurred because when the primary key was updated in Sutton Coldfield, the change was not made at Boldmere or Walmley meaning that the integrity (truthfulness and correctness) of the data was compromised. It is therefore necessary that any changes to the primary key in one fragmented part of the database are also made to the other fragmented parts of the database.

Horizontally partitioned databases

With horizontally fragmented databases, each record is kept in its entirety at a single site and therefore it is only updated at that one site. There are no potential conflicts with the data being updated elsewhere.

Replicated databases

This is where there is most potential for the integrity of the data to be compromised. Imagine the following scenario where there are two replicas of the database. In reality there would be more, but for the purposes of this example, only two are used.

< Example >

REPLICA A IN DURHAM

Account Number	Surname	Forename	Balance (£)
JKL123	Adams	Frank	− 25
STU123	Braid	David	50
GHI789	Brown	Jonathan	50
YZA789	Brown	Jonathan	10298
MNO456	Burns	Joanne	39
VWX456	Cooper	Martin	250
DEF456	Jones	Michael	2039
PQR789	Lloyd	Susan	258
ABC123	Smith	Wendy	5827

REPLICA B IN NEWCASTLE

Account Number	Surname	Forename	Balance (£)
JKL123	Adams	Frank	− 25
STU123	Braid	David	2,800
GHI789	Brown	Jonathan	50
YZA789	Brown	Jonathan	10298
MNO456	Burns	Joanne	39
VWX456	Cooper	Martin	250
DEF456	Jones	Michael	2039
PQR789	Lloyd	Susan	258
ABC123	Smith	Wendy	5827

David Braid started the day with £300.

David Braid withdraws £250 from his bank account in Durham. The balance therefore changes from £300 to £50 in Durham.

Replica B is now out of date and thus the integrity of the data has been lost.

David's salary of £2,500 is then paid in to his account in Newcastle giving him a balance of £2,800.

David needs to withdraw another £250 from Durham but he has no overdraft limit. Therefore, he is told he cannot withdraw the money. He knows his salary has been paid in so he cannot understand what has gone wrong.

Explain security issues of distributed databases: interception of data, physical access to data, consistency and integrity of data and describe methods of overcoming these issues

In order to resolve the inconsistency issue, updates need to take place regularly between the replicas. Let's imagine these take place every four hours. We can see what might happen below:

REPLICA A IN DURHAM

Account Number	Surname	Forename	Balance (£)
JKL123	Adams	Frank	– 25
STU123	Braid	David	300
GHI789	Brown	Jonathan	50
YZA789	Brown	Jonathan	10298
MNO456	Oakley	Joanne	39
VWX456	Cooper	Martin	250
DEF456	Jones	Michael	2039
PQR789	Lloyd	Susan	558
ABC123	Smith	Wendy	5827

REPLICA B IN NEWCASTLE

Account Number	Surname	Forename	Balance (£)
JKL123	Adams	Frank	– 25
STU123	Braid	David	2,800
GHI789	Brown	Jonathan	50
YZA789	Brown	Jonathan	10298
MNO456	Burns	Joanne	39
VWX456	Cooper	Martin	250
DEF456	Jones	Michael	2039
PQR789	Lloyd	Susan	158
ABC123	Smith	Wendy	5827

Susan Lloyd started the day with £258.

Susan deposits a cheque for £300 in Durham at 1 pm giving her a new balance of £558.

While she is out shopping in Newcastle, she realises she has no cash, so withdraws £100 from the cash machine. It only took here two hours to get to Newcastle and so no updates have taken place yet. Therefore, according to Newcastle her balance is £158.

Newcastle sends its updates across the network first. Durham therefore receives the following updated data:

REPLICA A IN DURHAM

Account Number	Surname	Forename	Balance (£)
PQR789	Lloyd	Susan	158

Now Durham sends its updates across the network. Newcastle therefore receives the following updated data:

REPLICA B IN NEWCASTLE

Account Number	Surname	Forename	Balance (£)
MNO456	Oakley	Joanne	39
PQR789	Lloyd	Susan	558

Joanne is OK because her name was only changed once. Susan is happy because she started with £258, deposited £300 (£558 so far) and withdrew £100 and so should only have £458. But the bank have lost £100 because the update from Newcastle to Durham was replaced by the update from Durham to Newcastle and therefore lost.

< Activity >

Martin Cooper starts the day with £250. He withdraws £50 from Durham and £100 from Newcastle. Assuming the update takes place from Durham to Newcastle first, identify what Martin's balance should be and what it will actually be due to the problem with updates. Explain how the problem occurs.

The distributed database management system (DDBMS) needs to be able to resolve these conflicts. It can do this by recording sending out transactions to the data rather than the results of changes to the data. If this had happened, then the following updates would have been sent:

Explain security issues of distributed databases: interception of data, physical access to data, consistency and integrity of data and describe methods of overcoming these issues

< Example >

Newcastle sends its transactions across the network first. Durham therefore receives the following transactions:

REPLICA A IN DURHAM

Account Number	Surname	Forename	Balance (£)
PQR789			– 100

Durham therefore updates its database replica to show:

Account Number	Surname	Forename	Balance (£)
PQR789	Lloyd	Susan	(558 – 100 =) 458

Durham then sends its transactions across the network. Newcastle therefore receives the following transactions:

REPLICA B IN NEWCASTLE

Account Number	Surname	Forename	Balance (£)
MNO456	(Change to) Oakley		
PQR789			+300

Newcastle therefore updates its database replica to show:

Account Number	Surname	Forename	Balance (£)
MNO456	Oakley	Joanne	39
PQR789	Lloyd	Susan	(158 + 300 =) 458

< Activity >

Frank Adams starts the day with an overdraft of £50. He gets paid £250 from his employer in Durham and withdraws £200 from Newcastle. Assuming the update takes place from Durham to Newcastle first, identify what Martin's balance should be and explain how transaction updates ensure that his balance is correct.

QUESTIONS

1 Describe **three** security implications of using distributed databases.
2 Why is encryption required with fragmented databases?
3 Describe how the integrity of data might be compromised within a replicated database system.
4 Describe how the integrity of data could be maintained within a replicated database system.

Explain what is meant by an expert system and describe its components and applications

■ What is an expert system?

An expert system, also known as a knowledge-based system (KBS) is a computer program made up of knowledge and rules that can be used to diagnose a problem. Expert systems are used for decision making and recommending particular courses of action. The system will try to replicate the role of the human expert.

It is called an expert system because the knowledge and rules are all defined by experts in a particular field. A popular expert system is that used by NHS Direct on their website. Experts (doctors) will have collated their knowledge about illnesses and the symptoms of those illnesses and identified the rules that state which symptoms suggest which illnesses.

A true expert system will:

- be able to make decisions based on uncertain data (e.g. 'don't know' answers from a user)
- be limited to a particular subject or area of expertise
- give advice based on the answers given by the user
- explain the reasoning behind its decision.

Figure 4.19 Expert

< Activity >

Go to Printers and Faxes on your computer (if you use Windows). Select a printer and click File on the menu bar, then Properties. Click Print Test Page. When asked if the page printed, answer 'Troubleshoot...'. Make up a problem and answer the questions. Eventually you will be given a diagnosis. This is a basic expert system.

■ Components of an expert system

There are three main components in an expert system: a knowledge base, an inference engine, and the user interface.

Knowledge base

The knowledge base consists of the factual knowledge and the rules gathered by knowledge engineers using methods such as interviewing experts.

Examples of knowledge are:

- the VAT rate is 15%
- a mobile phone needs a battery or power lead to work
- a human has two hands.

Examples of rules are:

■ if the product is food, then VAT should not be applied
■ if the battery not inserted, the phone will not turn on
■ if the phone is plugged in, the phone should turn on
■ if a patient has a cut on their hand and the bleeding can be controlled by putting a finger on the cut, then antiseptic cream and a plaster should be used.

Inference engine

The inference engine is the software that makes the decisions based on the answers given by the user and the knowledge and rules stored in the knowledge base. It will also decide which questions the user should be asked next based on the previous answers given. If the answers given by the user are uncertain, the inference engine will ask other questions to try to eliminate possible diagnoses. It will then identify a diagnosis and give a reason for the diagnosis. At a basic level, an inference engine uses a decision tree that might look like this:

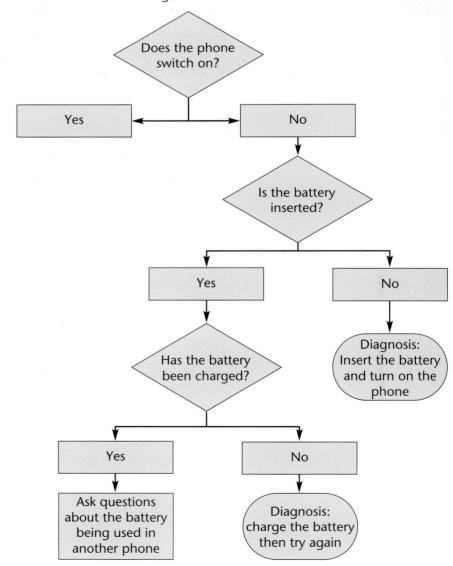

Figure 4.20 Example of a decision tree

Expand on the decision tree by asking questions about the battery being used in another phone and see if you can get to a diagnosis as to whether it is the handset or the battery that is faulty.

User interface

The user interface is the part of the expert system that asks the user the questions and then gives an answer with a diagnosis.

Figure 4.21 shows part of the print troubleshooter in Microsoft Windows. You can see how instructions are given and then questions are asked as part of the user interface.

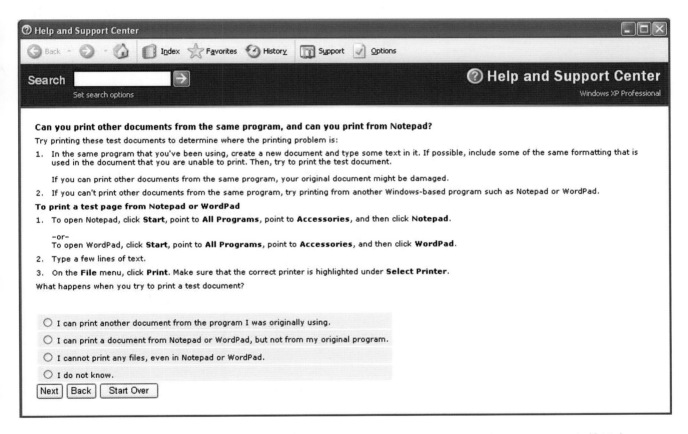

Figure 4.21 Microsoft Windows Help and Support Center

Figure 4.22 shows the user interface of NHS Direct Self-Help where questions are being asked about the type of cough that an adult has.

Once the user interface has asked all the questions and used the inference engine to determine the diagnosis, a result is given to the user. Figure 4.23 shows part of the diagnosis given by the NHS Direct Self-Help system.

Please select an answer

Are you:

- experiencing a severe pain in your chest, upper back, shoulder, arm or jaw,
- so short of breath that you are unable to talk in sentences, or
- turning blue or pale around your lips or at your nail beds?

 YES NO

Please select an answer

Are you struggling to dislodge a piece of food, or another object that is caught in your throat?

 YES NO

Please select an answer

Have you recently breathed in smoke or chemical fumes, for example from:

- any household cleaning products,
- glue or paint,
- hairspray or deodorant spray cans,
- petrol or car exhausts,

Figure 4.22 NHS Direct Self-Help questions

It is safe to manage this problem yourself at home.

These symptoms suggest you have flu.

Most people with flu do not need to see a doctor, as flu is usually a 'self-limiting' infection. This means that the body normally fights off the infection without medical treatment. The symptoms of flu usually clear within 4-10 days.

However, you should call **NHS Direct** on **0845 4647** if:

- you are elderly or frail and your symptoms are severe, or they do not improve within 48 hours,
- you have a child over 6 with flu and their symptoms are severe, or their symptoms do not improve within 48 hours (if you have a child under 6 with flu, see our Fever in children self-help guide), or
- you feel breathless, you have a stiff neck that is painful when you bend your head forwards, or light hurts your eyes.

You can manage flu symptoms using the following self-care advice:

- Take simple painkillers such as paracetamol (for children use children's liquid paracetamol, available from your local pharmacist. Read our information on Can I give my child painkillers?). If you have a high temperature this will help to bring it down. Always follow the manufacturer's instructions for the correct dose. If you are pregnant, you should only take paracetamol as instructed by your GP or midwife.
- Make sure you drink enough fluid to keep yourself hydrated — water is best. This is particularly important if you have a high temperature. Also, warm drinks can be soothing.

Figure 4.23 NHS Direct Self-Help diagnosis

Applications of expert systems

So far, you have seen three uses of expert systems which are:

- medical diagnosis
- mobile phone fault diagnosis
- printer troubleshooting.

Here are some other examples of how expert systems might be used:

- Fault diagnosis for a car engine – a car mechanic can plug in a laptop computer into the engine management system and it will run various tests. Based on the results of the tests, it will identify what the fault is with the engine. During the tests, the mechanic may be asked certain questions about sounds and emissions.
- Broadband Internet service provider (ISP) fault diagnosis – when you phone up your ISP to report a fault, the operator is likely to be using an expert system. The operator will ask the questions that the expert system tells them to ask you and will input the answers you give. The expert system will then suggest possible solutions that could be tried out. The results of all the tests will be stored and a diagnosis of the fault will be given if a solution is not found.
- Social services can use expert systems to determine what benefits are due to a claimant. All the answers that the claimant puts on the forms are input into a computer and the expert system will then determine the benefits that are due and will give a reason why those benefits apply.
- Her Majesty's Revenue and Customs expect some tax payers to file a 'tax return'. The tax payer answers lots of questions using an online form. The inference engine will then determine which taxes are due based on the answers given and calculate the amount of tax due. The user interface will then respond to the tax payer by explaining how the tax was worked out.

QUESTIONS

1 Identify the **three** components of an expert system.
2 Describe the purpose of each of the components of an expert system.
3 Give an example of knowledge and of a rule for somebody claiming income support (the knowledge and rule do not have to be real).
4 Describe **two** things that an expert system should be able to do.

Describe how the following ICT tools can be used to assist decision making: management information systems (MIS) and expert systems

■ Management information systems (MIS)

A management information system (MIS) is designed to organise information within an organisation in such a way that it can be used to produce useful information to the management of the organisation. Managers don't need to see all of the data that exists within an organisation, but will need to see summaries of data in the form of charts and reports.

A MIS organises data and creates links between sets of data that are inter-related. For example, your attendance at school might be unrelated to your attendance at lessons. An MIS can anlayse this data and produce summaries of which students were in school but did not attend a lesson.

A common misconception is to think that a MIS is solely computer based. A MIS needs a human information manager to ensure that the right type of data is collected in order to produce the information that managers require. The information manager will also produce standard reports that can be used by managers to see summaries of the information. Managers at different levels within an organisation need different types of information and it is important that a MIS can provide information that is useful to all levels of management.

Management information systems can provide information that will help managers with tasks such as:

- monitoring budgets to see how actual expenditure is comparing with planned expenditure
- identifying trends in sales for different products and at different times of the year
- gathering intelligence about other organisations
- identifying information about demographics and the types of customers that buy the products
- monitoring cash flows within the organisation
- analysing the effectiveness of a market campaign (e.g. did sales go up during the marketing campaign?)
- monitoring labour input into the production process and overall productivity per employee.

< Activity >

Find out what sort of data is collected by your school's MIS and what sort of information is used by managers and leaders within your school.

Information is only useful if it is then used to make decisions. An MIS provides information that can then be used to decide on appropriate courses of action based on the information provided. The MIS does not make the decisions itself – it just provides the information. It is then up to managers to make the decisions. Information reports can be produced at regular intervals so that managers can decide how to react to the current information, or managers can request unscheduled reports when they feel that there may be a problem that needs solving.

Given the following examples of information provided by a MIS, here are some types of decisions that might be made by managers.

< Example >

Information provided by MIS	Decision to be made
The marketing department has already spent 90% of its budget in September.	Senior management need to ensure that the marketing department cut down on expenditure as there are another six months of the financial year left to go. Plans need to be put in to place to ensure value for money is being achieved by the marketing department.
More nappies are being sold during April and May than other months and there was a shortage towards the end of May.	Production managers need to decide whether to increase production of these during next year in time for April and May. Marketing managers need to decide whether to repeat marketing campaigns that took place during those months.
Babies' dummies produced by a competitor have been selling for 80% of the price of the company's own dummies but are of a similar quality. Sales of dummies have not changed.	Sales managers need to decide whether to maintain or reduce prices as it seems the competitor's lower price is not having an effect. They will probably request further reports over the next couple of months to monitor the situation more closely.
The number of children born in Somerset increased by 20% during 2008.	Production managers need to consider increasing the amount of products that are produced for children of these ages in the area over the next few years.
The amount of money available in the company's current account has dropped from £384,000 to £1,500 in the last two months.	Finance managers need to consider whether the current account needs extra funds to avoid it going overdrawn and interest being charged. They also need to consider how a smaller deviation in funds could be maintained.
A marketing campaign for the company's brand name took place during June and July. A 1.5% increase in sales was noticed during July, 2% in August and 0% in September.	The marketing managers need to compare the cost of the marketing campaign with the increased profits due to the increases in sales. Consideration then needs to be made as to whether or not to repeat the marketing campaign.
Employees in the dummy assembly department have been making dummies at the rate of 25 per hour on average. One employee has only been making 10 dummies per hour.	The production manager needs to consider re-training the employee, or whether to terminate their employment.

■ Expert systems

Expert systems contain expert knowledge and rules so questions can be asked and a solution with reasoning suggested. This enables decisions to be made. Hypothetical questions can be asked and the expert system will give answers as to what the likely outcome will be. This is effectively modelling 'what if?' questions simulating the effect of the data and responding with a diagnosis or solution based on that scenario.

Some examples of how an expert system could be used to make decisions include:

< Example >

Scenarios	Decisions to be made
Answering questions about the type of person you are, what you like doing and what you are good at. The expert system suggests a future career.	You decide whether to follow that future career, or try putting in other information such as different things that you like doing.
Entering suggested prices for a product, quantities that can be produced and information about the local demographics. The expert system suggests how many products are likely to be sold.	How many products to make and what price to sell for. Different production quantities and selling prices can be experimented with.
A gas engineer enters symptoms regarding a gas leak at a house. The expert system suggests what might be causing the leak.	The gas engineer has to decide how to fix the problem based on the suggestion given.

The difference between expert systems and management information systems when it comes to decision making is that management information systems provide the information and the manager must make the decision, whereas an expert system suggests what the decision (solution) might be.

< Activity >

Consider the NHS Direct Self-Help guide introduced earlier in the chapter. How might this be used by a patient for decision making?

■ Reliability of data

When using an expert system or MIS to make decisions, the decision is based on the information provided by the expert system or MIS which in turn is based on the data stored in the expert system or MIS. If the data is out of date, incorrect or unreliable, then the information provided to make the decisions will also be unreliable meaning that the decision made as a result of the information provided could be misguided. The data in an expert system is only as good as the experts who provide the data.

Revise what you studied at AS Level about the quality of information and discuss the effect this would have on decision making using an expert system or MIS.

QUESTIONS

1 Describe how a management information system (MIS) might be used to help a construction company decide whether to build a new block of flats.

2 Describe how an expert system might be used to help a construction company decide whether to build a new block of flats.

Discuss the range of services offered by digital television networks and the impact of these services on individuals, television companies and broadcasters

When answering questions linked to this learning objective, you will need to consider the impact to a specific group. Individuals are the viewers that watch programmes and use services on digital television networks. Broadcasters are the companies that distribute the programmes, such as cable TV broadcasters (e.g. Virgin), satellite TV broadcasters (e.g. Sky) and radio waves broadcasters (e.g. Freeview). Television companies are the organisations that make the programmes and own the TV channels (e.g. Channel 5).

■ Pay per view

This is a facility whereby viewers can pay to watch a particular programme. These programmes are usually sporting events or movies but can include other special events or programmes. The viewer can book the programme in advance or at the time of viewing and will then be charged on their next bill.

Impact

Individuals	Television companies	Broadcasters
■ Viewers will have to pay for each programme that they watch and may build up a large bill without realising the potential total cost. ■ Viewers can watch individual events, such as a football game, without paying the full subscription price for a channel such as a sports channel. ■ Some programmes such as films can be watched at any time rather than specified start times meaning that the viewer can arrange their viewing around their life rather than the other way around.	■ The television companies may receive extra income by allowing customers to buy a particular event or programme. ■ The television companies may lose out on revenue for their subscription channels as customers will only buy the programmes they are interested in rather than a whole package of channels.	■ Broadcasters have got to make the facility for 'pay per view' available which could be costly. ■ Broadcasters have got to have a facility whereby payments can be made for 'pay per view' programmes. ■ Broadcasters have got to put encryption and other security in place to ensure that the programmes cannot be hacked. ■ A high bandwidth is required, particularly if viewers are allowed to watch a programme at any start time rather than a specified start time.

■ Voting

This feature allows viewers to vote as part of participating in a television programme. This could include voting for their favourite performer in a competition, voting for somebody to be removed from a reality television show, or voting for their preferred ending to a television programme. The voting facility can be made available in different ways:

■ Dialling a telephone number or sending a text message
■ Using a website
■ Using the interactive feature of the set-top box.

Impact

Individuals	Television companies	Broadcasters
■ The telephone numbers and text message numbers are often premium rate numbers which can be very expensive for the viewer. ■ The viewer feels like they are participating in the programme and are able to have an influence on an outcome. ■ If the viewer's vote is not part of the winning vote, then the viewer could be very frustrated by the outcome.	■ Using premium rate numbers will significantly boost revenue for the programme makers – imagine two million people voting at £1 per vote. ■ If viewers are voting for a preferred ending to a television programme, then either two endings need to be produced and recorded, or a live performance needs to take place. ■ The television company is at the complete mercy of the voting viewers who may not be the majority of the viewers. This means that an unpopular decision may be made.	■ If the interactive feature of the set-top box is being used, then the broadcaster will have to make this facility available which could be costly to implement; for satellite and radio wave broadcasters this will also involve the need for a telephone line to send back the viewer responses.

■ Game show participation

Some game shows allow viewers to take part by answering the questions along with contestants. This can be achieved either by the viewer answering the questions using the Internet or by using multiple-choice options with the remote control for the set-top box.

Impact

Individuals	Television companies	Broadcasters
■ The viewers feel part of the game show and will be more interested as they are participating. ■ It can be very frustrating if the viewer has answered lots of questions and then the wrong button is pressed meaning all the answers are lost.	■ If this is popular with the viewers then the television companies are likely to receive more revenue from advertisers if there are more viewers. ■ The television companies have got to set up the facility to receive viewers' answers and to give feedback which could be costly.	■ If the digital set-top box is used for answering the questions, then the broadcasters have got to ensure the facility is available which could be costly; for satellite and radio wave broadcasters this will also involve the need for a telephone line to send back the viewer responses.

■ Choosing camera angles

Some programmes allow the viewers to choose which camera angles they want to watch or which games they want to watch for a sporting event. For example, in a reality TV show, viewers could choose to watch a particular room within a house or for a football game, viewers could choose to watch a bird's-eye view, a particular player or the director's cut. For sporting events such as Wimbledon, viewers could choose which match they want to watch.

Impact

Individuals	Television companies	Broadcasters
■ Viewers get a choice meaning that they do not have to rely on the director to show them the best parts of a programme – they can choose the parts they prefer to watch. ■ Viewers may miss something exciting within a television programme if they are watching a particular picture and the exciting event happens on a different camera angle. ■ The viewer can choose to watch replays of parts of sporting events, such as tries in a rugby match, meaning that if they missed them, they can choose the replay viewing option.	■ The television companies have got to ensure that all the camera operators involved are constantly shooting a good picture as the director cannot switch to a different camera if the viewer has chosen a particular camera. ■ If this is popular with the viewers, then more viewers will subscribe to the channel increasing revenue and more advertising revenue will raised. ■ In live programmes, the television company has got to ensure that all content being shown from all cameras is appropriate rather than just the director's cut. For example, if a streaker was to run across a cricket pitch then this might need to be blocked meaning that more moderators are required.	■ Normally the broadcaster would only broadcast the director's cut (i.e. the final programme), but more bandwidth will be required to broadcast the extra camera pictures. ■ Broadcasters have got to ensure that advertisements are all shown at the same time, whichever camera picture is being watched.

Feedback comments to TV studio

Viewers can interact with a television programme by feeding back comments on live shows. The viewer can send a text message and it may be shown scrolling along the screen. Viewers may be able to phone in to the show and their comments may be read out or they may be able to talk themselves on the show. Emails can also be sent which may be read out. Set-top boxes could be used by the viewer to send a comment to the TV studio if the facility is available.

Impact

Individuals	Television companies	Broadcasters
■ The telephone numbers and text message numbers are often premium rate numbers which can be very expensive for the viewer. ■ Viewers may have a very strong opinion on a topic and will feel relieved if they can share this opinion with other viewers. ■ There are likely to be lots of viewers feeding back and so most viewers will be frustrated that their comment has not been included in the programme.	■ The television companies will need to moderate any messages that are sent in to ensure that they are not offensive or libellous. ■ Thousands of comments may be received and it may be very difficult to find the best comments to include on the programme. ■ In documentary-style programmes, the programme makers are less likely to be accused of bias if they include a variety of opinions from viewers.	■ If the interactive feature of the set-top box is being used, then the broadcaster will have to make this facility available which could be costly to implement; for satellite and radio wave broadcasters this will also involve the need for a telephone line to send back the viewer responses.

Interactive recording and live pause

The viewer can pause live TV using some digital set-top boxes. This means that the set-top box immediately starts to record the programme on a hard disk and when the viewer resumes watching the programme, the programme is played back from the disk rather than live while the live programme continues to be recorded. Viewers can also record television programmes for later viewing. The recorder can either be set to record manually when the programme starts, or an electronic programme guide (EPG) can be used to select programmes to record in advance. Some EPGs allow viewers to set a 'series link' which means that all programmes in the television series will be recorded without having to select each one individually. The EPG will usually include a schedule for at least seven days in advance and programmes on the screen in a tabular format with times in one direction and channels in the other. A synopsis of the programme might also be available as an option. The viewer can select or record a programme from the EPG.

Impact

Individuals	Television companies	Broadcasters
■ This facility usually incurs a monthly charge which adds to the total bill for digital television. ■ Viewers won't miss part of a programme if they answer the telephone or answer the door because they can pause the programme and return to it after the telephone call. ■ Viewers can watch one programme and record another being shown concurrently on a different channel meaning they will not miss one of the programmes. ■ Viewers do not have to be at home to watch a programme because they can set up recording in advance using the EPG and then watch the programmes at a time convenient to them. ■ Viewers are less likely to miss a programme by using a series link feature.	■ Television companies that use advertising as part of their revenue may lose revenue if people are not watching programmes live as these viewers can skip the advertisements. ■ This type of feature is attractive to viewers who are therefore more likely to buy digital television with more channels which will result in more revenue for the television companies.	■ Broadcasters need to ensure that the EPG is regularly updated. ■ Set-top boxes that include hard disks with the ability to play and record at the same time need to be produced. With strong competition between broadcasters, this may be costly if no monthly charge is made to the viewer.

< Activity >

If you have digital television at home, experiment with the set-top box to see what other facilities are available, including digital teletext. Complete the table below for each facility.

Impact

Individuals	Television companies	Broadcasters

QUESTIONS

1 List **seven** services available on digital television.
2 Identify **two** advantages of pay per view to the individual viewer.
3 Identify **two** impacts to broadcasters of enabling viewers to choose camera angles.
4 Identify **one** disadvantage to a television company that provides viewers with the facility to vote for their favourite performer.
5 Describe **three** features of an electronic programme guide.

Describe the internal resources of a system: human, technological and accommodation

▢ Human

Human resources are the people that use and maintain a system. They are either employed by the organisation or contracted to do particular tasks. Some tasks that may be carried out by human resources include:

- entering data into a system (e.g. entering details of orders received by post)
- maintaining the computer systems (e.g. an ICT technician)
- programmers who develop new software or produce web pages
- managing people within an organisation (e.g. a personnel director)
- managing the finances within an organisation (e.g. a finance director who would use spreadsheets and other financial modelling software)
- researchers who find out about and develop new products with new ideas.

▢ Technological

This consists of electronic or equipment with moving parts within an organisation. It could include:

- computers, peripherals, servers and communications links
- computer-aided manufacture (CAM) machines (e.g. lathes)
- electronic point of sale (EPOS) machines (e.g. tills)
- arcade games.

▢ Accommodation

These are the buildings, offices and other property owned by an organisation. People and equipment need to be situated somewhere (i.e. accommodation). The location of the accommodation can be important: shops need to be accessible to public transport and cars; manufacturers prefer out-of-town business parks where rental costs and council taxes are cheaper; car parks that are underground are expensive to build but take up less ground space. Accommodation could include:

- offices for people to work in – some may be private offices for managers, while other offices may be open plan for general employees
- factories for machinery and workers
- retail outlets (shops) to sell products
- a car park.

< Example >

A church might include the following internal resources:

Human

- A vicar who is responsible for organising services, the welfare of their congregation and a vision for the church's future.
- A curate who is training to be a vicar and will support the vicar in the pastoral care of the congregation.
- An administrator who is responsible for the administration of the church including taking bookings for rooms, dealing with enquiries, receiving correspondence and providing information.
- Church Wardens who are responsible for the accommodation and organising services in the vicar's absence.
- A congregation who are the people who worship at the church and will carry out various tasks voluntarily within the community.

Technological

- A computer and printer connected to the Internet for the administrator to use.
- A laptop computer for the vicar to use while at the church or in the office at the vicarage.
- Projectors and LCD screens for showing the words to worship songs and the liturgy.
- Microphones for singers, readers, vicar and curate.
- Speakers, amplifier and mixing desk to enable the congregation to hear what is being said and sung.

Accommodation

- The sanctuary where the congregation meet to worship.
- A lounge where the congregation meet to drink, eat and chat.
- A kitchen for making drinks and preparing food.
- Toilets for members of the congregation to use.
- An office for the administrator.
- A vicarage for the vicar to live in with his family.

< Activity >

Identify some of the internal resources within your school or college.

QUESTIONS

1 Identify **three** types of internal resources.
2 Describe **two** different human resources that may be required to work with ICT within a bank.
3 Describe a technological resource, other than computers, that might be required by a retail outlet.
4 Describe the type of accommodation that might be required by an estate agency.

Explain the importance of ensuring that information is exchanged accurately and in a timely manner within an organisation and describe how this is achieved

▪ Importance

Information which is not accurate is not useful because it means that decisions might be made based on incorrect facts. Imagine looking at a train timetable and seeing that the train from Birmingham New Street to London Euston leaves at 08:30 so you arrive at 08:25 only to find that its real departure time was 08:13. Therefore information needs to be accurate in order to be useful.

Some examples of the importance of information being accurate and on time are given below.

< Example >

The operators of an air traffic control system need to know exactly where each aircraft is positioned at any time so that they can direct aircraft to the correct positions within the sky as they approach for landing. The position of each aircraft must be accurate so that the air traffic controllers know not to allow an aircraft to go near another aircraft. The position must be in real time so that the controllers can ensure they are sending aircraft to a space that is currently unoccupied. If the information was provided 30 seconds after the aircraft was in that position, then the controller could send another aircraft to that position and this could cause a collision.

< Example >

When an ambulance is despatched to an emergency, information about the location is sent directly to an on-board computer in the ambulance. The paramedics need to know exactly which address to go to in order that they can deal with the emergency quickly when they arrive. If a house number of '30' was given instead of '13', then it could add several minutes to their response time which could result in the death of a patient. If the information is received by the ambulance dispatcher but not passed on to the paramedics for another 2 minutes, then this is wasted time which could also result in the death of a patient.

< Example >

A pizza company take orders from customers by phone. The orders are then passed to the kitchen to cook and prepare the food and the pizzas are then delivered to the customers by a delivery driver. It is important that the customer receives what they ordered because this is what they are expecting to eat. If the order passed to the kitchen is incorrect, then the customer may be unhappy, might refuse the pizza and refuse to pay for it (losing the pizza company money), might not use the pizza company again or might be allergic to an ingredient used that they were not expecting causing potential harm to the customer. The customer also expects their food to arrive on time and so it is important the order for the food is passed to the kitchen as soon as possible so that it can be cooked and delivered. If the kitchen does not receive the order for 30 minutes after it has been taken or the delivery driver is not told the pizza is ready until 30 minutes after it has been cooked, then the customer will be kept waiting and will become hungry and therefore disappointed. The pizza could arrive cold resulting in a dissatisfied customer which could potentially lose the company future sales.

< Activity >

1 Discuss the possible consequences of receiving inaccurate examination results.

2 Discuss the possible consequences of receiving examination results one week late.

How this is achieved

There are many ways to ensure data is exchanged accurately. This section will focus on two of these methods.

Validation can be used to ensure that data entered matches a pre-defined set of rules. This prevents some incorrect data from being entered into a system but does not prevent incorrect data that matches the rules from being entered into a system.

< Example >

Consider the example of the ambulance despatch. The operator could enter '30' as the house number and then enter the street address. A validation lookup could then be used to see if number 30 does exist on that street. If it does not, then the operator can check the house number with the caller. However, if 30 does exist, then this inaccurate data would still get through this validation rule.

Verification can be used to reduce data entry errors that are made. Verification is the process of checking that the source data matches the data entered. At AS Level, you studied the double entry method and the proof reading (manual) method.

< Example >

Consider the example of the ambulance despatch again. The operator enters the data and then asks the caller, 'Could you please confirm, you need an ambulance sending to number 30, three zero, London Road?' The caller can then say, 'No, I said 13, one three, London Road.' This is a form of manual verification.

Data also needs to be exchanged in a timely manner. There are two main ways that this can be achieved.

Real-time systems can be used that ensure that the data used on the computer matches the data in the real world at any precise point of time. This would be particularly important with the air traffic control scenario where the correct positions in the sky must match the positions on the screen precisely and at the same time. If a customer is booking a ticket for a concert and there is only one left, then the data must reflect this by storing the data in real time rather than updating the data every couple of hours, otherwise, the customer might book two tickets and be disappointed when they only receive one.

Procedures need to be put in to place within an organisation that ensure data is passed on to the next functional area on time. In the pizza example, there must be a procedure that ensures the only thing the telephone operator does after taking an order is take the order to the kitchen immediately and ignore any further telephone calls until this has been done.

QUESTIONS

1 Identify **one** example of how information for share prices could be inaccurate.
2 Describe **one** consequence of share prices being inaccurate.
3 Identify **one** example of how information for a bank may be provided too late.
4 Describe **one** consequence of information for a bank being provided too late.
5 Identify **three** methods that could be used to ensure data is transferred in an accurate and timely manner.

Describe the characteristics of the following systems: personnel, finance and stock control

Figure 4.24 Employees

Personnel

People are very important within a business. All resources need to be maintained by people and decisions are made by people. The purpose of a personnel system is to help with the management of all the people within a business.

The major part of a personnel system will be a database containing information about all employees. This database will include information such as:

■ contact details for each employee for times when the employee needs to be contacted at home, and next-of-kin details for emergencies
■ attendance of each employee on each day including planned holidays
■ salary details showing how much each employee has been paid during their employment at the organisation and any pay rises that have been awarded
■ qualifications for each employee – this will include information about qualifications the employee possessed before joining the organisation and any that were gained while at the organisation
■ a training record that shows all the training courses each employee has attended
■ outcomes of appraisals showing what targets were set for each employee and how well each of those targets were met.

The personnel system must comply with the Data Protection Act and so must include appropriate security to prevent unauthorised access. It must be regularly reviewed in order to ensure that data is accurate and up to date. Some personnel systems include features to help the organisation with Data Protection Act compliance, such as reminders when a certain time period has lapsed since personal information was last checked or automatic notification if attendance information has not been entered or automatic reminders if no appraisal or training updates have been made for an employee after a period of time.

Often personnel systems are part of a management information system (MIS). Whether the personal information system is a separate system or within an MIS, it will be able to produce reports which can help decision making. Some examples of these include information about:

- booked holidays, so that if an employee wishes to book a holiday, the availability of other employees can be considered before granting the request
- employees who have been absent because of sickness more than a certain number of days, or have been absent regularly on a particular day of the week, so that a decision can be made about whether to discuss the matter with the employee, involve occupational health or even start disciplinary action
- the total cost of employees within a particular department so that decisions can be made as to whether that department is profitable
- the skill sets of employees so that teams can be chosen to complete a project
- which employees have met their appraisal targets and which have not so that decisions can be made about whether employees can earn bonuses or need extra training or whether disciplinary action should be taken.

Figure 4.25 Money

Finance

The purpose of a financial system is to store data about all the finances of the organisation and provided information about the financial status at any time. A financial system may or may not be part of an MIS, but like a personnel information system it must still provide useful information that can be used for decision making. It must also be able to carry out day-to-day tasks such as making payments. Tasks that are performed by a financial system include:

- placing orders for products, parts, materials and services from other organisations
- paying invoices that are received from other organisations
- monitoring orders that have been placed and identifying any that have not been received or have not been charged for

- setting budgets at various levels within the organisation and comparing actual expenditure against budgeted expenditure
- storing information about any products or services that the organisation provides and the prices that should be charged for these
- receiving orders from other organisations for products or services
- producing invoices to other organisations
- monitoring the payment of invoices by other organisations and sending out automatic reminders when invoices are overdue
- providing information about the status of cash flow including how much money is available in all bank accounts and a graphical analysis of the cash flow over a period of time
- reports showing profit and loss that can be used to make decisions about future production and price setting as well as being used to give the required information by law to the government
- simulations of what might happen if prices of a particular product are changed or if additional sales representatives are employed
- forecasting of future cash flows based on historical patterns and planned expenditure and revenue
- analysis of overhead costs and fixed assets so that decisions can be made about whether to find more cost-efficient methods and their contribution to overall costs and ultimately profit
- providing information about the financial performance of each product produced or service provided by the organisation and its contribution to the profits of the organisation
- providing information about the total costs of running each department.

If a financial system is part of an MIS then it is likely to share data with a personal information system which will allow analysis of personnel costs such as salaries, training and absence. Types of financial system can include spreadsheets, off-the-shelf financial systems for a particular type of organisation (e.g. for schools, hospitals, charities, manufacturing, retail) and bespoke systems for larger organisations.

Stock control

The main purpose of a stock control system is to ensure that stock levels are maintained so that either production can continue as planned, products are available for sale or to be used for services. A stock control system will store information about:

- minimum stock levels that should be maintained for each product – these will depend on how quickly stock is used and how long it takes to order new stock
- up-to-date current stock levels of each product
- re-order amounts for each product – how many of each product should be ordered when the minimum stock level has been reached – these will depend on how quickly stock is used and any discounts that are applied for bulk purchasing

Figure 4.26 Stock

- planned deliveries of replacement stock
- the cost of purchasing each product and for the retail industry the prices to be charged for each product
- dates that each batch of stock was supplied so that the oldest stock can be used first
- suppliers that can be used to supply each type of product
- location of each product in stock so that it can be found when needed.

Whenever an item is removed from stock (either purchased or used) then this should be recorded so that the current stock level stored in the database can be reduced. With an electronic point of sale (EPOS) system in the retail industry, each time a product is scanned at the POS (till) the stock level will be reduced in the database. When the stock reaches its minimum level in the database, an automated order for replacement stock will be invoked. The amount to be ordered will be determined by the re-order amount for that product which will ensure that acceptable stock levels are maintained. When the delivery arrives, the current stock level stored will be increased by the amount of stock that has been delivered.

Some stock control systems are part of a MIS and will also link to a financial system so that data does not have to be repeated. This allows profits and losses to be calculated.

< Activity >

1 Create a simple database that includes a table with the following fields:
   - Stock description.
   - Current stock level.
   - Minimum stock level.
   - Re-order amount.
   - Supplier code.

2 Create a table that includes information about the supplier.

3 Create a query that lists any items of stock that are below the minimum stock level.

4 Create a report that is based on the query above that is a purchase order for replacement stock from each supplier. It should be grouped by suppliers and include a row for each product that needs to be ordered from that supplier and the quantity to order.

5 Create an update query that will add the re-order amount to the current stock level. This query can be used when the ordered stock arrives.

QUESTIONS

1 Describe **two** characteristics of a personnel system.
2 Describe **two** characteristics of a finance system.
3 Describe **three** characteristics of a stock system.
4 Describe how a stock control system maintains stock levels automatically.
5 Identify **two** characteristics that a stock control system and financial information system may have in common.

Summary

Telephone systems
- Voicemail
- Menus
- Ringback
- Videophone
- Caller display
- Conference call

Banking
- Automated teller machines
- Credit/debit card
- Cheques

Production control
- Computer Aided Design
- Computer Aided Manufacture

Global positioning systems
- Satellites
- Navigation software
- Route planning

Navigation
- Route planning

Weather forecasting
- Measuring and recording data
- Modelling a forecast
- Producing a forecast

Software based training methods
- Trainee logon
- Feedback to trainee and tutor
- Pre-assessment
- Target setting
- Assignment setting
- Advantages and disadvantages to:
  - Trainee
  - Tutor

Limitations of using ICT
- Battery life
- Bandwidth
- Portable screen size

- Wireless network connectivity
- Input devices
- Users

Use of networks
- Work
  - Small business
  - Large enterprise
- Home

Distributed databases
- Horizontal partitioning
- Vertical partitioning
- Replication
- Central database with local remote indexes

Discuss the use of distributed databases
- Storage
- Queries
- Data availability
- Local control
- Database design
- Back-ups

Security issues of distributed databases
- Interception of data
- Physical access to data
- Consistency and integrity of data

Expert systems
- Knowledge based systems
- Knowledge and rules
- Components
  - Knowledge base
  - Inference engine
  - User interface
- Applications, including:
  - Medical diagnosis
  - Fault diagnosis
  - Predicting outcomes

Decision making
- Management Information System
  - Provides managerial information
  - Decisions made by managers
- Expert system
  - Can ask 'what-if?' questions
  - Suggests a solution
- Reliability of data
  - Quality of data can affect quality of decisions

Digital television networks
- Features
  - Pay per view
  - Voting
  - Game show participation
  - Choosing camera angles
  - Feedback comments to TV studio
  - Interactive recording and live pause
- Consider the impact on:
  - Individuals
  - Television companies
  - Broadcasters

Internal resources of a system
- Human
  - Technological
  - Accommodation
- Exchanging information accurately and in a timely manner
  - Importance
    - Safety
    - Customer satisfaction
    - Profits
  - How it is achieved
    - Validation
    - Verification
    - Procedures
- Characteristics of systems
  - Personnel
  - Finance
  - Stock control

Test 1

A television company has decided to upgrade its ICT systems.

1   Describe how the television company could make use of a modern telephone system when receiving calls. [6]

Global positioning systems (GPS) are to be installed into the television company's vehicles.

2   Describe how GPS might help reporters arrive on time to a live television show. [4]

Before GPS was available, the television company used navigation software from the World Wide Web for planning journeys.

3   Explain the limitations of navigation software without GPS. [4]

The television company employs a weather forecaster.

4   Identify **four** measurements that the weather forecaster might use. [4]

5   Describe **three** advantages to the television company of installing a local area network. [6]

The television company will be opening two new studios. They have decided to use a partitioned database at each of its studios to store details about employees.

6   Discuss whether a horizontally partitioned database or a central database with local index should be used. [7]

The television company is going to provide digital television services to its viewers.

7 Discuss the impact on the television company of providing digital television services. [7]

Test 2

Frank has just retired and has decided to use his spare time to learn about new technologies and to invest his lump sum payment in buying some new hardware and software.

1 a) Explain how Frank might make use of an expert system if he feels ill. [4]
  b) Describe **two** components of an expert system. [4]

2 Discuss the impact on Frank of pay per view and being able to pause live television. [7]

3 Describe how Frank might make use of ICT with his bank. [4]

Frank passed on his ball bearing manufacturing company to his son Melvyn. Melvyn has been told that it would be a good idea to invest in a management information system (MIS).

4 Describe **two** ways in which Melvyn could use a MIS to make decisions. [4]

5 Describe **three** different types of internal resources within Melvyn's company and give an example of each. [6]

Software-based training methods will be used to help Melvyn learn the new MIS.

6 a) Describe **four** advantages to Melvyn of using software-based training methods. [4]
  b) Describe **two** disadvantages to the trainers of using software-based training methods.

7 Explain how a stock control system could help Melvyn's company ensure that enough parts are always available for the manufacturing process. [4]

5 Implementing computer-based information systems

Introduction

This chapter covers the implementation of computer-based information systems. The implications of the many decisions needed here must be carefully considered. You will need to make sure that you understand the different approaches that could be taken to make an informed decision. You should also be able to apply your knowledge to a specified scenario.

This chapter covers:

- Custom-written and off-the-shelf approaches
- Upgrading systems
- System installation
- System maintenance

Describe the involvement of a client when a custom-written computer-based system is produced, from the initial meeting with the client to the installation of the system

The client must be involved at every stage of the development of a custom-written information system. Initially the client will need to provide details to the development team about what the client would like the new system to do. These details form the basis on which the development will take place.

If the details are either incomplete or inaccurate, then this may lead to a system being developed which does not fully meet the needs of the client and the organisation. This will result in a system being developed that has wasted the money and the time of both the client and the development company.

Figure 5.1 shows the importance of the client being involved at all stages.

Clients must be involved at all stages of the systems life cycle. If the client is consulted at all stages, then errors, inaccuracies and omissions could be found in time to correct them. Consulting the client only at the installation stage is too late to rectify any issues.

What the client wants

What the development team thought the client wanted!

Figure 5.1 The importance of involving the client

Clients should be consulted at the end of every stage of the systems life cycle. During the consultation the developers should listen to any concerns that the client expresses, with the client being given the opportunity to suggest modifications that they feel are needed or to raise any concerns about any inaccuracies.

The extent that a client is involved might depend on the methodology being used during the development of the system. Some methodologies, such as the waterfall model, enable the developer to return to the previous stage in the cycle to correct any issues. Other methodologies, such as the prototyping methodology, enable the client to see a 'prototype' of the system which may enable a fuller and clearer understanding of it.

The developer, however, irrespective of the methodology being used, must ensure that the client, and the end users of the system, are consulted at each stage.

> **QUESTION**
>
> Describe why the client should be involved at all stages of the development of a custom-written software system.

Describe the involvement of a client when a custom-written computer-based system is produced, from the initial meeting with the client to the installation of the system

Discuss the implications of selecting, implementing and supporting the installation of custom-written and off-the-shelf solutions

▨ Selecting a custom-written or off-the-shelf solution

The selection of either custom-written or off-the-shelf system solution will depend on many factors. What is important is that the appropriate system solution is selected to fully meet the needs of the client.

A custom-written solution is when the software has been written to meet the specified needs of the end user – usually an organisation. It is developed by a software provider who works with the user to determine the requirements of the system design. The software provider builds the system to meet these requirements, and then implements and tests it.

The advantage of custom-written software is that it meets the requirements of the user exactly. The user will specify the functions of the software and the system will be developed to incorporate those functions. A lot of off-the-shelf software has many features that are not required by the user. This is known as 'bloat ware' – many of the functions of the software are not required and may never be used by the user. These functions increase the memory footprint (the amount of hard drive space taken up by the software). With custom-written software there are no extraneous functions because the software has been written to meet specific requirements.

Once the system has been developed, installed and paid for, then the user owns it and can sell it to other companies, which may cover the cost of development. However, the initial cost of the development may be very high.

Specialist back-up and support will be available from the system provider who developed the software. This back-up may involve correcting bugs, training users or assisting in extending the functionality of the program. There will not, however, be the wider support available, such as books, discussion groups etc.

One of the disadvantages of having custom-written system is the long time it takes to analyse, design, develop, test and implement it. The end-user requirement might even change during the process.

If mistakes are found in the code, then it may take some time to find and fix them. Problems might even occur when the system is being used in a live environment after implementation.

Off-the-shelf software is a term used to define any software that can be purchased, installed and used immediately. One of the main advantages of off-the-shelf software is that it is generally cheaper than having software specially written. The cost is a one-off purchase price.

Also, because off-the-shelf software has a large number of users, it is likely to have been tested by many people and a lot of the bugs will have been removed. It must be remembered that a piece of software can never be fully tested but the more testing that is done the more likely it is that it will work.

Another advantage of implementing a system that includes off-the-shelf software is that the choice of software manufacturers is sometimes greater. For example, word-processing software is available from companies such as Microsoft, Corel and Lotus, and as open source. The software is readily available, and can be installed and used almost immediately.

Off-the-shelf software is widely used, and this means that support can be got from books, discussion groups, websites and trainers. Bug fixes and patches are often released by the manufacturer and registered users can often upgrade to the latest version at preferential rates.

There are disadvantages to using off-the-shelf software in a system solution. Among these is the fact that there are likely to be many features and functions included in the software that are not needed by the user, and which cannot be removed because ownership of the software stays with the software manufacturer. The software may also not fully meet the needs of the user and so compromises will need to be made.

The software is also more likely to have a large memory footprint.

The table below shows a comparison of the main features that should be considered when deciding whether to install a custom-written or off-the-shelf system solution.

	Off-the-shelf	Custom-written
Cost to the end user	■ Either a one-off cost or a yearly rental cost, possibly thousands of pounds plus additional costs for each station it is used on.	■ Need to hire the company/person to write the software which could cost many thousands of pounds. ■ The end-user owns the system and can sell it to recoup some of the development cost.
Support	■ Discussion groups, online help, books and training courses are readily available.	■ Only likely to get support from the people who write the software – problems may arise if they choose not to support it or go out of business.
Purpose	■ May have to be altered and edited to fit the purpose. May never meet the purpose precisely. ■ Will have many additional features that may or may not be used. Better to have them there and never use them rather than to want them and not to have them?	■ Will fit the purpose precisely and do exactly what was asked. Possible problems might arise if the analysis was wrong. ■ If something it is not specified then it will not be there in the final product.
Testing	■ Will have been tested by many individuals. Bug fixes will be released regularly by the company.	■ Will only have been tested by a few people and there may be many bugs. Correcting them will take time.
Availability	■ Immediately available.	■ Will take time (possibly a few months) to complete the analysis etc.
Choice	■ Choice between packages available – but none may be an exact fit.	■ There is choice of who to get to write the software and the end user will have a lot of influence over the end product.
Upgrade	■ Likely to use a standard file format and the company is likely to release upgraded products. ■ Support for new peripherals and operating systems as standard.	■ New printers and drivers for peripherals may not be supported and major upgrades might not happen. If the software does not use a recognised file format it may not be possible to upgrade.
New staff	■ May be already familiar with the new software.	■ Unlikely to be familiar with the new software.
Memory footprint	■ Likely to be larger than bespoke solution.	■ Likely to be smaller that off-the-shelf solution.

QUESTIONS

1 What is meant by custom-written software?
2 What is meant by off-the-shelf software?
3 What are the advantages of custom-written software over off-the-shelf software?
4 What are the disadvantages of of-the-shelf software over custom-written software?

Implementing and supporting the installation of custom-written and off-the-shelf software

The staff who will be using the system will need to be involved during the implementation and installation stages. There may be some staff who feel that the new system might lead to job losses. There might also be staff who feel that they do not have the skills required to use the new system. Staff will need to be involved in discussions that should enable them to voice their concerns and to have their worries addressed. If staff feel supported, then they are more likely to accept the changes and to feel confident when using the software.

Staff should be offered training sessions to ensure that they are confidently able to use the system. This should be appropriate to both their job role and the level of skills they already possess.

Staff need to be reassured that their jobs are not in jeopardy and the benefits of the new system should be emphasised, so they feel more loyal towards the organisation and, hopefully, use the system efficiently.

Staff should be given easy access to user guides and documentation to help them use the new system effectively. The user guides, and associated documentation, should also be readily available after installation so that staff can refer to them if any problems occur. This means that staff should become more independent and confident, which in turn will make them more efficient in their work.

> **< Activity >**
>
> Investigate the different types and format of software user guides that are available, indentifying the strengths and weaknesses of each.

Most organisations have customers (clients). The needs of the customers should also be considered during the installation of new system solution. The new system may cause some problems for the customers. It may be that, despite testing having taken place during the development of the solution, some teething problems are still present.

This may have an impact on customers, for example, incorrect invoices being sent out or details not being transferred to the new system correctly.

The organisation, and the staff dealing with the customers, should offer some explanation to the customers and attempt to rectify any issues as quickly as possible.

The implementation and installation of the new system should be managed carefully with the needs of the staff and customers of the organisation being considered as much as possible. By considering these needs there should be no loss of confidence in the organisation for either the staff or the customers.

Explain how the expertise of staff, costs, benefits and current systems affect decisions about upgrading or installing software and hardware

The decision about whether or not to upgrade or install new software and hardware should be taken during the analysis stage of the systems life cycle. The decision should be taken after considering the expertise of staff, the costs involved and the budget given by the organisation, the benefits the system will bring and the system currently in use. A cost–benefit analysis should be completed with the results influencing the decision.

The cost–benefit analysis should consider the costs incurred. These will include the costs of any staff training which will be needed. If the software and hardware is being upgraded, then the staff are likely to already have some of the skills that will be required to competently use the software and hardware, but it is likely to be dependent on how much the versions differ. It is also possible that the planned changes may affect the administrative and operational procedures currently in place in the organisation. This may lead to extending the training required by the staff.

If new software and hardware are to be installed, then the training costs are likely to be high. If the software is custom written, then the training will have to be bespoke because it is unlikely that any commercially available training courses will be appropriate. Any training, however, will cause some disruption to the organisation. This means that when training takes place and which staff receives it needs to be carefully planned.

If the software to be upgraded or a new package is to be installed, then the cost of licences needs to be considered. Sometimes a software upgrade might have a smaller licence cost than that of a new software package. Another cost with off-the-shelf software is for the time that will be needed to tailor and test the package in the new system environment.

Irrespective of whether the software is to be upgraded or a new package is to be installed the issue of hardware must be considered. The new software must run successfully on the old system and, in addition, the existing hardware must run the new software. Upgraded versions of software invariably add new features and as a result tend to use more memory and require faster processing speeds. To ensure that the software operates at optimum performance, the hardware may, therefore, need to be upgraded to meet these requirements. In addition, the upgrading of software may enable the organisation to use newer or additional hardware. If this is the case, then the cost of the hardware should also be taken into account when making any decisions about whether to upgrade or install new items.

In addition to the issues with software and the impact this may have on hardware, it may be that the hardware currently being used by the organisation has become obsolete or outdated. New hardware may also be required by the organisation. For example, a change in type of printer may be needed due to a change in business function of the organisation. The upgrade of new hardware may, however, require some changes to the software being used within the organisation. This is likely to be achieved by installing drivers or downloading the software patches from the hardware vendor's website. It is important, however, that the software and hardware are compatible and cause no problems to the organisation. To ensure this compatibility the hardware and software must be thoroughly tested.

If the software to be upgraded was initially custom-written, then any upgrades to the software may be covered by the maintenance contract that is in place with the software development team. However, there is likely to be a limit on the number and level of revisions that can be made without incurring extra costs.

If the software to be installed is an addition to the software currently used, then the compatibility of the new software with the old must be considered. If the new software does not interact or is incompatible with current software, then it may be that the data held by the organisation will need to be transferred or reconfigured. This may add to the costs in terms of the time and personnel needed to carry out the process.

Explain how the expertise of staff, costs, benefits and current systems affect decisions about upgrading or installing software and hardware

Other issues that will have to be considered, and require decisions to be taken, include the method of implementation and the available timescale.

The method of implementation must be selected carefully. (The different methods of implementation that are available are discussed later in this chapter.) The method of implementation should take into account the extent of the upgrade or installation and the impact on the organisation.

The timescale available will, in some cases, have an impact on whether an upgrade or fresh installation would be appropriate. A short timescale may not be appropriate, especially if the software has to be custom written.

The upgrading or installation of a system must, ultimately, ensure that the benefits of the new outweigh the advantages of the old. In addition, the long-term benefits need to outweigh the costs and inconvenience/disruption of the installation.

QUESTIONS

1 Describe how the expertise of staff affects the decisions about the upgrading of software.
2 Identify **two** factors affecting decisions which must be made when upgrading hardware.

Describe a range of methods for installing a new computer-based system: parallel, phased, direct, pilot

Discuss the choice of a particular installation method or methods for a range of applications

Once a new computer-based system has been developed and tested it needs to be implemented.

In this stage of the systems life cycle, the system will be installed, new equipment will be put into operation, software will be installed and set up, data files will be created and end users will be trained.

There are four main strategies that can be taken when implementing a new system. These are:

- parallel
- phased
- pilot
- direct.

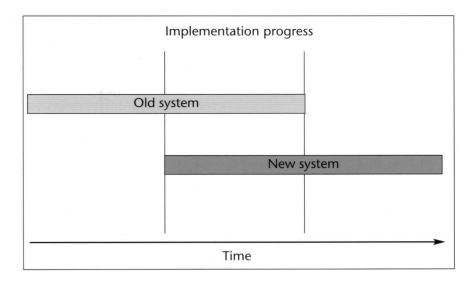

Implementation progress

Old system

New system

Time

Figure 5.2 Parallel implementation strategy

◼ Parallel

The old and new systems are run concurrently during a parallel installation. The results from each are compared for accuracy and consistency. The old system is not discarded until there is complete confidence in the reliability and accuracy of the new system. Figure 5.2 shows the old system being used in parallel with a new system for a time and then being withdrawn, leaving the new system being the only one in use.

This strategy has some disadvantages. Staff are effectively doing their work twice meaning that data is duplicated and inconsistencies can occur between the old and new systems. The inconsistencies have to be rectified which might be very expensive in terms of staff and time costs.

However, if a problem is found with the new system, then it is possible for the organisation to function as the old system is still in place and can be used. This means that there are no detrimental effects on an organisation.

Phased

Phased implementation is used with larger systems where the system to be put in place has several smaller subsystems. Each subsystem is introduced one at a time, making sure that each one is working before the next is commissioned. The actual implementation method can be direct or parallel.

The advantages are that each subsystem can be introduced with a minimum of disruption and if a subsystem fails to work, it is small enough to correct the errors.

The disadvantages are that the changeover may take a long period of time and create an extended period of unsettlement.

Pilot

The pilot implementation strategy requires selected departments to use the new system before other departments which continue to use the old system until the pilot has been proven to work correctly. Once confidence in the new system is high, then the new system can be implemented in another department. This continues until all the departments within the organisation are using the new system.

For example, a retail chain could implement the new system in one of its shops. When confidence in the new system is high, the rest of the shops can begin to use the new system.

The disadvantages of this strategy is that it can take a long time and is, therefore, very expensive in terms of staff and time costs.

An advantage is that the old system can still be used in parts of a company if a problem is identified with new system. These problems, or bugs, can then be rectified before implementation is continued. Using this strategy limits the detrimental effects on an organisation.

Direct

The direct or 'big bang' implementation approach is the riskiest strategy. The new system completely replaces the old system, on a given time, with no interim parallel, phased or pilot implementation. Figure 5.3 shows the old system being withdrawn and the new system beginning to be used immediately!

The disadvantages of using this strategy are great and may have potential consequences for the organisation. Any problems or bugs in the new system may lead to complete loss of data and the failure of the organisation. If this strategy is chosen, then these risks need to be minimised by careful planning by the analyst. The new system must be thoroughly and completely tested prior to

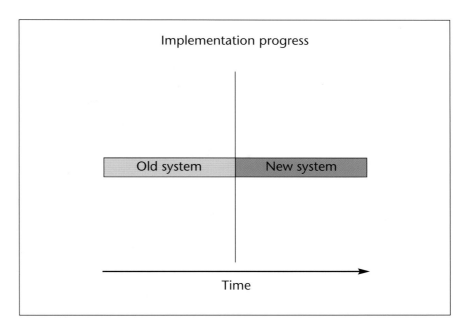

Figure 5.3 Direct implementation strategy

implementation. Staff also need to be fully trained to use the new system. It may also help if the direct implementation is carried out during a slack period to ease the stress and pressure that will be placed on the staff at the switch over to the new system.

A carefully managed direct strategy that ensures a seamless transition, both in terms of the new system working correctly from the word go, and staff being adequately trained, is potentially the cheapest in terms of staff and time costs, but the analyst must consider the advantages and disadvantages of using this strategy very carefully otherwise the consequences might be very expensive.

A summary of the advantages and disadvantages of the different implementation methods are given in the table below.

Implementation method	Advantages	Disadvantages
Parallel	■ If a problem is found with the new system it is possible for the organisation to function as the old system is still in place and can be used. ■ There is little or no detrimental effect on the organisation.	■ Data is duplicated. ■ Staff undertake tasks twice. ■ Inconsistencies have to be checked and errors have to be located.
Phased	■ Problems or bugs are found within small subsystems making it easier to find the error and correct it. ■ Limits the detrimental effect on the organisation.	■ Slow to commission the complete system. ■ Very expensive in terms of staff and time costs.

Implementation method	Advantages	Disadvantages
Pilot	■ If a problem or bug is found with new system, these can be recitfied before implementation is continued. ■ Limits the detrimental effect on an organisation.	■ Implementation can take a long time. ■ Very expensive in terms of staff and time costs.
Direct	■ Potentially the cheapest in terms of staff and time costs.	■ Problems or bugs could lead to complete loss of data and/or the potential failure of the organisation.

QUESTION

1 Identify the advantages and disadvantages of the phased and direct methods of implementation.
2 Identify a situation where the parallel method of implementation could be used. Explain your choice.

QUESTION

Identify a situation where the parallel method of implementation might be used. Explain your choice.

Explain the role of reviews during the life of a computer-based information system, describing how reviews may be planned for and carried out effectively

During the life of any system reviews need to be undertaken to ensure that the system continues to operate effectively.

Reviews should be scheduled to occur on a regular basis. Using a planned, scheduled review strategy will ensure that the system continues to provide satisfactory levels of performance to the users. Scheduled regular reviews will allow users to report any problems they have had with the system. The reviews can also ensure that the system does not become out-of-date or be perceived by the users to be 'old fashioned'.

Reviews of a system can also be scheduled to coincide with any planned changes in the operation of the organisation using the system. Planned changes may include external and/or internal changes.

External changes may include legislation changes (including tax and VAT) and data protection updates.

Internal changes relate to the organisation itself, such as, for example, a change in the mode of operation whereby new functions performed by the system will need to be included.

Other internal factors that may be considered during a review include checking that data is being processed efficiently and that there is still sufficient storage space for the number of, for example, new customers/orders. If a data entry system is part of the system being reviewed, then this should also be checked during a review to ensure that it is still working effectively and accurately.

< Activity >

Investigate different types of external and internal changes which could result in a system having to be changed.

Another role of a review is to enable developments in hardware and software to be incorporated into a system. Developments in hardware and software occur very frequently. New software might not be compatible with the system. As hardware becomes obsolete and/or needs replacing then a review of the system must take place to make any necessary changes to ensure that the new hardware works successfully with the system.

During a review of a system, users must be asked for their views on how well the system is performing. This will also enable the users to suggest improvements to the system – they are the ones using the system on a day-to-day basis so they will be able to provide relevant suggestions as to the overall system performance from a user's perspective.

Describe perfective, adaptive and corrective maintenance

Explain the need for perfective, adaptive and corrective maintenance during the life of a computer-based information system

Over the life of a system (post-implementation) it may be necessary to perform maintenance on it. There are many different reasons for maintenance.

The main reason for post-implementation maintenance include:

- errors/bugs that may not have been identified during the testing process but become apparent when the system is being used
- users finding that parts of the system are not working as they would like
- tasks that were not included at the design stage but now need to be incorporated into the system
- the emergence of security issues that mean the system requires an extra level of protection
- the software developer/vendor may find a way to make the system run more efficiently – this will usually result in the release of a patch/fix
- new hardware or other software may be purchased which needs to be integrated into the existing system resulting in changes needed.

Adaptive

This type of maintenance usually occurs when the organisation using the system has a new need that the system must fulfil. The system may need to be adapted due to changes within the organisation using it, external changes such as legislation (i.e. tax/VAT rate changes) or to enable the system to operate with new hardware.

Perfective

This type of maintenance usually occurs when it may be advantageous to make changes to enhance the performance of the system or to make it easier for end users to use. This type of maintenance should turn a good system into a better one. This type of maintenance is generally completed at the request of the end users.

These requests could include:

- the addition of shortcut keys to help carry out processes
- an improved screen design where the colours/layout of the existing system might not be appropriate
- increased levels of online help
- the rewriting of procedures to reduce the response time of the system
- the restructring of data to reduce storage requirements.

It is important, however, to remember that perfective maintenance does not change the overall functionality of the system.

Corrective

Corrective maintenance is also known as remedial maintenance. This type of maintenance is usually completed if there are errors in the software. These errors or 'bugs' can be of two types:

- Programming errors. These occur when the programmer/s have made a mistake. This type of error should have been discovered and corrected before the system was released.
- Logic errors – These are more likely to be undiscovered during the testing stage of the systems life cycle. With this type of error the system will appear to work as it was intended but does not process the data and/or produce the output as it was designed to do.

Corrective maintenance is usually resolved through the use of patches. The Y2K problem in 1999–2000 was solved through the use of corrective maintenance and the release of software patches.

> **QUESTIONS**
>
> 1 Describe perfective maintenance.
> 2 For each maintenance method identify a situation when it could be used.

Summary

Client involvement during the development of a custom-written software system
The implications of:
> selecting
> implementing
> supporting

Custom-written and off-the-shelf software
Decisions about upgrading or installing software and hardware may depend on:
> expertise of staff
> prices
> benefits
> current systems

Installation methods
Parallel
Phased
Direct
Pilot

Factors to be considered when selecting implementation methods
Impact on:
> organisation
> staff
> data/information

Reviews
Scheduling

Maintenance
Perfective
Adaptive
Corrective

Test 1

A company wants to introduce a stock ordering system. The system can be either custom-written or an off-the-shelf package.

1 Explain the implications of selecting a custom-written software solution. [6]

2 During the life of the system reviews will need to be carried out. Describe the role of these reviews. [6]

3 Maintenance will be carried out on the system. Describe perfective maintenance. [4]

Test 2

A boat company is updating the booking system that it currently uses.

1 Describe **two** different methods the company could use to install the new booking system. [4]

2 Identify and describe **two** different types of maintenance that might be required during the life of the booking system. [6]

3 Describe **two** factors which should be considered when managing the change in the booking system. [4]

6 Implications of ICT

Introduction

This chapter is about the effect of ICT on people and organisations. The majority of learning objectives are about discussing impacts. This means that you need to consider all points of view rather than focusing on just positive or negative outcomes. The word 'impact' might sound negative, but it is actually more about the effects on people and organisations – these can be neutral, positive or negative. You will consider the impact of ICT in the following areas:

- External change
- Managing change
- Ethics, codes of conduct and professional bodies
- The need for confidentiality of data
- Security methods
- Hardware and software developments

The last section requires you to keep up to date with hardware and software developments as they are changing all the time. You will need to read computer magazines/journals/newspapers or online articles in addition to the ideas given to you in this book.

Discuss the impact of external change on an organisation, individuals within the organisation and on the systems in use

■ External changes

External changes for an organisation are those changes over which the organisation has no control. Some examples include:

- the government changes the VAT rate or income tax bands
- interest rates are changed by the Bank of England
- competitors bring a new product to the market or offer discounts
- the government changes to a different political party following a general election
- the price of shares for a company changes
- demographics of the area in which the organisation is based change, such as the number of people in particular age groups

- fashions in clothing change
- environmental changes, such as global warming
- the introduction of the updated Data Protection Act in 1998
- the development of a new manufacturing tool
- trade union action, such as a strike or work to rule
- a variation in the exchange rate between the pound and other major currencies
- developments in ICT
- pressure groups, such as the boycott against Nestlé products due to their marketing of breast milk substitutes in the third world
- development of new transport links, such as a new motorway or railway station.

■ Impact of external change

When external changes occur that have an effect on an organisation, it is essential that the organisation responds to that change. The response may only need to be small, but some changes will require a whole change in working practices. Some external changes must be implemented by organisations, otherwise they will not be complying with the law. Some external changes require organisations to update their practices and procedures in order to remain competitive.

Some examples of the impact of external changes are given below:

< Example >

A new manufacturing tool is developed that can produce ball bearings three times faster than the previously best tools available. The organisation has got to decide whether to purchase this new tool, otherwise its competitors may be able to make ball bearings more cheaply if less manufacturing time is required. It may be that less employees are required if less tools are being used to develop the ball bearings in which case redundancies may be needed. The organisation will also need to consider whether it needs to make redundancies.

< Example >

Figure 6.1 The millennium rollover problem

An example of external change that affected organisations all over the world was the new millennium in the year 2000. Many computer systems used two-digit dates (e.g. 94 for 1994) which needed to be updated to use four-digit dates. The problem centred around the fact that when each new year arrives, 1 was added to the previous year. For example, in 1995, 1 was added to 95 to change it to 96 for the new year. When it came to changing from 99, 99 plus 1 equals 100. There was therefore a lot of concern as to whether systems would be able to cope and automatically revert to 00. There were also other issues as the year 00

(2000) needed to appear bigger (i.e. after) the year 99 (1999), whereas 00 is in fact smaller than 99. Therefore, computer software had to be changed to work with four-digit dates and data needed to be updated to include four digits rather than two digits. Organisations had to spend a lot of money employing people to update their software and hardware in order to ensure that their systems remained operational. This was commonly known as the 'millennium bug', but because organisations responded to the forthcoming change, there were very few problems experienced when the calendar changed from 1999 to 2000.

< Example >

If the government changes the VAT rate, businesses have to pass this on to their customers. Computer systems need to be able to cope with a change in the rate of VAT. Properly produced systems will easily be able to deal with this, but sometimes the VAT rate is 'hard coded' into software which means that software developers are required to rectify the problem. The business has no choice but to comply with the new VAT rate and so must respond to this change immediately. In December 2008, the government changed the VAT rate from 17.5% to 15%. Many shops experienced a lot of difficulty because prices were printed on products and computer systems were unable to develop new prices easily. Therefore, many stores had to give a discount to customers once the bill had been calculated to match the reduction in VAT.

< Example >

During 2008, the UK started to experience a recession. Demand from consumers for products and services reduced and this resulted in less income for many businesses. As a result, fewer employees were required and many experienced redundancies or a reduction in working hours. Those who kept their jobs would have been de-moralised by their friends losing their jobs and the potential that their own job may not be safe for much longer. Interest rates were reduced monthly during the latter part of the year which meant organisations were able to borrow more money to invest in capital funding.

< Example >

If a competitor to a business introduces a new product to the market, such as a new games console, that is better or different from those produced by the business, then the business must respond. It can either continue to market its own product and hope that consumers will still purchase its product, or it needs to develop an even better product. This will impact on the systems as new computers may be required to cope with more complex programming methods or manufacturing techniques. The individuals within the organisation will need to change the way that they work – new programming skills will need to be learnt, new marketing campaigns will need to be developed and new manufacturing processes may need to be introduced.

Figure 6.2 Product competition

< Example >

The introduction of the Data Protection Act in 1984 had a massive impact on organisations, individuals and systems. Systems had to be updated to include increased security and back-up facilities where they did not already exist. Organisations had to change their procedures to ensure that they complied with the rights of data subjects. Individuals within organisations may have felt more satisfied that their data was being managed better but were also made more aware of the dangers of personal data being handled incorrectly.

< Activity >

List **three** rights of data subjects under the Data Protection Act. Consider how the introduction of each of these rights would have affected organisations, individuals and systems.

< Activity >

Discuss with your peers what external changes have happened that have affected your school and what external changes may happen that may affect your school. How did your school react to the changes that have happened?

QUESTIONS

1 Give **two** examples of external changes that may affect an organisation which are not already given in this book.
2 The government has decided to reduce the lowest band of income tax from 20% to 15%. Describe the impacts that this will have on organisations, individuals and systems.
3 Give **two** reasons why organisations should react to external change.

Describe change management and factors that must be considered (staff capability, staff views, systems, equipment and accommodation) when managing change

■ Change management

Changes are a necessary part of any organisation that wants to progress its aims. Change management is all about making the process of change as smooth as possible. Change is not just about implementing a new computer system; it affects people too. Therefore, later in this chapter you will learn the importance of consulting with people, involving them and communicating with them when managing change.

There are a number of stages involved with change. These include:

- identifying the need for change and deciding whether the change is necessary
- sharing the reasons for change with people within the organisation so that it is a shared vision
- planning the change, including a detailed implementation plan that includes changeover and training
- implementing the change that may involve changes in working practices.

■ Staff capability

Depending on the amount of change that is involved, some staff may need re-training in order to work with changed systems. Staff will need to learn new procedures and changes in working practices, and often this will involve learning how to use new ICT equipment.

Some staff will be highly skilled, and the introduction of systems that perform skilled tasks that were previously carried out by employees will leave these staff with less demanding work to do. Similarly, some employees may have been involved with many stages of manufacture or service, and with a new system, they may only perform a small part of the whole process. This is known as de-skilling and can lead to demoralisation among the work force.

Some staff may not be capable of using new systems that are introduced and therefore will need to be re-deployed elsewhere within an organisation. This will involve re-skilling which means the employees learn a completely new skill that leads to a new career path.

Staff are also only capable of managing a certain amount of change at a time. If too many changes are implemented in a short period of time, then this can cause staff to become unsettled and confused. They will feel that they have no stability within their job and that they are constantly having to develop new methods of completing tasks. This can often be the case when a new government is elected and it decides to implement lots of new policies that its been waiting to do for many years. Staff become overworked and tired.

< Example >

Secondary school teaching staff in England faced enormous and continuous changes from September 2008 when the government introduced 14–18 reforms and a new 11–14 curriculum. In the academic year 2008–09, teachers had to deliver new AS Levels, a new curriculum to Year 7 and many were involved with introducing functional skills and diplomas as part of pilot courses. Immediately following this, during the academic year 2009–10, teachers had to deliver new A2 Levels, a new curriculum to Year 8 and on top of this had to deliver new GCSE courses too. In addition to this, the second year of functional skills and diploma courses needed to be planned and implemented, and some schools were implementing these for the first time. During 2010–11, things are a bit quieter as teachers now only have two new courses to introduce – the second year of GCSE and Year 9. The amount of change that was introduced over such a short amount of time was beyond staff capability in terms of their work–life balance.

Figure 6.3 Change can be worrying

■ Staff views

People are naturally resistant to change that they are not in control of because they become comfortable in the environment they are working in. Therefore it is necessary that people within an organisation are made aware of the need for the change, otherwise they will believe it is change for the sake of change rather than for genuine reasons that will benefit the organisation and maybe the people within the organisation too. Staff will be concerned that they may lose their jobs if tasks that they previously completed are now completed by computer systems.

Staff who have worked for an organisation for a long time will find it very difficult to change their working practices because they will have become accustomed to a particular way of doing things. Some staff will be scared of new equipment, particularly computers, that may be introduced to their job role and may believe that they are incapable of operating the equipment.

There may be a need for re-location or a change in working hours, so staff will need to be consulted about this to ensure they are willing to co-operate.

People are a very important and valuable part of an organisation, so it is important that their views are listened to and taken into consideration when managing change. Change will fail if the people within the organisation resist it.

■ Systems

Any new software that is to be installed must be fully tested before it is implemented. Staff within an organisation will be apprehensive about using new software and therefore if it does not work as it should do, then they will resist the change.

Any data needs to be transferred to the new system. This will have to happen at a particular time on a particular date because once it is transferred, the new system will have to be used in order to keep the data up to date. Everybody needs to be aware of the time and date when the data transfer will take place.

A new system is not just about software and, therefore, procedural changes need to be communicated to all staff through training sessions so that staff know how to do things differently. Methods of monitoring the changes in procedure need to be planned by management. There needs to be a set of clearly defined actions that should be taken to help staff who are having difficulty with new systems and procedures.

If anything goes wrong with new systems, then management need to be able to have contingency plans in place and will need to maintain the confidence of staff.

■ Equipment

Figure 6.4 Introduction of new equipment

Any new equipment such as machinery, computers and peripherals will need to be purchased. The people responsible for procurement will need to ensure that it is all capable of completing the tasks it is designed for and fit for its purpose. They will also need to ensure that it arrives in plenty of time to be configured and fully tested. Any telecommunications equipment required will need to be installed and working. As with any new software or systems, faulty equipment is likely to lead to resistance to the change.

■ Accommodation

Any equipment that is purchased will need to be located. Often, temporary accommodation, such as storage, will be required for equipment as it arrives and is configured ready for use. Offices will need to be re-designed to enable the inclusion of any computers and peripherals and this will include cabling as well as furniture. Staff will be wary about changing location within an office where they may have felt quite comfortable with the people in their immediate vicinity.

Figure 6.5 New premises

If lots of computers are to be installed, then it will be important to ensure that the temperature in the rooms does not become too high and therefore air cooling systems such as air conditioning may need to be installed.

With large-scale changes, the existing accommodation may not be large enough, and more offices may need to be built, purchased or leased. Staff may need to be relocated and this may cause resistance because they may have to travel further or may not be as conveniently located to a nearby bus stop or train station.

It's not just computers that may be installed. Any machinery is likely to need even bigger accommodation and if this needs to be installed while existing machinery is still being used, then new permanent accommodation will be required and existing accommodation will need to be vacated.

< Activity >

Imagine you are turning an ordinary classroom into a computer room. Consider the changes that will need to take place and discuss the factors that will need to be taken into consideration, including staff capability, staff views, systems, equipment and accommodation. You may want to do this as a group exercise.

QUESTIONS

1 Describe the process of change management.
2 Describe the purpose of change management.
3 A new CAD/CAM system is to be installed at a company that manufactures bicycles. Describe **three** factors, other than staff capability and views, that need to be considered when making this change.
4 Staff at a telephone call centre usually answer and deal with any incoming calls. A new system is to be introduced that will direct calls to specific members of staff who will be trained to deal with specific enquiries. Describe **three** factors related to staff that need to be considered when making this change.

Discuss the importance of consultation, participation and communication when managing change

■ Communication

When change is necessary, those people who manage the change must ensure that the changes are explained clearly to other people within the organisation. Before anything is communicated, they need to plan how the communication will take place so that it is done considerately and takes into account all potential concerns that people within the organisation may have. However, it must not be kept secret for too long in case rumours are spread which could suggest the changes are worse than they really are. A common example of rumours being spread is when a department within an organisation (e.g. cleaning, ICT support or buildings maintenance) is outsourced to another company. If the workers find out before they are consulted, they might start worrying about losing their jobs, when in fact their jobs will be safe because the new company will have to retain all existing staff in the short term.

Managers must start by explaining the need for the change so that people will recognise the reasons for making the change. If people within the organisation do not see a reason for the change, then they will not be motivated and will believe it is change for the sake of change. When explaining the need for change with people within the organisation, the benefits must be illustrated very clearly, particularly if the people within the organisation are likely to benefit from the change.

Once everybody is aware of the need for change, they will need to know how it is going to affect them. They need to be reassured that their jobs will be safe and that if any new skills are required that they will be provided with a full training programme. If redundancies are necessary, then staff need to know if this will be on a voluntary basis and if it can be accommodated through natural wastage – this means people who would be retiring or leaving the company any way.

< Activity >

Imagine your school decides to change the uniform or introduce one if you do not currently have one. How would you feel if you were not told about this until the last day of term? How would you react?

Consultation

You have already read about how staff views need to be considered when managing change. People are a very important part of an organisation and they have emotions that must be taken into account. Telling staff about the reasons for change is only a small part of effective change management. Communication should be a two-way process and so includes listening to staff views about the changes.

If staff are consulted about a change, they are more likely to support that change. It is commonplace that when staff are not consulted about change, they tend to resist change as they feel unvalued. In large organisations where trade unions have an influence, it is important that the trade unions are consulted as they represent the views of the staff.

People within an organisation may want to express concerns about proposed changes and if they are given this opportunity, it will go someway towards believing they are being listened to. If staff are given the opportunity to ask questions of management directly, then they will feel even more valued and are more likely to be supportive of the change. Some people may have useful suggestions and if these are taken on board then they will be more motivated to change and likely to encourage others to support the change too. However, if suggestions are not taken on board, then the people that made those suggestions may become resistant to changes suggested by other people.

Participation

Staff need to be motivated to change and different people require different motivation factors. Some staff need to be told that they will be rewarded for the extra work that they put in to making the change successful. The reward could be a financial bonus or earning time off in lieu or a staff away day. Some staff will be excited by the change and these people can be used to help shape the changes that will happen. Staff who are likely to be particularly resistant to change can also be used to help introduce changes because if they become part of the task force that is introducing the change, they will feel valued and more likely to be supportive of the change.

While some staff may claim that it is not within their job description to be helping management, others will see it as an opportunity to show what they are capable of. If new ideas come from the people within the organisation, then they will take ownership of those ideas and the changes that are necessary. This will then lead to much less resistance to change.

Figure 6.6 Participation

There needs to be a balance of how many people should be allowed to participate with the change process. If too many people are involved, then there will be too many opinions and this will lead to conflict and dissatisfaction. If there are not enough people participating, then there may not be enough of them to encourage other people at their level within the organisation that the change is worthwhile and those who were not allowed to participate may be deliberately obstructive when it comes to the change. Similarly, some people who are not asked to be involved may feel that their contribution to the organisation is not valued.

Participation is a very important part of a user-centred approach to the systems life cycle. There is more explanation of how the client should be involved with the development of a new system in chapter 5.

< Activity >

Imagine a new community hall is to be built in your local area and you have been asked to be on a committee to decide how it should look and how it should be used.

1 What contributions could you make to the discussions?

2 When the community hall is built, do you think you will be more likely to use it if you've been part of the committee? Explain your answer.

QUESTIONS

1 Describe **three** reasons why employees might be resistant to change.
2 Describe **three** aspects of change that people within an organisation should be told about.
3 Explain why consultation is an important part of change management.
4 Describe **two** ways in which people within an organisation could participate with the management of change.

Discuss ethics relating to ICT with reference to codes of conduct, for example, the British Computer Society (BCS) code of conduct and the Association for Computing Machinery (ACM) Code of Ethics and Professional Conduct

■ Codes of conduct

There are a number of laws that cover the use of ICT and these are covered in module G061 at AS Level. These laws cover a variety of issues such as copyright, protection of individuals about whom data is stored, misuse of computers, freedom to seek information and investigation of data. These are all laws which everybody in the UK must follow. Codes of conduct provide a voluntary extension to these laws that determine how individuals should conduct themselves when using ICT, predominantly in the workplace. An example could include rules about the use of a workplace computer during a lunch break and what social activities are allowed and are not allowed.

Codes of conduct are usually related to ethical and moral issues that are not defined in law. A code of conduct therefore has no legal standing. However, people who sign up to a code of conduct are bound by the rules or the organisation's code and are subject to the organisation's disciplinary procedures.

Codes of conduct can be put into place by an organisation for its own employees, or an individual employee can sign up to a code of conduct provided by a professional body, such as the British Computer Society in the UK or the Association of Computing Machinery in the USA.

Some of the reasons for having a code of conduct within an organisation include:

Reason	Example
Setting boundaries for what can and can not be done using ICT so that both employers and employees know what is allowed or not allowed.	■ What the World Wide Web can be used for during working hours and what it must not be used for. ■ A company's computers should not be used for personal gain, such as running a private business. ■ Not being allowed to install software for personal use. ■ Being allowed to send private emails up to a maximum of 300 words per day.
Setting out expectations of what behaviour is acceptable and unacceptable when using ICT so that employees can not plead ignorance if disciplined for unacceptable behaviour.	■ Not sending emails that could be interpreted as flirting, bullying or gossip. ■ Not accessing inappropriate websites such as those with pornographic, racist or violent material.
Giving employees rights and responsibilities so that employees feel they are a valued person within the organisation and so that they realise their employer and other employees also have expectations of them.	■ The right for employees to request to see any emails that have been written about them by others. ■ The responsibility of employees to keep passwords private so that confidential data is not accessible by unauthorised personnel. ■ The responsibility of employees to regularly delete old files and emails to save storage space.
Giving employers responsibilities so that employees feel more valued and have confidence that their employer takes their responsibilities seriously.	■ A regular audit of health and safety for all computer equipment and users. ■ The provision of training courses about new software or equipment for employees.
To provide a method of applying disciplinary procedures if the code of conduct is breached by an employee so that appropriate and fair disciplinary action can be taken if necessary.	■ When an employee is caught sending inappropriate emails, they could be given a verbal or written warning, have pay deducted, be demoted, be suspended or dismissed from the organisation.
To give an organisation a good image within the industry so that they are seen to be responsible employers, manufacturers, retailers or service providers.	■ Customers, particularly other organisations, may be impressed by the fact that a potential supplier conforms to a code of conduct beyond the statutory laws.
Setting out required levels of competence for employees so that employers can expect good quality work and employees know what they are required to achieve.	■ Employees will be expected to attend training courses for any new software or equipment that is installed within the organisation that directly affects their own working practice.
To set standards of confidentiality so that information of a sensitive nature is not accessible outside of the organisation.	■ An employee needs to be aware that if they are privileged to know about a proposed take-over bid then they must not discuss this with their family or friends.

< Activity >

Other than the examples given above, give **six** other examples of how boundaries of what can and what cannot be done, and expectations of acceptable and unacceptable behaviour could be represented in a code of conduct.

BCS Code of Conduct

The full British Computer Society (BCS) Code of Conduct can be viewed on their website www.bcs.org. It is more general than an organisation's code of conduct because rather than covering specific responsibilities, it covers general responsibilities that a member should abide by. Individuals who join the BCS are compelled to comply by its Code of Conduct. Membership of the BCS is voluntary but formalises an individual's level of experience and commitment to good ethical practice. It covers the areas below:

- The public interest – This is about behaving in a way that is responsible towards the health and safety of oneself and others and having respect for the environment.
- Duty to relevant authority – This is about having respect for an employer or client or other organisation that has authority over a member's activities. It covers the need for members to carry out duties with diligence and to use professional judgement appropriately. Members are expected to avoid conflict between themselves and their relevant authority and to ensure that confidential information is not disclosed to a third party or used for personal gain.
- Duty to the profession – This is all about behaving in a professional manner within the ICT industry and in particular with other BCS members. It covers the promotion of ICT, supporting other users of ICT, behaving with integrity, and the extra care that should be taken when making public statements.
- Professional competence and integrity – This is about ensuring members regularly update their ICT knowledge and skills and only claim levels of competence that they possess. It also covers the need for members to encourage colleagues to act within the Code of Conduct and the need for members to take full responsibility for the work of sub-ordinates.

< Activity >

Read the full BCS Code of Conduct at
http://www.bcs.org/server.php?show=nav.6030

ACM Code of Ethics and Professional Conduct

The ACM Code of Ethics and Professional Conduct is designed to help members to make ethical decisions and to provide a framework for formal complaints. It is for individuals within the USA. It covers the following areas (note the American spellings are quoted directly from the ACM in accordance with their copyright conditions):

General moral imperatives

- Contribute to society and human well-being.
- Avoid harm to others.
- Be honest and trustworthy.
- Be fair and take action not to discriminate.
- Honor property rights including copyrights and patent.
- Give proper credit for intellectual property.
- Respect the privacy of others.
- Honor confidentiality.

More specific professional responsibilities

- Strive to achieve the highest quality, effectiveness and dignity in both the process and products of professional work.
- Acquire and maintain professional competence.
- Know and respect existing laws pertaining to professional work.
- Accept and provide appropriate professional review.
- Give comprehensive and thorough evaluations of computer systems and their impacts, including analysis of possible risks.
- Honor contracts, agreements, and assigned responsibilities.
- Improve public understanding of computing and its consequences.
- Access computing and communication resources only when authorized to do so.

Organizational leadership imperatives

- Articulate social responsibilities of members of an organizational unit and encourage full acceptance of those responsibilities.
- Manage personnel and resources to design and build information systems that enhance the quality of working life.
- Acknowledge and support proper and authorized uses of an organization's computing and communication resources.
- Ensure that users and those who will be affected by a system have their needs clearly articulated during the assessment and design of requirements; later the system must be validated to meet requirements.
- Articulate and support policies that protect the dignity of users and others affected by a computing system.
- Create opportunities for members of the organization to learn the principles and limitations of computer systems.

Compliance with the Code

- Uphold and promote the principles of this Code.
- Treat violations of this code as inconsistent with membership in the ACM.

< Activity >

< Activity >

Compare the BCS Code of Conduct with the ACM Code of Ethics and Professional Conduct.

a) Identify similarities between the two.

b) Identify anything that exists in one code, but not the other.

Discussing ethics

All of the requirements of the BCS and ACM codes are related to ethical practice. You can see many examples of ethical issues related to ICT from these codes, in particular the general moral imperatives in the ACM code. In an examination, you would be expected to discuss some of these ethical issues and relate them to the BCS and ACM codes. This means that you would need to look at the advantages and disadvantages of following ethical practice.

The main problem with following ethical practice is when competitors who do not do this gain a competitive advantage because they are not bound by the same voluntary terms and conditions. However, if they do not behave in a moral manner, then this will be noticed and eventually they may lose customers and thus profits. Behaving morally may seem difficult in the short term but it has long-term advantages when it comes to being noticed as a trustworthy person or organisation.

Employees within an organisation can be disillusioned if a code of conduct is introduced that they have not had to follow before. Hardworking employees who have worked diligently and probably worked beyond their working hours but have also taken advantage of using their employer's facilities may feel restricted by a code of conduct and that there is no longer a relationship of trust between the employer and employee. For example, an employee may have a laptop that they use at home and regularly carry out work in their own time for their employer using the laptop. They may also use the laptop to keep financial accounts for their own small business. When a code of conduct is introduced, the use of the laptop for personal gain may be banned and therefore the employee will not be allowed to use the laptop for their financial accounts. The employee may become disgruntled, particularly if other benefits such as being able to use the World Wide Web for personal shopping is banned, and as a result may withdraw their own goodwill of doing extra work for the employer beyond the terms of their contract.

< Activity >

An example of unethical practice is when working as a network cable installer for a contractor, the organisation the contractor is working for recognises you are a skilled professional and offers you a direct contract for some additional cabling work and you accept. What could be the consequences of this unethical practice?

Another example is that you have done some software installation work for a company and during this time you had access to information that showed the company would soon be going into administration. You withdraw your services, but behave unethically by advising the company to use one of your competitors. What could be the consequences of this unethical practice?

In a group, think of **four** other scenarios where you might be able to behave unethically to gain advantage and discuss the consequences. Report back to your class about your scenarios.

QUESTIONS

1 Describe **three** reasons why an organisation might introduce a code of conduct for its employees.
2 Describe **four** ways that the ACM code of ethics and professional conduct promotes ethical practice in the ICT industry.
3 Describe the essential difference between an organisation's own code of conduct and the codes of conduct provided by the BCS and ACM.

Describe the purpose and activities of professional bodies (e.g. BCS)

The British Computer Society (BCS) is used as an example here. A small selection of other professional bodies include:

- Intstitution of Engineering and Technology (IET, formally IEE)
- Institute of Electrical and Electronics Engineers (IEEE)
- Irish Computer Society (ICS)
- Österreichische Computer Gesellschaft (OCG) – Austria
- Information Processing Association of Israel (IPA)
- Korean Institute of Information Scientists and Engineers (KISS)
- Institute of Information & Computing Machinery (IICM) – Taiwan

The BCS itself claims, 'Its objects are to promote the study and practice of computing and to advance knowledge of and education in IT for the benefit of the public.' (see http://www.bcs.org/server.php?show=nav.00100c). The ACM 'delivers resources that advance computing as a science and a profession. ACM provides the computing field's premier Digital Library and serves its members and the computing profession with leading-edge publications, conferences, and career resources' (see http://www.acm.org/).

Some of the purposes and activities of professional bodies are summarised below:

Purpose	Examples of activities
To provide recognition of a person's experience in the ICT industry.	■ Allowing members to use letters after their name (e.g. MBCS, CITP). ■ Allowing members to use the organisation's logo on curriculum vitae or other documents. ■ Provision of a free email address with the professional body's domain name.
To provide opportunities for career development.	■ Training courses (e.g. e-type offered by BCS). ■ Advice on seeking jobs. ■ Methods of seeking prospective employees such as a website that advertises jobs and enables members to upload their curriculum vitae. ■ Career newsletters.
To enable members to discuss issues relating to ICT.	■ Discussion forums about general issues or specialist topics. ■ Special interest groups that meet to discuss that particular interest. ■ Online conferences. ■ Face-to-face conferences/lectures.
To provide knowledge and information services.	■ Provision of access to online books. ■ Provision of access to journals and magazines. ■ Provision of access to market research. ■ Provision of regular publications such as newsletters and magazines. ■ Publication of books (e.g. the BCS Glossary of ICT and Computing Terms).
To provide financial benefits to members.	■ Discounts for training courses. ■ Free legal helpline. ■ Discounts for professional indemnity insurance. ■ Discounts on software and hardware.

QUESTIONS

1 Describe the purpose of professional bodies.
2 Identify **four** activities of professional bodies.

Explain the advantages and disadvantages of belonging to a professional body

■ Advantages of belonging to a professional body

The advantages of belonging to a professional body are directly related to the purpose of the professional body. Each of the purposes is taken in turn below and the advantages explained.

To provide recognition of a person's experience in the ICT industry

- Using letters after their name or the BCS logo on stationery enables members to be recognised as an experienced ICT professional who has met a set of stringent criteria for membership to the organisation. This helps the member when applying for jobs or when securing contracts.
- Using an email address with the professional body's domain name gives instant recognition that the person is a member of that professional body and this will give a good impression to potential employers or organisations seeking the member's services.

To provide opportunities for career development

- Members have access to advice on how to seek jobs or contracts within the ICT industry. This advice will be offered exclusively to members and will increase their chances of future employment.
- Some training courses may be offered free as part of the membership which will enable members to improve their skill and competence levels.
- Exclusive access for members to job advertisements means that they will be competing only with other professional members when applying for certain jobs. They will also be confident that their employer acknowledges that professional membership recognises the experience of the member as being important.
- The ability to upload a curriculum vitae to the professional body's website means that members can offer their services as an employee or contractor and be found by organisations requiring their services without having to advertise using conventional methods.

To enable members to discuss issues relating to ICT

- Members will be able to participate in discussion forums about general issues related to ICT or specialist topics. This enables them to seek advice and opinions from other members which will increase their knowledge.

- Members can join specialist interest groups where they can meet with like minded people to discuss their interest or to participate in their interest. For example, somebody interested in geospatial technology might find it difficult to find other professionals to share experiences with, but a professional body provides this opportunity.
- Members can participate in either online or face-to-face conferences or lectures which gives them the opportunity to network with other professionals and to find out about new developments in the ICT industry.

To provide knowledge and information services

- Members will have access to online books, journals, magazines and newsletters that will enable them to keep up to date with the most recent developments in ICT as well as increasing their knowledge and understanding of ICT issues by reading about what experts have written.
- Members will have access to market research that has been conducted about issues to do with ICT meaning that they will not have to carry out their own market research or pay for statistics from other sources.

To provide financial benefits to members

- Members will be able to get discounts for training courses, hardware, software and other services related to ICT. This will reduce expenses and make more money available for other expenditure.
- Members will have access to a free legal helpline which will enable them to seek initial legal advice if required. This could be important, for example, if a client has not paid and the member needs advice on how to secure that payment. It could also be useful if a client takes legal action against the member.
- Members who work freelance or own their own company will need professional indemnity insurance. Professional bodies will be able to provide details of insurance services available and give discounts to the members.

< Activity >

Go to either the BCS or ACM website and look through the membership benefits section.

■ Disadvantages of belonging to a professional body

While there are many advantages to belonging to a professional body, there are only a few disadvantages. These include:

- The cost of membership to a professional body can be quite expensive and is a recurring annual cost. Members have to consider whether the benefits they receive outweigh the cost.

- Professional bodies have a code of conduct which members must abide by. While this is morally and ethically correct, it can put restrictions on the way members conduct themselves which non-members do not have to do. Members who own their own business and quote or tender for contracts, may find that their competitors behave unethically in order to secure the contract. The member in this situation has to act ethically and morally in accordance with the code of conduct of the professional body and may lose out as a result.
- Similarly, members who abide by the code of conduct will have extra responsibilities in relation to their clients and the environment which may cost them extra in time and money compared with non-members who will 'cut corners'.
- Members need to keep themselves updated with current developments in ICT by reading and maybe attending conferences. This can take a lot of time and while it can be beneficial to their professional competence, it can put a strain on their work–life balance.

QUESTIONS

1 Describe **two** reasons why an ICT professional would want to join a professional body.
2 Describe **two** disadvantages of ICT professionals belonging to a professional body.

Discuss the need to keep data confidential and explain how this can be achieved

Figure 6.7 Security of data

■ Discuss the need to keep data confidential

As with other discussion sections, you need to be able to look at different view points of arguments. You will need to be able to explain why data should be kept confidential and consider the problems that might occur if it is not kept confidential. You will also need to consider the problems that occur if data is kept secret and not revealed.

There are two main reasons for keeping data confidential:

- To comply with the Data Protection Act in terms of the privacy of information relating to individuals.
- Organisational, whereby information is commercially sensitive, such as plans for a new product.

The Data Protection Act states that all data stored about individuals must be kept secure. It is also a moral obligation of organisations to ensure that personal information is not revealed.

If you work for an organisation, then they will store personal information about you, such as date of birth, national insurance number, bank details (for paying salary), absence records, qualifications, disciplinary records and appraisals. This information is very private to you and you would not want your colleagues to know all of it. While it might be reasonable for a personnel administrator to enter and check your absence records, you would not want them to see details about your appraisals because they are private (known only to you and your manager). A correct balance needs to be made between ensuring people who are not entitled to see your information do not see it and ensuring that certain employees are able to carry out their duties if this requires using personal data.

Organisations also store information about customers or people linked with the organisation and this must remain confidential too. For example, your doctor's surgery will store all of your medical records. These could be very sensitive and so must be kept secure. If you purchase some products from a company, then you may or may not choose to receive emails from other companies that they select. If you choose not to, then they must ensure that other companies do not see your email address or any other data about you.

However, there are occasions when personal data may need to be accessed. For example, the Regulation of Investigatory Powers Act enables organisations to view emails that are being sent to and from employees within the organisation. The organisation may be suspicious that an employee is giving away company secrets and will therefore monitor emails being sent and received by that employee.

< Example >

The growth of social networking sites has caused controversy about the privacy of data. People sign up to join social networking sites and often do not realise that their profile can be seen by other people unless they specify that they want it to be private. Even if it is private, if you have allowed one of your friends access to view your profile, then one of their friends may also be able to see your profile without you being aware. People also use these sites to discuss issues, some of which might be about other people. The issues being discussed may be private and the individual who is being talked about may not want these details to be made available to other people. For example, one person may be talking about her friend having just broken up with her boyfriend, but her friend did not want anybody to know about this. Even information that you make freely available about yourself, such as a blog about what you did at the weekend, may seem quite harmless; but in 15 years' time you might not be happy about what you had done and written about but it could still be available on the internet for everybody to know about and so cannot be kept confidential.

Discuss the need to keep data confidential and explain how this can be achieved

Some information about people may need to be made publicly available or may be kept confidential when it would be in the public interests to reveal that data. There is a lot of debate as to whether details of the addresses of individuals on the sex offenders' register should be revealed. Some people would like to know this information so that they can ensure their children do not go near those addresses and are frustrated if they are denied access to this information. However, making this information available could cause vigilantism against the sex offender which does not allow the offender to live a normal life after they've served their punishment and causes disorder in the community.

< Example >

A potential employer may want to be able to see their potential employee's past employment records so that they can look at attendance records and disciplinary records to see if the person is reliable. The employer would consider this to be very useful information because it would help to determine whether to offer the person a job or not. However, if a person was suspended following a false allegation that was proven to be untrue, then this could be looked on unfavourably. Similarly, if the person had experienced a long period of illness due to an operation, then this could also go against the person. The employer might not want to risk employing the person, but the person would feel that this does not give them an opportunity of a fresh start.

Organisations will have data that is sensitive, such as plans for a new product or details of financial difficulties that are being experienced. In these situations, they will want this information to be kept secret so that their competitors do not find out and try to produce a better product or spread rumours about the financial difficulties. Other sensitive information may include market research statistics which have cost a lot of money to collect and if they are made available to other organisations, then they will gain an advantage at no cost to them.

■ Explain how to keep data confidential

A very important method of keeping data confidential that is often missed by many organisations is a security policy. This will include procedures that employees will be expected to abide by in order to keep data secure. Some of these procedures are explained below.

Employees need to be given guidance on how to use passwords. This should include:

- Choosing a password that can be remembered but is not obviously linked to you (such as your child's name) so that it is not easy to guess.

- Choosing a password of a minimum length (e.g. six characters) so that there is a larger combination of characters to make it harder for hackers to crack, and that includes letters, numbers, lower case, upper case and special characters to increase the number of combination of characters; some useful ideas include using 0 (zero) for the letter 'O' or 1 (one) for the letters 'L' or 'I'.
- Changing passwords regularly (e.g. at least every two months) in case somebody has found out your password.
- Not giving your password to anybody else, not even your manager or a colleague you think you can trust.
- Not using a password that has been used previously.

Employees need guidance on how to prevent unauthorised access to their workstation. This could include:

- 'Locking' the computer (not physically) so that it cannot be accessed without entering the password.
- Using a screensaver with a password so that if you forget to 'lock' your computer, then the screensaver will take over after a couple of minutes and 'lock' your computer for you.
- Ensuring nobody is looking over your shoulder or across the table when you enter your password.
- Anti-spyware should be installed so that malicious software cannot be installed on a computer that would gain access to the data on the computer and send it to the spyware originator. Spyware software can also track a user's keystrokes to find out what is being typed, including passwords.
- A firewall should be installed between a computer network (or an individual computer) and the internet or WAN. The firewall will ensure that only data of certain types are allowed in to the network and it will prevent some applications from sending data out of the network to prevent spyware attacks.

Other methods of keeping data confidential are discussed in the next section.

<table>
<tr><td colspan="2">QUESTIONS</td></tr>
<tr><td>1</td><td>Explain why it is necessary to keep data about employees confidential.</td></tr>
<tr><td>2</td><td>Describe two reasons why an organisation would want to keep information that is not about people secret.</td></tr>
<tr><td>3</td><td>Give three pieces of advice for choosing a secure password.</td></tr>
</table>

Discuss how encryption, authorisation, authentication, virus checking, virus protection and physical security can be used to protect data

■ Encryption

Figure 6.8 Encryption

Encryption is where data is scrambled so that if it is accessed unlawfully, then it will be meaningless to the person viewing it. However, it does not prevent an unauthorised person from intercepting the data, but it does make it difficult for them to decrypt it. When encryption is used, only the intended recipient of the data will be able to decrypt (unscramble) the data. The user probably won't be aware that the data is encrypted as the encryption and decryption is carried out automatically by computers.

> ### < Activity >
>
> Using the very basic encryption method below, decipher the message.
>
> A = Z, B = Y, C = X etc.
>
> **IVNVNYVI GL IVERHV**

The process of encryption (known as cryptography) uses a cipher (algorithm) to scramble the data. A decipher algorithm is required to unscramble the data. Random encryption keys are used to encrypt the data so that the same algorithm is not used each time. Therefore, anybody trying to intercept the data not only needs to be able to view the data, but must also have access to the decryption key. This also means that the intended recipient must also have the decryption key which can be problematic as the decryption key that is sent could also be intercepted. One way of overcoming this is to use public key encryption.

< Example >

Public key encryption

If Joanne wants to send a private message to Adrian, she (or rather her computer) uses Adrian's public key to encrypt the message. Adrian then uses his private key to decrypt it. This means that the decryption key does not need to be sent to the recipient. Even if somebody knows the public key, they can not work out what the private key is.

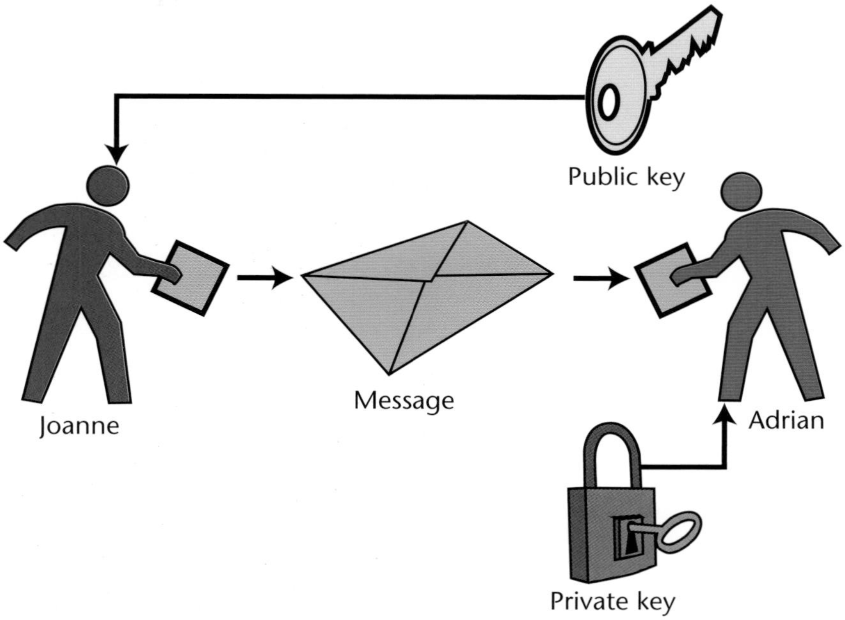

Figure 6.9 Public key encryption

Data that is sent across communication links that is not encrypted could be intercepted and viewed. This is a particular problem with wireless networks. Many home wireless networks now have encryption enabled as default, but there are still a lot out there that are not encrypted. Not only does this mean that somebody else can gain access to the wireless network, but they can also view all the data that is being sent across the network.

< Activity >

Find out what HTTPS is used for and how it links with TSL.

Authorisation

< Activity >

Think of as many words as you can that mean the same as 'authorise' or 'authorisation'.

Authorisation is all about giving permission for users to access data. Some users are allowed to see different aspects of data. For example, a personnel department may be able to see data about employee qualifications but not about their salaries, whereas a finance department may be able to see data about employee finances. There are four main levels of access to data:

Discuss how encryption, authorisation, authentication, virus checking, virus protection and physical security can be used to protect data

225

■ Read only – a user is allowed to read data.
■ Create – a user is allowed to create new data.
■ Write – a user is allowed to make changes to data.
■ Delete – a user is allowed to delete data.

Other access levels exist, such as being allowed to give permission to other users to access the data, but it is sufficient to focus on the four above.

< Activity >

Consider different file storage areas of your school or college network. What sort of access do you have to each storage area of the network? What sort of access do you think your teacher has to each storage area of the network?

Permission can be given to users to gain access to particular storage areas on a network. Similarly, permission can be given to different groups of users to gain access to data within a database.

< Example >

Your school or college will use a management information system to store and use data about you. Groups of users may have the following permissions to access your personal data.

	Teacher	Data clerk	Nurse	Parent (for own children)
Name	R	RCWD	R	R
Address	R	RCWD	R	R
Assessments	RCW	RCWD	–	R
Medical	R	–	RCW	–
Behaviour	RCW	–	R	–
Special needs	R	–	R	R

Key: R = Read only, C = Create, W = Write, D = Delete

To gain authorisation, a user must identify themselves. This is usually done by using a username, but there are other methods, such as a magnetic stripe on the back of a card, a smart chip on a card, a phone number, an email address, voice recognition, a fingerprint and a retina scan. On its own, authorisation only tells the computer who the user is and then gives the user the permissions required. However, it does not prevent somebody from pretending to be a different person.

Authentication

Figure 6.10 Identification

< Activity >

Think of as many words as you can that mean the same as 'authentic'.

Authentication is used to prove a person is who they say they are. The most common method of authentication is a password. A user will usually use a username to state who they are (e.g. paul_long) and then use a password to prove they are that person. As only that person knows the password, it is accepted as proof that the user is genuinely that person (i.e. authentic). Personal identification numbers (PINs) are often used instead of passwords, for example with credit cards and cash cards.

However, passwords and PINs do have weaknesses. These include:

- People write down their passwords or PINs which mean that they may be easily found, especially if a PIN is kept with a cash card.
- People choose passwords and PINs associated with themselves (e.g. the last four digits of their phone number), making it easy for hackers to guess.
- Default passwords set by a system are often used (e.g. 'password' or '12345') with the user not being required to change them, meaning that a hacker can easily try the default password.
- Passwords and PINs often are not changed by people, meaning that there is more chance of a regular observer learning and then using them in the future. Hackers can watch people typing in their passwords (e.g. by looking through a window) or entering their PIN (e.g. by looking over the person's shoulder).

Discuss how encryption, authorisation, authentication, virus checking, virus protection and physical security can be used to protect data

227

- A person may use the same password or PIN for everything because they find it difficult to remember many different ones, meaning that if a hacker discovers one password or PIN then they know them all.
- Software can be used to keep trying out character combinations until the correct one is found.

Some authentication methods perform the process of authorisation and authentication in one go. These are known as biometric authentication methods because they use parts of a person's body that are unique. Fingerprints can be used to identify a person. A fingerprint is unique, so it alone identifies who the person is. It can only belong to that person because it is unique, and therefore the person is obviously who they say they are. Similarly retina scans can be used for this purpose.

Fingerprint recognition is becoming much cheaper to implement, but there are many concerns about privacy. Some people think that if their fingerprint is stored for checking against when using an ATM, then the record of that print could also be used without permission to identify them if they commit a crime. Other people say that it should not matter because that person should not have committed a crime in the first place. Retina scanners are not as cheap as fingerprint recognition scanners, but they are not as controversial among human rights activists. Some people are also concerned that a thief may cut off a person's finger or take out their eye. However, nobody can forget their finger or eye, but it is very easy to forget a password or PIN. Fingerprint and retina recognition can also be used for authentication, so it means that a person does not have to carry around a cash or credit card.

Voice recognition can also be used for the dual purpose of authorisation and authentication. However, a voice can easily be recorded and then played back. There are also technical difficulties with voice recognition when a person has a cold and therefore a different sounding voice.

< Activity >

Complete the following table:

Authentication method	Advantages	Disadvantages
Password/PIN		
Fingerprint		
Retina scan		
Voice recognition		

Virus checking and protection

In computing, a virus is a piece of software that is designed to:

- cause deliberate harm to data stored on a computer
- replicate itself so that it transfers to as many computers as possible.

A virus will have an effect on a computer immediately purely by its presence, but then it can start to cause problems. Some viruses do silly things like minimise your window when you're not expecting it or send a picture of an ambulance across the screen. Other viruses deliberately cause harm to data on a computer. They may delete files in particular folders, make changes to application files so that they will not run, or they could systematically destroy all the data on a computer's disks.

Computers can be infected by viruses when new data is introduced to the computer. This can be through USB storage devices, memory cards, CD-Rs, DVD-Rs, across a network, via the internet or any other method where data is transferred. One method of avoiding viruses is to isolate a computer so that it does not receive any new files. However, this is often not very practical, although it can be sensible if a computer is only used for a single purpose and never needs to receive new data (e.g. to control a lighting system in a house). The main method used to avoid viruses is anti-virus software. This has two main elements. The first is to have a resident shield that will detect any viruses as soon as they try to enter the computer system and stop them from doing so. The other is to scan a computer to see if there are any viruses and then to remove them.

Scanning is only required the first time anti-virus software is installed as the resident shield will keep viruses out of the system after that time. To give you an idea of how important a resident shield is, if a computer has no resident shield and no operating system updates and is connected to the internet, it will be attacked by several viruses within minutes. It is therefore advisable to download anti-virus software using a different computer and then install the software on the unprotected computer before it is connected to the internet.

The main problem with anti-virus software is that new viruses are being introduced all the time. While the anti-virus software can look for patterns, it can not guarantee that it will not spot a new virus. Therefore it needs to be regularly updated. If a computer is connected to the internet, then the anti-virus software should automatically update itself. Some companies charge an annual subscription for this service. The anti-virus software installs its resident shield in memory and uses up processor power which means that other applications can be slowed down and file access is slower due to each file being checked before it can be opened.

< Activity >

1 Find out what the Trojan virus 'Dica-Kit' does.

2 Find out what the malware '78Crack-A' does.

3 Find out what the worm 'Sdbot-ZY' does.

4 Find out about the 'footmouth' and 'nastyfriend' hoaxes.

5 Why do you think people create hoax virus alerts?

6 What signs are there that an alert is a hoax?

7 Discuss with other people in your class any hoaxes you may have received.

■ Physical security

Figure 6.11 Physical security

Physical security can take many forms. Some of these are discussed below.

Surge protection

Computers, servers and other storage devices are all electrically operated and therefore prone to electrical surges. An electrical surge can not only damage the device, but also affect any data that is stored on disks. All these devices should therefore be plugged in to sockets that include surge protection which will cancel out the surge.

Locks

Passwords, encryption and other methods of preventing access to data will help to keep data secure, but there is also the chance that the data on storage media could be stolen too. Therefore, all data must be kept under lock and key. This means putting servers in secure rooms with only those who need access having keys/codes. Many organisations forget to keep their back-ups secure. These should also be kept under lock and key, which could include a secure room, secure cupboard or safe. This should apply to back-ups that are stored off-site too.

Different types of locks can be used. Code number locks are useful if a few people need access and it saves a key being copied, but often people will write down the code or forget it. It's also possible for somebody to look over your shoulder as you enter the code. On some locks, you can see the numbers that have been used as the buttons will be worn. It's also important to remember to change the code regularly. Where keys are used, this requires copies to be made and if somebody loses a key, then the whole lock needs replacing and new keys issuing. Electronic methods can be used such as magnetic stripe cards, although there is the danger of these being cloned. However, if a card is lost or stolen, it is very simple to cancel it so that it no longer works.

Security guards

Some organisations store extremely sensitive data and therefore will employ security guards. Guards may be used to check every single person that enters the building or they might be strategically placed by a server room.

Flood and fire protection

It's not just thieves that can cause damage or loss to data. A flood or fire can wipe out all data that is stored on servers and on back-up tapes. Server rooms should never be on the ground floor in order to reduce the chances of flood damage. Server rooms should be fire proof so that fire in other parts of a building cannot spread to the server room. Smoke detectors should be used within server rooms so that a fire can be detected quickly and CO_2 (carbon dioxide) fire extinguishers that only expel a gas should be available. Back-up tapes should be stored in fire-proof storage such as a fire-proof safe.

Portable security

Data is not just stored on servers. It also exists on removable storage. In 2008, there were many stories in the media about lost disks and laptops with personal data on them. Many laptops include a Kensington security slot into which a standard Kensington security cable can be attached. This will deter the opportunistic thief, but a determined thief will just break the laptop and make a lot of mess. It's also important for people carrying portable data to keep it safe in a locked briefcase although this could be easily broken.

Figure 6.12 A Kensington lock

Discuss hardware and software developments that are changing, or might change, the way we live. Examples might include advances in treating injuries or disease, leisure activities, the environment, the home, education and freedom of speech and movement. This list of examples is not exhaustive as questions will reflect the current use or abuse of ICT in society

For this learning objective, you are expected to keep up to date with new developments in ICT. You should be regularly reading computing magazines or computing newspapers and watching television programmes such as *The Gadget Show* in order to keep up with developments. This might sound like a bit of a burden, but some new technologies are fascinating to find out about. If you find a useful article in a newspaper or on the internet, then it is worth sharing it with your class by uploading it to your virtual learning environment (VLE) or emailing it to the class.

The focus for this learning objective is on the hardware and software developments and the effect that these are having or might have on our lives. Some examples of topics are given, but questions could be asked about any new developments. Examination papers are written between 18 and 24 months before you sit the exam, you will not be expected to answer a question on a specific development that has only happened in the last 6–12 months. Examiners will try to make exam papers interesting and so something that was a major development while they were writing the paper may be a topic that is used for a question.

As long as you keep up with your background reading, you should have plenty of material that you can use to answer questions because they will be asked in such a way that you can contribute different experiences. You should also try to be imaginative and you could discuss possible developments that have not yet taken place but might do in the future. In this situation, the examiner will nearly always give you a mark because they can not assume that it will never happen.

To gain the most marks, you will need to discuss the effect the developments will have. You might be given a target group, such as employees, children or the government, about which you should discuss the effect. If the question does focus on such a group, then ensure that your answer also focuses on the group. When you discuss the effect of the developments, ensure that you give a detailed and balanced argument. Balanced means that you must look at different points of view, usually advantages and disadvantages. Detailed means that you must explain why something is an advantage. For example, if you were to say 'an interactive classroom wall will make learning more exciting for students' then you have not given enough detail. You would need to say something like 'an interactive classroom wall would mean that students could approach the wall and answer questions by touching it and the pictures displayed would change depending on answers given; this will engage and motivate students to learn.'

Each of the topics suggested in the specification are included below. Each one will be structured in a different way to give you a variety of different ways of learning. At the beginning of each topic, there will be a short explanation as to why the topic is presented in the way it is.

▓ Treating injuries or disease

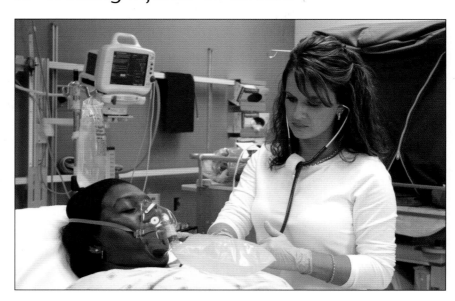

Figure 6.13 Medical technology

< Activity >

There are many ways in which ICT is being used to treat injuries and disease, and many new developments, so the best way to find out about them is to do a bit of research. Therefore, visit http://www.teach-ict.com/news/news_stories/news_medicine.htm for up-to-date news stories about how ICT is being used in medicine. Produce a short (4–6 slides) presentation to your class about **two** innovative ways in which ICT is used to treat injuries or disease.

■ Leisure activities

Figure 6.14 Games technology

For this section, you are going to be given a question and an answer. The question will be as if it was an examination question and the answer will be written as it should be in an examination.

< Example >

Question: Discuss how developments in hardware and software are changing the way people play computer games.

Answer: A new style of console game playing has developed that enables game players to use hand-held movement sensors in three dimensions (3D) in mid-air. The Nintendo Wii games console was the first to introduce this technology. Rather than playing games using a joystick or simple game pad, players can move the sensor in all three dimensions. This has enabled players to play games such as tennis and ten-pin bowling where they mimic the motions of a player to compete against the computer or other players at home. It's also possible to compete against other players across the internet using a wireless connection to a wireless router in the home. The physical aspect of the game has meant that players are no longer stuck to sitting in front of a computer or games console just using their fingers, but instead are jumping up and down and moving around physically which will have a positive impact on their physical health and reverse part of the trend towards obesity. However, the sensors have to be tied to the player's hands because there have been many occasions when the player has moved too quickly and the sensor has 'flown' out of their hand and caused damage, particularly to televisions. The regular movement of hands and jumping around is also likely to cause damage with spillages of drinks and damage to ceiling lights and ornaments. The next development was a board that could be used for fitness training. This is capable of weighing a person and monitoring their balance. There are various games that people can use to improve their levels of fitness which is a great improvement on the old style of game playing where the player is sat down for long periods of time. It's possible that in the future, small sensors could be attached to the hands, feet and head and the whole body could become part of game play. This would be part of developments in virtual reality and the player would feel a real part of the game. A headset that shows the image on a screen giving a 3D view could be used or just a special pair of glasses. However, there are risks that this could cause nausea due to moving about but not physically seeing what is happening in the real world. It's even possible that sensors could be injected into the body so that nothing has to be worn and implants could be used that send the images directly to the eyes. This could be very risky because there might be side effects that are not known for many years until they develop, similar to the problems that asbestos caused when it wasn't realised it would cause lung problems for people who breathed in the dust particles. Holograms could be used in the future which would provide an interface, such as a cockpit, that could be seen and the player could use the controls by interacting with the hologram. As the player moves the virtual controls, the hologram image could change so that the player gets a real sense of interaction using the movements that a real pilot would use.

Notice how a number of different ideas have been given: some are technologies that have already been developed, and some are potential new technologies. Different points of view have been given looking at both the excitement and realism that the new technologies could give to games as well as some of the potential problems the new technologies could cause.

■ The environment

In this section, you are given a set of bullet points on how developments in ICT have affected the environment. You can use these for revision, but you would need to identify the advantages and disadvantages and turn them into a full discussion in an examination.

Advantages	Disadvantages
■ Video and teleconferencing reduces the need to travel and thus CO_2 emissions. ■ Wireless technologies and satellites mean there is less need for cables which can be unsightly. ■ Sensors can be used to monitor the weather and software can forecast what is going to happen, which can mean floods and hurricanes can be prepared for causing less damage. ■ In the future, weather could be predicted and gases could be emitted to change the pattern of undesirable weather. ■ Farmers can use sensors that detect how much rainfall there has been and then automated sprinklers water the crops when extra water is needed. ■ Developments in solar-powered technology mean that less coal and oil has to be used for producing electricity.	■ Unsightly cables that can be seen and ruin landscapes. ■ Mobile phone networks that have potential health risks. ■ Hardware uses up a lot of electricity which will run out one day if new generation methods are not found. ■ Computers tend to require air conditioning which requires yet more electricity. ■ Increased use of electric devices causes more CO_2 emissions from electricity generation which contributes to global warming. ■ Equipment which is thrown out becomes waste in landfills.

■ The home

Figure 6.15 Technology in the home

In this section, you are going to be given a framework for answering a question in an examination. You will be prompted with parts of the answer and you should develop a full answer.

< Activity >

Use the table below to structure your answer to this question. Discuss how hardware and software developments could change the way in which people live in their homes. The first one has been done for you.

Idea	Advantage	Disadvantage
An electronic fridge could know exactly what products are inside it by using remote frequency identification (RFID) tags. The user could programme the fridge using a touch screen or wireless connection using a laptop to identify what the minimum stock levels should be.	When the fridge starts to run out of a particular food, an automated order could be sent to the supermarket which will save having to remember what to buy. An audible and visual warning could be given if a product reaches its use-by date meaning that there is less chance of food poisoning. If the fridge suffers a power failure then a battery-operated device could send a text message to the owner which means they could return home to save the food.	As different food will run out at different times, this could result in several orders being sent to the supermarket at different times and so there will still be a need to either go and collect the food or arrange a delivery. If the owner is a long way from home when they receive the text message, it could be too long before they return home and so there would be no benefit to the text system. There might also be false alerts which mean wasted journeys back home.
Electronic books could be used on a foldable screen that could be carried around in the pocket. Developments in solid state memory could mean that thousands of books could be stored on one device.		

Idea	Advantage	Disadvantage
Lights and curtains in the home could be controlled by signals sent through the electrical circuit so that they turn on/off or open/close at pre-defined times.		
Television could be watched by means of a hologram that follows you around the house with an ear implant that means only you can hear what you are watching.		
A glass dining room table could turn into a touch screen when required that enables interactive games to be played, the Web to be surfed, and different images and videos to be displayed that can be used as a background during dinner times.		

■ Education

In this section, you are going to consider how ICT is used at your school or college and then try to be imaginative about the future. Visit http://www.teach-ict.com/news/news_stories/ news_education.htm for news stories about how ICT is being used in education.

< Activity >

Fill in the table below by listing **three** different ways in which ICT is currently used innovatively at your school or college. Then explain what the advantages and disadvantages of each are.

Innovative use	Advantage	Disadvantage

Now do the same, but for **three** ways in which ICT could be used in education in the future. Explain what hardware and software developments would be needed to achieve each new idea.

Future use	Hardware developments	Software developments

Figure 6.16 Technology in society

■ Freedom of speech and movement

In this section, you are going to be set a question that could appear on an examination paper. Remember all the things that you have learned above about focusing on hardware and software developments, the impact on society and being imaginative about the future.

QUESTION

Discuss how hardware and software developments could affect the freedom of speech and movement of criminals. You should not limit your answer to existing systems and the way in which they could be advanced, but allow an imaginative approach given possible trends and directions of hardware and software development in the future.

Summary

Impact of external change on:
- Organisation
- Individuals
- Systems

Change management
- Good change management
  - Identify need for change
  - Sharing reasons for change
  - Planning the change
  - Implementing the change
- Staff capability
- Staff views
- Systems
- Equipment
- Accommodation

Good methods of managing change
- Communication
- Consultation
- Participation

Ethics
- Codes of Conduct
  - Voluntary extension to the law
  - Sets out expectations
- British Computer Society Code of Conduct
  - Public interest
  - Duty to relevant authority
  - Duty to the profession
  - Professional competence and integrity
- ACM Code of Ethics and Professional Conduct
  - General moral imperatives
  - More specific professional responsibilities
  - Organisational leadership imperatives
  - Compliance with the code

Purpose and activities of professional bodies
- Purpose
  - Recognition of experience
  - Opportunities for career development
  - Enable discussion and collaboration
  - Knowledge and information services
  - Financial benefits

Disadvantages
- Cost of membership
- Abiding by code of conduct
- Extra responsibilities
- Work-life balance

Keeping data confidential
- Need
  - Data Protection Act compliance
  - Sensitive data
- Regulation of Investigatory Powers Act

Keeping data confidential
- Passwords
- 'Locking' the computer
- Screensaver password
- Vigilance and awareness
- Anti-spyware
- Firewall

Protecting data
- Encryption
  - Scrambling data
  - Public and private keys
- Authorisation
  - Read only
  - Create
  - Write
  - Delete
- Authentication
  - Passwords and PINs
  - Biometric security
- Virus checking and protection
  - Virus scan
  - Resident shield
  - Updating software
- Physical security
  - Surge protection
  - Locks
  - Security guards
  - Flood and fire protection
  - Portable security

Discuss hardware and software developments
- Treating injuries or disease
- Leisure activities
- The environment
- The home
- Education
- Freedom of speech and movement

Test 1

Bill runs a factory that makes teddy bears. Several employees are required to make them by hand as part of the production line. He has decided to use an automated production line that will make the teddy bears instead of them being hand made.

1 a) Describe **two** new jobs that may be required.   [2]
   b) Describe why it is important to consider staff views before making this change.   [4]
   c) Describe the how accommodation should be considered for this change to happen.   [4]
   d) Explain the importance of communicating and consulting with the employees
       before the change.   [6]

Bill has decided to join the British Computer Society which is a professional body.

2 Describe **three** benefits of Bill joining the British Computer Society.   [6]

Bill has decided to introduce a code of conduct for all his employees that use computers at work.

3 a) Describe **three** rules that might be included in the code of conduct.   [6]
   b) Describe **one** benefit to Bill's employees of having a code of conduct.   [2]
   c) Describe **two** benefits to Bill of having a code of conduct for his employees.   [4]

Bill uses a database to store data about his employees.

4 a) Explain the importance of keeping the data about his employees confidential.   [6]
   b) Describe **three** different methods that could be used to keep the data confidential. [6]

Test 2

The Chancellor of the Exchequer has decided to increase the basic rate of income tax by 2%.

1 Discuss the impact of this change on the individuals and systems within a school.   [7]

The Director of ICT would like to have all lessons taught through the virtual learning environment (VLE).

2 Discuss the importance of participation when managing this change.   [7]

3 Discuss how encryption, authorisation and authentication could be used to protect
   data on the VLE.   [7]

The Director of ICT is considering joining a professional body which has a code of conduct.

4 Explain some of the ethical practices that the Director of ICT will be expected to
   abide by.   [6]

The school runs an annual Geography field trip to the Lake District. Some parents find it very difficult to pay for the trip and some students find some of the activities on the trip boring.

5 Discuss how hardware and software developments could change Geography field trips
   at the school. You should not limit your answer to existing systems and the way in which
   they could be advanced but allow an imaginative approach given possible trends and
   directions of hardware and software development in the future.   [11]

Introduction to the project

Introduction

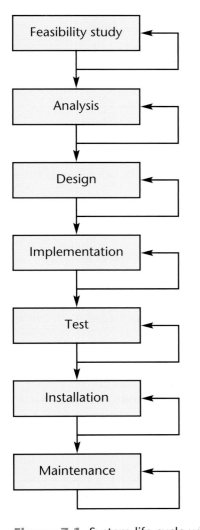

Figure 7.1 System life cycle with recursion

The project is based on the systems life cycle.

You need to, in conjunction with a third-party user, choose a well-defined client-driven problem that enables you to demonstrate your skills to:

- analyse a problem
- design a solution to the problem
- develop the software solution
- test the solution against the requirements specification
- document the solution
- evaluate the solution.

What makes a suitable project is a key question to consider before starting the project. If you make the wrong choice of project, you could waste weeks of work by having to start again. In the very worst case scenarios, it might not be possible to do anything about it and as a result your grades will suffer.

The project is worth 20% of your final grade (40% of the A2 grade) and it is vital to get the choice correct from the very beginning. The project should take approximately 80 hours to complete – this is the recommendation from the examination board and you should try and stick to this amount of time.

Some points to consider in the selection of appropriate projects are given below and should be looked at and read before beginning the project.

1 The project should fit the specification

This is a general statement but important. The project should be able to meet all the requirements of the specification and be of sufficient complexity to allow the top marks to be reached. If you read the marking scheme for the specification, it is possible to achieve all the required elements with a relatively simple project. It is because of this that the problem itself must have a certain degree of complexity – it must be of A-level standard.

2 How complex must the solution be?

The complexity of the solution is a difficult question. The specification does not give specific information on complexity. The project must be logically correct – the flow from 'analysis' to 'design', to 'creation', to 'documentation' and to 'evaluation' must be correct. Each section is based on the previous and it must reference and follow it – you cannot add something in 'creation' that has not been designed and appeared in the analysis. The complexity of the project is based, to a degree on the analysis, however the solution developed must need a level of complexity greater than a simple linear-type solution. This means that a simple singular problem with one output is not sufficient to gain full marks.

- In a database, a single table, form, query and report is a linear solution.
- In a spreadsheet, data entry, formulae and functions based on a single output is a linear solution.
- In websites, a purely content-driven information website, even if hierarchical in nature, is a linear solution.

To get into the higher band, your project will need to be:

- a database which uses the data from the tables to create different queries and reports
- a spreadsheet which can use functions and formulae to provide different outputs on different sheets
- a website that takes data from the user and can store and use it in some way, such as sending documents, log-on areas etc.

The complexity should be there from the beginning and included in the analysis. It should not be 'bolted on' when you get to development.

3 The project should enable the student to achieve all areas of the marking criteria

In the evaluation section, there are marks available for 'a range of possible extensions'. If your project is a complete unit with no extensions, you will not be able to achieve marks in this area. Therefore, you must make sure that when you are stating the problem you do not solve all of it, but leave room for extension at a later date.

4 A stand-alone problem or a redevelopment of an existing solution?

Projects do not need not be stand-alone; the enhancement or modification of an existing system provided that all these elements are covered is acceptable. They are more likely to be a real-world situation. Unfortunately projects of the type 'a shop has a paper-based system that it wants to computerise' are unlikely to exist nowadays. It is still perfectly acceptable, if you can find one, to computerise a manual system. It may be, however, that the system has a computer system and you are updating a part of it.

5 A suitable problem with end user interaction

The project work ideally requires user interaction, that is there should be a 'real' problem to solve and people to help you. It is recognised that it is not always possible for you to solve a real problem, but you should try and get 'real' people to help you. 'Real' people refers to people who actually work in the area where your problem lies. The people need to be prepared to help you with questionnaires, interviews and testing of the final solution.

You need to involve a client and/or third-party user, who may be different people. The people will need to provide information for the analysis, use the solution and contribute towards its evaluation.

A teacher could act as the third party, but this arrangement is far from ideal and if you can find a person who is involved with the organisation that has the problem you will produce a better solution. Ideally, you should try and look for projects beyond school life and into business and organisations in your community.

It is a good idea to inform the individual of the level of involvement that you will require from them. They should be willing and able to assist:

- in the analysis of the problem, (where their requirements are obtained) – this will include an interview
- at the design stage to comment on the designs that you produce
- at the software development, testing and installation stages, (where they may be involved in prototyping)
- at the evaluation stage (where they are involved in checking that the system is completed as specified).

Leading on from these, they should be willing to critically comment on the system.

6 The project should demonstrate the complete system life cycle

You need to show the successful completion of a whole task from its initial definition involving a third-party user, to its acceptance and evaluation by that third party and other possible users. This starts with the definition of the problem, through to designing, creating, testing, documenting and evaluation the solution that has been created.

7 Work within the limits of the available hardware, software and personal skills

You may have an excellent problem and brilliant design, but unfortunately find that you do not have either the hardware or the software to implement it. It is a balancing act to make sure that the solution does what you want within the resources available.

The solution may be implemented using one or more of

- a standard generic applications software package
- prewritten modules
- toolkits/authoring/publishing software, interface/client software (including HTML/Java).

You need to ensure that you have the skills to use the packages to create the solution. You do not want to have to learn how to use new software as you will not have the time.

8 An organisation or a person?

The size of the organisation is always a question that arises. You can create a project that gets full marks even if there is only one person. The size of the organisation is not important – it can be a multinational company or just one person. What is important is that you differentiate between the end user and the person in charge. Even if there is only one person in the organisation, they may have to 'put on different hats' to help you with different parts of the project – some parts require an end-user response, some require a 'management' contribution. Even if this is the same person, there will be no problems as long as you make this distinction.

9 Evidence to submit

You need to submit a report on what you have done. This report is the evidence that is sent to the moderator, so if any evidence is not included in the report, it cannot be marked.

The project report should contain:

- a title
- a contents list
- page numbers.

The report should be spellchecked and appropriately formatted. There are three marks available for the presentation of the final report. You must have created the report yourself. If you use a report template supplied to you by a third party you will not be able to gain these marks and effectively your project will be marked out of 77.

You should not submit magnetic or optical media as supporting evidence, but you can make references to web pages available over the internet or to photographs where appropriate. Ideally, all evidence will be submitted on paper and it will follow the sequence laid out in the following chapters. You want the moderator to be able to sit down and read the report sequentially (rather than to have to flip backwards and forwards through it) confirming the marks.

10 Final points to consider

■ Interest

You will be working on this project for a considerable period of time. It must be something that will hold your interest for that length of time. If you become bored of it after three months and still have another five months to go, it may affect the quality of the work you produce.

■ Teacher supervision

At all times, the teacher must be convinced that the work you are producing is your own work and nobody else's. This can be a problem if you do the majority of work at home. It is essential that throughout the project each component is monitored by your teacher.

■ Teacher expertise

Although your teachers will have many skills, they will not be an expert in every piece of software written and every problem. You must be aware that if you require assistance and support, but have chosen software in which your teachers are not experts, then you will need to find it from elsewhere. This may affect how well your teachers are able to supervise the project, so choose carefully and weigh up the advantages/disadvantages of using specialist software.

■ Reference to real data

You must be careful not to enter real data into your system. For example, if you are entering names and addresses, one way around this is to pick a name from an address book, a different address and a different telephone number. This way the data entered will not relate directly to a 'living identifiable human being' and contravene any of the principles of the Data Protection Act.

■ Programming and customisation

A common question is 'how much programming must I do in the project?' The answer, unfortunately, varies. It will depend on the project. It may be none or it may be a fair amount. You are more likely to customise an existing software package.

The course is ICT, it is not computing, so the examiner is not expecting a custom written solution in a programming language. They will be expecting you to take an existing package (spreadsheet, word processor, database etc.) and tailor it to your solution. This may involve creating menus, toolbars, macros and *some* programming.

Types of problem

There are many different types of problem that you could choose, but in general, they can be divided in four categories:

■ Database

This involves accessing a database, and sorting and searching data. You will be required to print reports and maybe mail merge a document.

Examples of database-type projects include:

- a video shop – for storing data on customers, on videos, and on hiring and reservation of videos
- a hotel – for booking rooms in a hotel and calculating the bill
- an employment agency – for matching job vacancies to people.

■ Data analysis/mathematics

This involves collecting data and then analysing it by producing graphs or tables of data. It may involve calculations of some kind.

- Data collection and analysis – collecting data via questionnaires and analysing it.
- Booking a holiday – holiday data entry and calculation.
- Budgets – working out a budget for an organisation.

■ Measuring/control

This involves monitoring or measuring using some form of control equipment. It may be a mock up of a real situation.

- Traffic control – setting up a sample of a traffic light sequence, questionnaires to see what to implement, analysing data and informing people of the new lights.
- Burglar alarm system – setting up a mock system, user instructions etc.

■ Internet/web-based

This involves the use of the internet in some way.

- E-commerce – selling goods over the internet.
- Setting up access to a database over the internet.
- Chatrooms and discussion boards.

These are only a few examples and are not complete. You would need to develop the project and complete all the sections to score marks.

You are better off choosing a topic where you will be able to complete all sections of the documentation with a database or spreadsheet that is fairly simple than having a very complicated database or spreadsheet and not being able to completely document it.

Log of events

You are required to keep a log of events for your project. This is a diary of when you worked on the project and what you did. This log is important because without it the number of marks you can get in the final section is limited.

It is an ongoing account of the project. It can be handwritten or typed on the computer. It should be logically correct – this means that the dates on letters in the project and the project plan should correspond with the log of events.

Two main questions asked about the log are:

- How long does each entry need to be? – It does not need to be an essay for each day, a few sentences about what you did that day is enough.
- Do I need to write an entry every day? – No you do not. You only need to fill in the log if you do some work on your project.

An outline for the log might be as shown here.

Date	Activity
4/9/09	Completed background to the problem
7/9/09	Wrote questions for interview
8/9/09	Planned date for interview

Make sure you get into the habit of filling in the log after working on the project.

Definition, investigation and analysis

Introduction

There are a total of 25 marks available for this section: three for the definition of the problem, 10 for the investigation and 12 for the analysis.

As this is the opening section of the project, first impressions are important. This is the part of the project the examiner will read first, so it is important to get it right. If it is vague, waffly, indistinct or incorrect it will set up an unfavourable impression in the mind of the examiner that may be difficult to change later in the project. Imagine opening up a project to find it untidy, with spelling mistakes, and different font types and font sizes all over the page. What would your initial impression be? Perhaps it is not fair that impressions contribute to the mark, but they do. It is in your best interests to follow the guidelines to gain the highest mark you can.

The amount of work involved in this first section is disproportionate to the number of marks available. However, much of the work done here will be re-used in the design and evaluation sections. From your point of view, this section is very important – it will let you to clarify, in your mind, what the problem is and what you will be developing as the solution. You will not be able to produce a good project unless you are clear about what the problem is and what your solution is going to be prior to attempting the design.

Overview

The section can be broken down into five stages.

1 **Problem definition and organisation:** A new computer system must have a purpose. There will be a problem, or perhaps several problems, that the system you create will be required to solve. You must first define the problem, so that you can select a system that will solve it. You must also outline the organisation that has the problem.
2 **The gathering and analysis of data about the current system:** This involves you in detailed fact finding and identification of why the problems with the current system have arisen.

3 **Establishing objectives for the new system:** Once you have defined the existing problem, and gathered data about the current situation, the next step is for you to decide what the new system will be designed to achieve.

4 **Analysing alternative systems:** There will always be several different ways of designing a system to meet the stated objectives. You need to think of, analyse and evaluate several different options. The alternative systems need not necessarily be computer systems.

5 **Hardware and software selection:** Having selected the system that best meets the system objectives, you need to compile a reasoned list of the hardware and software required.

There should be a continuous process of re-examining and re-assessment of each stage of the system selection process, until the preferred system is eventually selected. In other words, you should be continually asking:

■ Have I properly defined the problem?
■ Have I correctly gathered and analysed all the relevant data about the current system?
■ Have I satisfactorily identified the objectives for the new system?
■ Have I identified and properly evaluated all the available system alternatives?

You should not be asking these questions in isolation, but in conjunction with the end user – the project should be a partnership. It is the end user – the client – who makes the decisions based on recommendations from you.

Everything you do must be documented. This includes interviews, questionnaires, subsequent analysis of the data collection and conclusions reached. If you make mistakes and the re-examining process brings these to light, it is very tempting to change the project to make it seem that you got it right in the first place. Don't do this, document the process and show what has changed. You will not lose marks for getting it wrong, as long as you show why and what you have done to correct it.

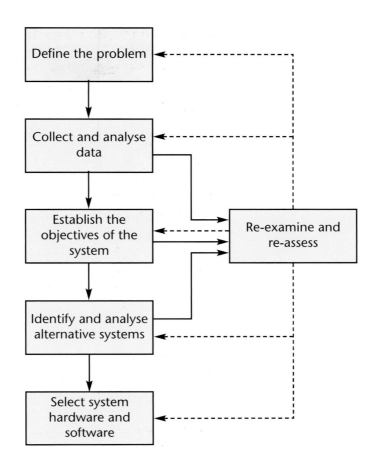

Figure 8.1 Diagram showing how re-examination fits into the life cycle

Definition – The nature of the problem to be investigated (3 marks)

There are many different problems and many situations and circumstances from which you can select your project. The examiner will not be familiar with all of them. This introductory section is your opportunity to make the examiner familiar with the particular scenario on which your own project is based.

You should begin with an introduction to the organisation.

< Example >

Sample questions that you might choose to ask in order to complete the section might include:

- What is the name of the organisation?
- What does it do?
- Where is it located?
- How many people does it employ?
- How many shops/head offices are there?
- What are the names and positions held of people who are going to be involved with the project?
- What is the problem that they have?

The level of detail required is not great, as long as you give enough information for the examiner to understand the outline of the scenario into which your project will fit.

Having obtained the answers you require you need to write it up in an easily understood way.

■ Marking

1 mark   A brief description of the organisation or group that has the problem.

1 mark   An introduction to the client and/or the end user(s) and their place within the organisation or group.

1 mark   An outline of the problem that needs to be solved.

Investigation (10 marks)

This section is about collecting information on the current system (that is the system that is in place at the moment). There are two main types of project:

- Those that put a new system into place – this may be a complete new system or adding new functionality to an existing system.
- Those that use ICT to replicate a manual system.

Both types of project need to have information on the current system in order to be successful in their use – that is 'how does the current system function?'

You need to plan the mechanics of the collection of information, decide on the questions to ask, carry out the collection and record the findings.

■ Investigation into the current system to find more information about the problem

In the previous section you gave a very basic outline of the company and the problem. It is necessary to do some more research and find out some detailed information about the system as it currently stands and the problem.

You will do this by investigating the current system, so you will need to find out the facts ('fact finding') and then record them ('fact recording').

Fact finding and recording

Methods of fact finding include using questionnaires and interviewing to find personal knowledge of the situation, observing the current system, and reading existing documentation and manuals. You may need to use more than one method in order to find out what you want. The main method will be an interview.

■ Interview

There are four components to the collection of information by an interview:

- Planning the questions.
- Planning the interview.
- Conducting and recording the interview.
- Post-interview analysis.

Planning the questions

Before conducting an interview, you need to plan a set of prepared questions, and have one or two follow-up questions for each that you may or may not ask depending on the interviewee's initial answers.

It is good practice to let the interviewee see the questions before the interview.

The questions you ask need to give you more information about what happens now, such as the inputs, the processes, the outputs and the storage in the current system. You may also ask questions about the personnel.

When planning the questions, think about the 'flow' through the system. For example, for a stock control system:

- How is the stock level updated?
- When is the stock level updated?
- How do you know when stock needs to be reordered?
- How do you know that stock has been reordered?
- How is the order to suppliers generated?
- What happens when an order from a supplier arrives?
- How many stock items do you have?
- How many different suppliers do you have?

This is not an exhaustive list of questions. Several of these questions might have follow-up questions.

Having established how things work within the current system, you need to get some more information on the problem and why it is a problem. This is likely to require a second set of interviews, at the end of which you should have enough information to be able to create a requirements specification.

Planning the interview

You need to plan the interview before conducting it. This involves thinking about who you are interviewing, and where and when the interview will take place.

You need to set up an interview – you cannot just turn up and interview people. There should be a set of letters or emails between you and the person you are interviewing setting the time, the date and the venue. As mentioned above, it is good practice to include a copy of the questions you are going to ask so the interviewees can make sure they have all the relevant information to hand.

OCR Systems
Birmingham
B7 4DR

23rd June 2009

Dear Mr Jenkins,

Further to our telephone discussion last week I am writing to you to arrange an interview to look in detail at the system that you currently have in place. If you could get back to me with times when you are available next week I can see when I am free and arrange to meet up.

Yours sincerely,

A Student

Figure 8.2 A example letter to arrange an interview

Conducting and recording the interview

You need a record of the interview as evidence that it has taken place. This can be in the form of a typed transcript. It should match the details you gave in the planning stage but some of the questions might be different. There should be a clear differentiation between question and answer. There needs to be a record that both the interviewee and the interviewer agree with the contents of the interview – this usually involves both people signing the transcript.

Name of Interviewee:	Mr Jenkins		Position in Company:	Manager
Date of Interview:	28/6/2009		Location of Interview:	Manager's Office
Purpose of Interviewee:	To gain a clearer understanding of the current system for stock ordering			
1 What is your role within the company?				
I am in charge of looking after the customers				

Figure 8.3 Record of interview with informative headings

Post-interview analysis

After the interview you need to analyse the responses and extract the important points.

Following the analysis you may be aware that you have not got all the information you need. If this is the case you will need to conduct additional interviews repeating the four steps above.

Document analysis

If the new system involves the use of existing documents, then it is useful to include copies of those documents in your project. Make sure that any personal information is obscured. You will also need to write a comment about each document – what it represents and how to will make use of it in your project.

▧ Marking

1 mark Thorough planning of the mechanics of the interview situation.

4 marks Reasoned set of questions to elicit important information (possible responses have been considered and follow-up questions have been planned).

1 mark Record of key responses of interview, demonstrating two-way discussion.

2 marks Additional information collection that has been justified as being sensible (this may take the form of additional interviews, the collection of currently used forms, observation of current system or other methods).

2 marks Clear presentation of the results of any additional information collection.

Analysis (12 marks)

You should now know what the problem is. It is now time to begin to develop the solution. There are four parts to the solution:

- Analysis of the information collected in the investigation.
- The requirements specification, that is the requirements of the solution.
- Possible approaches to solving the problem.
- The justified approach you are going to use to solve the problem and what software and hardware are involved.

Analysis of the information collected

In the previous section you collected information, hopefully from more than one interview and more than once source (e.g. observation, documentation analysis, questionnaires etc.).

The first part of analysis is collating and summarising all of this information into a single document that is then agreed by the client. It will contain:

- a summary of the current situation
- identification of the problem to be solved
- details of the problem to be solved.

If there are any gaps, then you will need to go back to the investigation stage and use a method of collection to fill them in – this must be recorded. You will not lose marks for making mistakes. The moderator will be able to see recursion in progress.

The summary document needs to be agreed by yourself and the end user/client – this is done in a formal manner, usually by both parties signing the document.

Requirements specification

The end result of the data collection is a list of requirements for the new system. This is a list of what the finished system must be able to do.

You must revisit the data collection section to check that is possible for the examiner to link each of the requirements listed to the conclusions you have drawn from the data collection, and to backtrack to the data itself. It may be necessary to redo this section several times, each time revisiting the system to find more evidence. This is acceptable as long as it is documented. Do not fall to the temptation of making it seem as though you got it right the first time. You will get more credit if you show your mistakes and how you have corrected them.

The requirements must describe the external behaviour of the system. You need to write it in terms understandable to the end user. The requirements should not contain too much information but describe what the system should do.

The requirements specification lists features of the system without saying how they are to be implemented.

If you are given any limitations or constraints, then you must include them as part of the requirements. For example, if you are told that it must be a menu-driven system, then one of the requirements is that it must be a menu-driven system.

It is essential that the requirements are detailed and get to the very core of the system. There may be several user requests that are ill-defined and difficult to clarify (e.g. the interface needs to be 'user friendly' or 'easy to navigate', or the design needs to include 'warm colours' or 'documentation' etc.). It is not useful to list these as part of the requirements specification without adding more detail. For example, you might replace 'easy to navigate' with 'no option is more than three mouse clicks away', or you might redefine 'user friendly' as 'appropriate error messages', 'readable user guides', 'screen tips on icons', 'accessible online help' etc.

How many requirements should there be? This is a totally open question. Some projects might have four or five detailed requirements, other projects may have 10–15 less detailed requirements.

It is vital that all the requirements are achievable because they will be used in the evaluation section of the project.

Once you have listed the requirements, you need to get them agreed (e.g. with a signed statement) by the organisation.

Here is an outline requirement specification agreement with some examples. The text in italics should be replaced with appropriate text.

Analysis (12 marks)

Requirement Specification Agreement

- To be able to find all members with overdue books.

- To print a list of overdue members.

- To order books using email.

I *name*, of *organisation*, have discussed the requirements and I am in agreement that a system that delivers these will fulfil our requirements.

Signed:

Name (printed)

Position

Figure 8.4 Example agreement of requirements specification

Approach to be used

Several alternative designs should be considered and compared. You should look at each from the point of view of:

- its feasibility (i.e. how will it operate and how it will succeed in achieving the system's objectives
- its expected costs and benefits.

Any alternative system you look at must be compared with the requirements specification.

You **must** compare at least three solutions. One can be the current solution and at least two others, or they can be three completely new ones.

The alternative approaches that you look at must be possible solutions. For example, if you are looking at a solution that requires data handling, it is not appropriate to look at the use of a word processor. You may be able to match it against the cost, training and other requirements but it is not a valid solution in the first place. Make sure that all the alternative solutions that you are looking at could be used to solve the problem and deliver the requirements.

There may be constraints put upon the solution by the organisation (e.g. the solution must be developed in a specific package). If this is the case, the alternative approached will be primarily based on differences in data structures (e.g. relational versus flat file, file sizes etc.), and you need to be take these into account.

Even if there is a limitation, this does not stop you from discussing alternative solutions. The discussion can still take place, it is only the conclusion that is affected.

■ System justification

You should not recommend a new system unless you can justify it. Criteria for basing your justification are an evaluation of:

■ the costs and benefits of the proposed system
■ other performance criteria
■ whether the system meets the requirements specification.

The costs of the proposed system

In making a recommendation for a particular approach, you need to make a full study of the economics of the proposed system(s). This is unlikely to be possible for you, but some attempt at financial justification should be made.

The costs of a new system may include:

■ equipment costs (capital costs, leasing costs etc.)
■ installation costs
■ development costs
■ personnel costs
■ operating costs

The benefits of a proposed system

You must also evaluate the benefits of a proposed new system. As with financial costs, this may be difficult for you to do, but some effort should be made. Benefits of a proposed approach can include:

■ savings, because the old system will no longer be operated
■ extra savings or revenue benefits, because of the improvements or enhancements that the new system should bring
■ possibly some one-off revenue benefits from the sale of equipment which the existing system uses, but which will no longer be required. Secondhand computer equipment does not have a high value but it does have some. It is also possible that the new system will use less office space (filing), and so there will be benefits from selling or renting the spare accommodation.

Some benefits might be intangible or impossible to give a monetary value to. These might include:

■ Greater customer satisfaction, arising from a more prompt service (e.g. because of a computerised sales and delivery service).
■ Improved staff morale from working with a better system.

Once you have a general analysis of the potential approaches to the problem, you can evaluate them against the requirements specification in the form of a grid.

Alternative approaches listed across the top

Requirements can be listed down the side

	Database	Spreadsheet	Paper system
To perform complex searches	Yes, both static and dynamic, can be given a forms interface	Yes, both static and dynamic, can be given a forms interface	Yes but very time consuming and difficult to guarantee results
To integrate with the Web	Yes – with ActiveX	Yes – with ActiveX	No automatic integration

Figure 8.5 Grid for alternative approaches

The approaches to be used are not names of specific packages but applications. The move from application to specific software is made in the next section.

You need to select a final solution giving reasons for the choice. Having assembled the evidence, you need to discuss your chosen solution with the client – this needs to be recorded. The end of this discussion should be an agreement to move forward with the selected approach.

Hardware and software choice

Once the solution has been agreed, you can specify the hardware and software required. This should be a justified selection, and not simply a list. The hardware and software specified should be all the items required for a full installation of the solution, even if you are not personally implementing all of the end product (e.g. a network installation on 20 PCs in an office where there are currently no computers will require 20 PCs, cabling, a server etc. and you are unlikely to fully implement this, however you do need to specify the complete requirement).

The software list must include the operating system, and if the internet is to be used, then you must state the additional software required (such as an email package, protocol etc.). You need to state the network software required if a network is being used as part of the end product.

The hardware list must also be fairly detailed. Make sure that you have covered the input, processing and output requirements. For input, you may need items such as a keyboard and a mouse, a scanner and an optical mark reader. If the system receives data via a network or the internet, then you will need a network card/router and appropriate software. Do not forget to specify what sort of disk is needed for input (e.g DVD, CD) and what type of monitor.

Output requirements may cover many of the same items as input (e.g. disk type, internet connection, network connection, printer type).

Processing requirements can include what is inside the machine (e.g. RAM, hard disk drive, processor).

You must justify all the hardware and software you specify. Here is a sample layout.

< Example >

Software/hardware	Justification
Micorosoft Windows 2000 with SP3	Operating system required to run Microsoft Access 2003 with minimal problems.
Microsoft Access 2003	Software selected to develop the system and required by the end user.
Microsoft Internet Explorer 7	Internet browser required to run Web elements of product.
TCP/IP	Internet protocol required to connect to the internet.
17-inch monitor	Required to see the data that is being entered into the system.
Keyboard	For manually entering data.
Mouse	To move the cursor around the screen in the WIMP interface that has been developed.
Router	To connect the computer to the internet so that Web access can take place.
128 MB RAM	Required for running Microsoft Windows 98, Microsoft Access 2000 and Microsoft Internet Explorer at the same time.
Intel Pentium 233 MHz processor	Required for running Microsoft Windows 2000, Micorsoft Access 2003 and Microsoft Internet Explorer at the same time.
Black and white laser printer	Black and white printing of invoices is required.
4.5 GB HDD	Required for storing of software and additional storage space for records.
CD writer	For loading software and creating back-ups.

Table 8.1 Table of software and hardware justification

Note that a specification has not been given that cannot be justified. The operating system is the minimum required to run Microsoft Access. The hardware is the minimum required. You may choose to go above the minimum but justification must be given.

■ Marking

3 marks   Evidence of analysis of the current system or of likely problem areas, arriving at reasoned conclusions that will show evidence of being agreed by client.

3 marks   A requirements specification containing a number of clearly defined objectives that the solution should meet. These must be arrived at through consultation with the client.

3 marks   A comparison of a number of different methods of solution, one of which may be the present solution and at least two others to allow a reasoned decision to be made in consultation with the client.

3 marks   A reasoned list of hardware and software requirements for the new system, providing clear justification for each choice in relation to the problem to be solved.

Introduction

There are a total of 12 marks available for the design:
10 marks for the nature of the solution, and 2 marks for the project plan.

Meeting the requirements of the Design section is difficult, particularly since you do not have a very detailed knowledge and understanding of systems analysis. Design is the link between the analysis and software development. It is important to match your stated requirements of the previous section (definition, investigation and analysis), with the design created in this section, and with the results of the next section (software development). In other words, what you say you are going to create in the requirements section is covered by the design in this section and created in the next. It is very tempting to get carried away with the design and create masterpieces of screen design, but if the reality of software development does not match the design you will lose marks. Keep the design functional and as simple as possible.

Overview

The section can be broken down into two stages. The first is the most important.

- **The nature of the solution:** This is where you create the designs of the input, output and processing, and files required to implement the requirements.
- **Project plan:** This will require a breakdown of the tasks and a time plan.

You will draw many diagrams as you undertake this section and it is very easy to get page numbers mixed up and out of order. You can draw diagrams by hand and there is no reason why you cannot add blank pages to the project and, once printed, draw in your designs. This will keep the correct page number order that is vital to the marking of the project.

Nature of the solution

This is where you create all the designs that will be used to develop the solution. The overall aim is that you should be able to pass all the design diagrams to a third party and they should be able to create the required solution.

You should actively involve the end user in the design process.

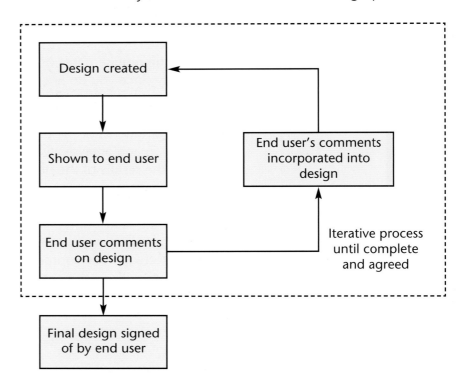

Figure 9.1 The design process

■ Design specification

The design specification is a document that shows how each of the elements in the requirements specification can be created and included in the end product. The design specification shows how the data gets into the system, what happens to it, where it is stored and in what format, the processing, the output and the user interface, as well as back-up procedures and any connections to other programs.

You will be required to draw up input documents, data entry screens, output documents and the user interface. There are three ways you can design the screens and documents:

- On paper (hand drawn).
- In the package in which you intend to create the final product (e.g. Microsoft Access, Microsoft Excel, Microsoft Word, Corel Paradox).
- In a package that will not be used to create the final product (e.g. by using Corel PaintShop Pro to mock up the screens).

Which method should you use?

The choice is yours. You will not be marked down whichever one you choose. However, the second option is the one to be wary of – designing in the package in which you will create the final product – because it is very easy to create the product and then print out a created, working form and claim that it is a design. The examiner must be sure that you have not done this. The easiest way to prevent any doubts is to choose one of the other options.

What to include in a design?

Any design needs to be annotated – you should not submit any design that has not been annotated. All final versions of designs **must** be signed off by the end user.

The following elements may or may not appear in your design. It may not be appropriate for your particular project to have all of the elements – choose the ones that fit your project.

The design specification comprises six elements:

- Input
- Processing
- Output
- User interface
- Files and data structures
- Error messages

Input

The input section can be broken down into two sections:

- **Input documents:** These are the documents that will be filled in as part of the manual system. They are paper-based documents: the data capture forms. The data collected on the forms will be entered into the computer system. There needs to be some correlation between the data capture forms and the forms on the computer where the user will enter the data. Look at all the data entry points going into the system, as identified in the data flow diagram, and if they are paper based, then there needs to be a data capture form.
- **Input interface:** This is the computer screen that will be used to enter the paper-based documents identified above. You will have one computer input form for every data capture form. If the form automatically looks up data (e.g. you enter a postcode and the system automatically returns the street name, town and county), then this must be detailed. If any data is calculated (e.g. you enter a hotel room number and a number of nights and the system calculates the price), then this must be documented.
  Where appropriate you need to specify any screen tips or associated help.

< Example >

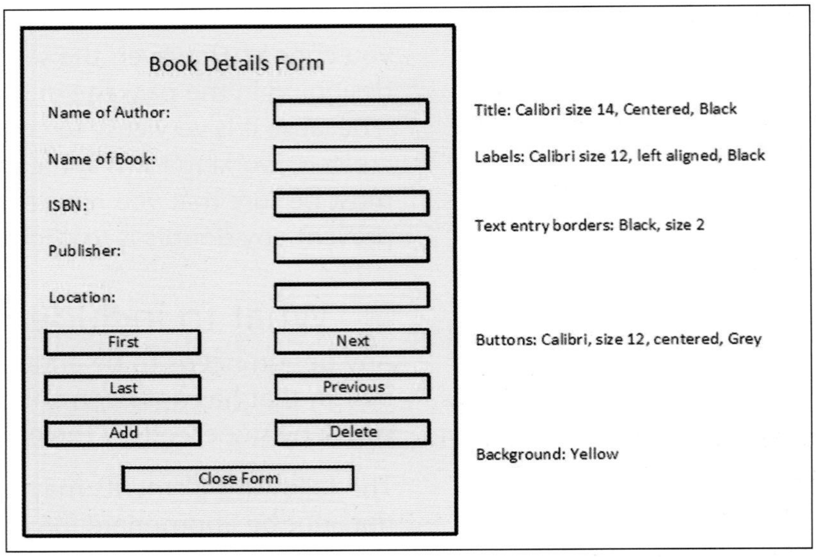

Figure 9.2 Sample design of a form

You must have considered how the data is to be collected and prepared for data entry. How is the paper-based data that is received to be sorted or changed to be suitable for data entry.

■ Are there any coding procedures that need to take place?
■ Does it need to be sorted by customer number?
■ Does it need to be matched with any other documentation (e.g. matching a dispatch note from the company to the order placed by the end user)?

Forms can be included in web-based, database and spreadsheet projects.

It is not anticipated that you will get the designs correct first time. Do not throw away any initial designs – the moderator will want to see the progression of the design. There may be user comments written on early versions of the forms: these will indicate that the end user is involved in the process.

Processing

The processing section must detail what happens at each stage. It can be written in text form, pseudocode or any other appropriate method. You must list:

■ the action that begins the processing
■ each action that occurs during the processing, indicating what data and files are being used
■ what happens to the data, that is, where it is saved to (variable, file, table etc.).

The processing is a logical list of what happens. Where necessary it must include queries (if in a database), formulae (if in a spreadsheets) etc.

< Example >

Processing example

This is an example is of the processing requirements of the hire component of a library system.

Enter code number of book to hire.
Look up code number of book to hire in book table and return book details to form.
> **If book does not exist, give error message.**

Look up customer number in customer form and return details to form.
Look up customer number in outstanding fines.
> **If there is a fine give the customer a chance to pay.**
>> **If they pay, flag fine as paid and continue.**
>> **If they do not pay, end transaction.**
> **If customer does not exist, give error message.**

Automatically enter the date (today).
Automatically enter the date+3 as the date of return.
Add a record to the hire table that includes customer number, book number, date of hire and date due back.
Flag the book record in the book table as being hired.

This can be completed as a diagram if necessary.

Where appropriate, you should specify the security procedures (e.g. what security is in place, how it is applied and on what areas it works). Each 'object name' is a table, a form, a query, a report etc. The 'access rights' are full, read only, write, edit and delete. The 'user' is the name of a user or a group who have the specified rights to the object.

< Example >

Object name	Access rights	User
Members Form	Read Only	Mrs Jones, Mrs Adams, Mrs Lee
Members Form	Read, Edit	Daily Managers
Members Form	Full	Administrator

Table 9.1 Security form

You must also include a back-up and a restore procedure for the files used.

Output

The output section is similar to the input section. There are three types: the output that appears on the screen, output documents (printed output) and other output such as email, files etc. You need to design and annotate each type (as you did with the input).

User interface

The user interface is what the user will see and it must remain consistent throughout the project. This section requires a specification of the general rules that you will apply to the user interface (e.g. the colours used, what buttons appear on all screens, menus and general layout of the screen). Remember to include items such as menus that do not appear under the input or output sections.

You must design and annotate the user interface in a similar way as for other designs.

Files and data structures

The design specification needs to contain details on all files and data structures that you will be using.

The file specification needs to include:

- the name of the file
- a description of the file's contents and the use of the file
- the location of file (if known)
- the name of fields contained within the file
  - a description of the contents of fields
  - the data type of field
  - the length of the field
  - an example of contents
  - validation on the field.

The following format can be used.

< Example >

Format of file details
File name: TbookHire
Location: C:\Program Files\A level project\book.mdb
Purpose: To hold details about a book hire in a library

Field name	Description of contents	Data type	Length	Sample values/ range/set	Type of validation expected
HireID	Primary key	Autonumber	3	45	Auto-generated
MemberID	Who has taken out the video	Number	3	121	Looked up
BookID	What the book is that has been taken out	Number	4	1065	Looked up
Date Out	When the book was taken out	Date	8	15/08/09	Calculated as today

Table 9.2 Format of files table

For data structures, you must specify:

- what the structure is (e.g. record structure, array)
- where it is used (list the names of the procedures, forms etc. where it is used)
- what it is used for (detail what is contains and why).

For a spreadsheet-based project, the data structure is likely to be combined with some of the processing. It will include the functions and formulae used and descriptions of variables (including type).

< Example >

Name of Item: *Drop-down list from items worksheet*

Price of Item: *Looked up using VLOOKUP from items worksheet and Name of Item to return price – formatted currency*

Number Purchased: *Entered by user – integer value only between 1 and 100*

Total Price: *Multiplication of Number Purchased by Price of Item – formatted currency*

VAT: *Multiply Total Price by VAT variable in Variables worksheet – formatted currency*

Total to Pay: *Add Total Price and VAT – formatted currency*

Figure 9.3 Part of the structure design for a spreadsheet

If appropriate, you must include security features (e.g. what access rights exist on the various files/cells/worksheets).

Error messages

You need to design a basic format for an error message box. A standard error message box should tell the user what has happened to cause the error, what they need to do to correct it.

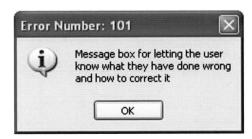

Figure 9.4 Custom error message

The message box should give a unique error number to help trace the error. You need to create a list of the error numbers and what they refer to. The following format is appropriate:

< Example >

Message ID	Error
101	Incorrect date entered into Hire form
102	No name entered in Customer form
103	No book entered into Add Book form

Table 9.3 Format for error message listing

System diagrams

You will already have completed several system diagrams that relate to the existing system. In the design phase, you need to draw the diagrams for the new system. The diagrams you may choose to include are:

- data flow diagrams
- entity relationship diagrams
- data structure diagrams

You should include a diagrammatic representation of data through the system.

Not all projects will include all items. The main projects will be:

- data handling (databases)
- calculations (spreadsheets)
- informative (web-based/Flash)

The following table gives examples of the different areas that could be included under each section.

< Example >

Example	Data handling	Calculation	Informative
Input forms	Forms	Forms or worksheet	Web form, buttons
File structure	Tables	Functions, formulae, variables	Navigation diagram, file locations
Output forms	Forms/Reports	Forms or worksheet	Web pages, display

Table 9.4 Representation of data in a system

All projects are likely to have:

- backup
- security
- error messages
- a test plan

It is entirely possible for a project to include more than one element (e.g. a Web-based project that stores customer information collected from a form in a database or a Web project that uses a spreadsheet to return quotation information).

Marking

4 marks Design of data handling, including capture, preparation and storage or design of website to include map and diagrammatic representation of links.

4 marks Design of inputs, processing and outputs, including error capture reports as appropriate, based clearly on the analysis of the client requirements.

2 marks Clear evidence of end user/client involvement in decision making and evidence that the options of the user/client have had an effect on the solution.

There must be evidence of redevelopment based on discussions with the client.

Each section must be agreed and signed off by the client.

Project plan

The task model is a list of the order that you will undertake the various tasks. You can complete this using a Gantt chart, timelines, tables or calendars. It should make some reference to the timescale for each task.

The task model needs to show the tasks in order, when you will begin and when they will end. The chart should also show predecessors. Predecessors are events that must be done before another particular task. For example, if creating a form in a database that is based on a table, you must have first created the table.

The task model needs to be detailed. (Do not, however, go into too much detail – you can specify when to create a procedure, but do not go into detail about the procedure.)

The date started and date ended do not have to be totally accurate – at your age and level of skills it is not expected that you will be able to correctly judge time plans.

< Example >

Task number	Task	Date started	Date ended	Predecessor
1	Create table of library members	12/6/09	13/6/09	
2	Create table of book genres	13/6/09	13/6/09	
3	Create table of books	12/6/09	13/6/09	2
4	Create form of members	13/6/09	14/6/09	1
5	Create form of books	13/6/09	14/6/09	3
6	Create form of genres	13/6/09	14/6/09	2
7	Create main menu	13/6/09	14/6/09	
8	Link forms to main menu	13/6/09	14/6/09	5,6,7

Table 9.5 Sample tasks and how they are related for a time plan

Gantt charts are a graphical method of displaying tasks and dependencies between tasks.

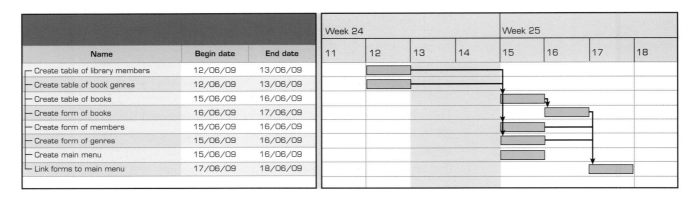

Figure 9.5 Sample Gantt chart showing the tasks in Table 9.5

Open source Gantt chart software can be downloaded from http://ganttproject.biz/webstart.php

Marking

2 marks Clear description, diagrammatic or otherwise, of the different tasks necessary to complete the solution and a clear timetable.

Software development, testing and installation

Introduction

There are 24 marks available for this section, 19 for the software development and testing, and 5 for the installation.

Overview

This section can be broken down into three main stages, of which the first is the most important:

- **Software development:** This is where you print out the project. You produce evidence of what you have actually created – including printouts of any programming, table definitions, HTML coding etc.
- **Testing:** You must test everything that can be tested using normal, extreme and incorrect data. Every test must be planned prior to running it and, once run, the results produced for the examiner to see.
- **Installation:** This requires the cooperation of the end user. They have to see the system and commented on it. The second half of this section is about the production of an installation plan.

Software development

This is the section where you document the finished product. The only things the examiner can mark are what you produce – if you have not printed it out, it did not happen and it does not exist.

The technical evidence is a very important part of the project. It should contain every screen (input, output and user interface), reports and any code written. The technical evidence is the only evidence you can produce of the creation of the project. You should not include any screenshots unless they are annotated or cross-referenced. A screenshot is only useful if it is referenced and the examiner is able to understand how it fits into the project as a whole.

It is not necessary to print out the design of a form unless it is unusual. Where possible you should group together a form and any related code. Annotation of individual items is not necessary as the design of the form details this, and any code will support the names of the objects.

It must be possible for a third party to copy the software development from your printouts, so you need to make sure that everything is included.

The following is a list of what you need to provide. Of course, it will depend on your exact project whether you have them all.

< Example >

Database	Spreadsheet	Web page
Tables	Worksheet(s)	The web page itself
Forms	Formula view	Associated data structures
Queries	Macros	(database, spreadsheet, text file)
Reports	User forms	Macro code
Macros		

Table 10.1 Evidence of software development

The printouts that you provide should show how the project meets the client's requirements. It should also show how you have met the stages in the project plan.

One method of producing the evidence might be to reproduce the tasks from the project plan and, this time, take a screenshot as evidence.

< Example >

For example:

Task	Evidence
Create Table of library members This is the design of the table created to hold details on the library members.	

	Field Name	Data Type
🔑	MemberID	AutoNumber
	Forename	Text
	Surname	Text
	Address1	Text
	Address2	Text
	Town	Text
	County	Text
	Postcode	Text
	Telephone	Text

Figure 10.1 Example of database fields used in Library Members table

Annotation

Note the additional notes in the Table 10.2. It is always useful to give as much additional information as you can – the annotation should refer to the screenshot.

Your printouts of procedures, modules and macros also need to be annotated. Ideally you should annotate the code as you write/edit it, but if this is not possible then you should write on the printout.

Annotation should tell the reader what is going on, therefore you need to strike a balance between annotating everything, and only those items that need annotating for clarity. Remember to annotate all variables.

It is not necessary to print and annotate every piece of code. For example if code is generated when placing a button on a worksheet to take the user to another worksheet, and this is recorded, it does not need to be printed. Wizard- or recorded macro-generated code does not need to be printed and annotated. If, however, you write your own code, then this must be annotated and printed.

It is good practice to begin each piece of your own code with a header section. The header should contain:

- a line that identifies where it is (makes it easy to find)
- the title of the procedure
- the final date of editing
- the version number (incremented after each edit), and
- the name of the editor (i.e. your name).

< Example >

```
`* * * * * * * * * * * * * * * * * * * * * * * * * * * * * * * * * * * * * * * * * *

`FINES FORM

`26/06/09

`Version 1.3

`Writer: G Millbery

`* * * * * * * * * * * * * * * * * * * * * * * * * * * * * * * * * * * * * * * * * *
```

Figure 10.3 Sample annotated header from a procedure

Testing

This is the section where you test the product. Testing needs to occur during the development of the solution and also once you have created a finished product.

Testing during development

You need to make sure you are testing a solution at the same time as you are develop it. For example, you need to enter data into a formula as you develop it, and make sure it works before moving on.

< Example >

For example, in a project involving delivery of items, the delivery price needs to be calculated:

			Delivery Prices Data Table		
Weight of final Products	1.30 kg		0	£	2.99
			1	£	4.99
			3	£	7.99
Price for delivery	£ 4.99		5	£	10.99
			10	£	25.00

Figure 10.4 Example of testing spreadsheet formulae

It is important to test that the function for the delivery price works before integrating it into the solution. The testing that occurs during development is informal and does not need a test plan.

There might be instances where the testing does not work.

< Example >

A form has been created to search for orders by customer. The customer name is selected from a drop-down list, but the query is not returning any values.

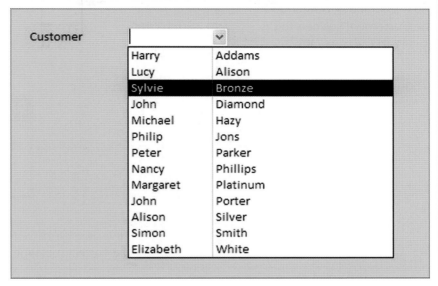

Figure 10.5 Example of drop-down list

A message box has been set up to identify the value being passed to the query.

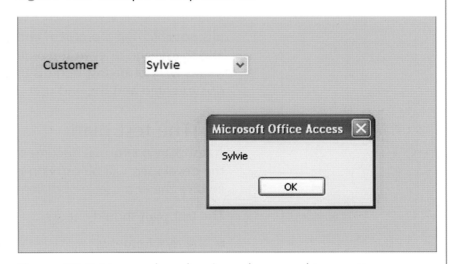

Figure 10.6 Message box showing value passed to a query

As can be seen, the value being returned is the forename and not the expected CustomerID.

In this instance, the testing has revealed a problem which can then be rectified. It is essential that where you need to rectify a mistake, you give evidence of this. It is very easy to find an error and correct it without writing down what you have done. If you do this, you will lose marks.

In this example, the primary key had been missed out when the combo box was created. The solution was to include the CustomerID in the row source as the first field.

Figure 10.7 Correcting the error

When a customer is selected, the message box now shows the CustomerID. When this is passed to the query it works.

Figure 10.8 The correct message box

After each major section that involves, queries, formulae, functions etc., test the solution and document the process.

It is possible that a problem encountered cannot be solved easily, and the design or even the requirements need to be revisited. Marks will not be lost if this is the case, so long as the procedure is documented and the end user is involved in the discussions.

The test plan

A test plan is a formal document that lists the tests that you, as the developer, will be carrying out on the system. You should involve the end user (your client) in the process.

The test plan should check:

- the requirements
- pathways
- validation routines.

There is no minimum or maximum number of tests that can be carried out. The rule of thumb is whether the solution has been tested against the requirement and that you can prove that it works.

The test plan needs to show normal, extreme and incorrect data.

- **Normal data** is the data that is used in every day usage. It is also known as correct data.
- **Extreme data** is data at the edge of tolerances. This is data at the ends of the ranges specified. For example, if a number is entered with a validation set of between 1 to 20, then extreme data would be 0 or 1 and 20 or 21.
- **Incorrect data** is data that is wrong. It is also known as erroneous data. This is data that, when entered into the system, should produce an error message and not be accepted by the system.

< Example >

This test plan layout is an example that could be used.

Test number	Description of test	Type of test	Data used	Expected result

Table 10.3 Example of a test plan layout

Column headings

- **Test number:** a unique identifier for each test.
- **Description of test:** an every day language description of what you are testing.
- **Type of test:** is the test 'normal', 'extreme' or 'incorrect'?
- **Data used:** the data that will be entered to run the test. It must be specific and, if appropriate, where it will be entered will be indicated. All data used must be given.
- **Expected result:** what you expect to happen when you run the test. For normal tests it should be a positive result; incorrect data should result in an error message.

Test number	Description of test	Type of test	Data used	Expected result
1	To test if correct price of delivery is calculated.	Normal	In E4 enter 3.6	In E7 £7.99
2	To test if the maximum weight allowed for delivery of 10 kg can be exceeded.	Incorrect	In E4 enter 12	Message: The Maximum Weight We Can Accept For Delivery is 10.0.

Table 10.4 Example test plan with sample entries

■ Test results

Having created a test plan, you need to run through the tests listed in it and provide evidence of the results. This is best done by giving the results under the test plan cross referenced to the 'Test number'.

< Example >

Test number 1:

3.6 has been entered into cell E4 and the result £7.99 is displayed in E8. This answer matches the expected result.

			Delivery Prices Data Table		
Weight of final Products	3.60 kg		0	£	2.99
			1	£	4.99
			3	£	7.99
Price for delivery	£ 7.99		5	£	10.99
			10	£	25.00

Figure 10.9 Sample test result 1

Testing

279

Test number 2:

12 has been entered into cell E4. The correct error message has appeared. The test has passed.

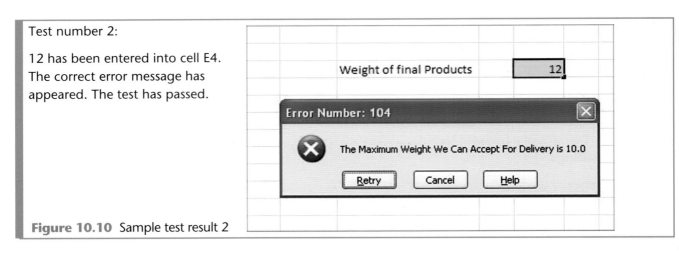

Figure 10.10 Sample test result 2

If a test fails, then you need to correct the error and run the test again. Remember to provide evidence of the correction and the re-test.

User testing of the system

There needs to be evidence of user testing as part of the testing process.

The user testing must be detailed and needs to cover the following questions (as appropriate):

- Are the buttons in the correct place?
- Are the colours correct?
- Is data entry easy to do?
- Do the help instructions (screen tips and labels) work?
- Are forms presented in the correct order?
- Are the output requirements correct?
- Is the correct data being stored?
- Do drop-down boxes/list boxes/option buttons work correctly?
- Are error messages useful?
- Does the security work?
- Are the user guides easy to follow and use?
- Is the main menu easy to use?

This list is not exhaustive and other questions may be appropriate for different systems.

It is possible to create a questionnaire for the end user to fill in. If there is more than one end user, then all (or as many as is practical) should test the system and the results summarised in a graph or table. Not all responses need to be 'pass' and 'fail'; some can have an explanatory comment.

< Example >

User test	Pass	Fail	Comment
Is the main menu easy to use?	✓		All required options are coved.
Do the labels on the button make sense?	✓		They are easy to understand.
Are all the error messages easy to understand?		✓	Error Message '531'.

Table 10.5 Sample questionnaire for user testing

The user must write a letter to you detailing the fact that they have tested the system. The letter needs to contain:

- their name, position and address
- a reference to the project
- a reference to you (your name)
- a date on which the system was tested
- some comments.

< Example >

This is a sample letter from the user. The italics are to be replaced with relevant details.

Their address
The date

Your name
Your address (or the address of the school)

Dear *Your name*

With reference to the system you are developing for us, I am writing to confirm that on **XXX** *date, myself/I and* **XXX** *(if others)* tested the system.

We/I have filled out and returned a questionnaire on the test and would like to make the following comments.

Enter comments here.

Yours sincerely,

Signature

Position within organisation

Figure 10.11 Sample letter from user

If the end user has any problems or comments, you must address them and, if necessary, re-test the system.

▨ Marking

4 marks A test plan that will identify a number of tests that will be carried out on completion of the work. Each test outlined should be clearly related to the relevant requirements stated in the requirement specification, all of which should feature in the test plan. The specific test to be carried out should be included in the plan together with the result expected. The tests specified in the test plan will be completed during the testing of the solution (some elements of testing should involve the end user(s)).

To obtain these marks you must have created a test plan that checks:

■ the requirement specification
■ pathways
■ valid/invalid data.

The test plan should include the expected results and involve the end user.

8 marks ■ 6–8 marks: the candidate has solved a problem that has needed a level of complexity greater than a simple linear type solution.
■ 3–5 marks: the candidate has attempted to solve a problem that has needed a level of complexity greater than a simple linear type solution and has been successful in some aspects.
■ 0–2 marks: the candidate has produced a solution that is a linear style of solution in the use of software.

If your project is a simple linear solution, you cannot get any more than two marks. A linear project is one that has a single aim and a straight path from data entry to output of results.

If you have created a complex solution, but some of the tests fail and you cannot make the solution work, then you will not be able to achieve more than five marks.

A complex solution that works can gain the full eight marks.

The evidence for the solution working comes from the test results and the screenshots of software development.

2 marks Hard-copy evidence of an effective HCI with annotations explaining its effective solutions for problems that had been highlighted in the requirements specification.

The screenshot evidence from software development needs to be annotated showing how it meets the requirement specification.

2 marks Evidence that the individual stages of the solution have been tested during the development of the solution and that failures in the design or implementation of the solution have been identified and corrected.

Testing must have occurred during development and not just once the solution has been finished. If there are problems, then the corrections to procedures and end user involvement need to be documented.

3 marks Evidence that each of the tests specified in the test plan have been carried out, that they are linked to the hard copy evidence, that the results have been analysed and that any necessary action has been identified.

These marks are awarded for running the tests from the test plan. If tests fail, the system must be corrected and a re-test carried out.

Installation

The specification recognises that it is not always possible to install the system. However, as long as the user is involved, it is still possible to gain full marks without actually putting the system completely into place.

The end result of this section should be a written installation plan that could be followed by a third party.

The installation section has three stages:

- User training
- Files, hardware and software
- Method of changeover

User training

It is likely that staff will need to trained to use the new system. You need to give details of the training that will be required and, if necessary, when and how this training will take place.

The dates for training need to be agreed with the client, and take place at a time appropriate to the method of changeover.

The types of training to be agreed include:

- One-to-one training.
- Using a start-up guide/user manual.
- A group presentation.
- Post-installation training.

You will need to consider the data that will be used for training purposes and how this will be created/entered.

Files, hardware and software

The system that you have created will require either:

- new data to be entered, or
- existing data to be transferred.

You need to indicate the volume of data that is to be transferred/entered and to make an estimate of how long it will take.

If data is entered into the new system too early, then by the time it is ready to be used, the existing system will have generated more data. This will need to be entered and a cycle is entered into. If the data entry is started too late then it may not all be completed in time.

You need to consider:

- the volume of data involved
- the number of people to be involved in data entry/data transferal
- the time taken for data entry/data conversion.
- how the process is to take place.

An organisation may not have in place the hardware and software required for the new system, so it may be necessary to upgrade or purchase them.

The hardware and software required needs to be listed along with the dates by when it is to be delivered and installed.

Methods of changeover

There are four methods available for changeover:

- Direct
- Phased
- Parallel
- Pilot

Direct changeover

Direct changeover is likely to be the most appropriate. It is where the use of the old system stops and the new one begins. There is a cut-off point when the old system stops working.

The advantage is that it is fast, efficient, requires the minimum duplication of work, only one system needs supporting and no interfaces between old and new systems are needed.

The disadvantages are that if the new system fails to work, there will be disruption. The new system has to be completely implemented during a period of time when the system is not required and there may be some disruption to customers while staff get used to the new system.

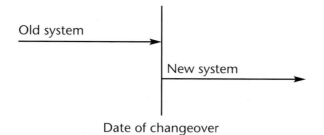

Figure 10.12 Direct changeover

Date of changeover

Phased changeover

Phased changeover is used with larger systems where the system to be put in place has several smaller subsystems. Each subsystem is introduced one at a time, making sure that each one is working before you begin with the next. The actual installation method can be direct or parallel.

The advantages are that each subsystem can be introduced with a minimum of disruption and if a system fails to work, the system is small enough to correct the errors.

The disadvantages are that the changeover may take a long period of time and create an extended period of unsettlement.

Parallel changeover

In a parallel changeover, the old system and the new are run side by side for a determined period of time.

The advantage is that if there is something wrong with the new system, the old system is still in operation and can continue to work. The disruption to the customers is minimised and the results from the old system (which are trusted and known to be correct) can be compared with the results from the new. This will establish trust and confidence in the new system.

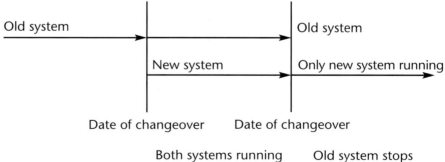

Figure 10.13 Parallel changeover

Pilot changeover

Pilot changeover is used in large organisations and involves the new system being tested in a small portion of the organisation for a determined period of time.

The advantages are that bugs can be worked out with the minimum of disruption, and training and testing can be completed in a small section of the organisation.

The disadvantage is that several changeovers need to take place.

You must detail the different methods of changeover, with advantages and disadvantages in such a way that the client can make a decision. You must give evidence of client consultation and of an informed choice being made and communicated to you by the end user.

< Example >

The installation plan should contain dates, which you need to agreed with the end user.

Date	Phase of installation
1/2/09	Acceptance meeting
2/2/09–5/2/09	Data changeover
6/2/09	Budget meeting for equipment
6/2/09	Delivery of user manuals
7/2/09	Group training
8/2/09–10/2/09	Individual training
9/2/09	Acquisition of equipment
13/2/09	Installation of equipment
15/2/09	Data changeover update
16/2/09	Direct changeover
18/2/09	Training session

Table 10.6 Sample format for calendar

Marking

2 marks Details of the training that will need to be available for the staff who must use the new system.

2 marks Details of the means by which the new files are going to be created, including some indication of the scale of the problem, and also the possible need for hardware installation and the installation of the software on the hardware.

1 mark Details of appropriate, different, methods of changeover explained so that the client can make a reasoned decision.

This information should be presented in a written installation plan.

11 Documentation

Introduction

There are 10 marks available for this section. Documentation is often an area that is not done particularly well. Guides are often difficult to follow and presented badly, and could not be used by the end user. Documentation should stand alone and be presented in a binder/section separate to the numbered page sections of the project.

Overview

The user guide is for the end user of your system. As such it so should tell the end user how to use the system you have created. It should not detail how to use any application software you might have used to create your system. You must include all routes through the system and how to troubleshoot errors.

User guide

There are 10 marks available for the user guide and all marks should be easily accessible. You should include a collection of screenshots and associated text, but you must never include a screenshot unless it is annotated in some way. You must also make sure that the user guide is a sequential document. This means that it follows the standard routes through the system that the user will use.

The guide must be easily used, that is, it should be an every day reference guide that will help users of all levels. To separate different aspects of the guide, it can extend to a manual containing more than one document.

In order to achieve marks for the highest band, you must include some documentation that exists only on the computer, such as on-screen help/electronic guide. It is possible that all the documentation exists only on the computer, and if this is the case there are two points to note:

- How does the system cope with novice users? – A novice user is unlikely to have the skills to begin by reading on-screen documentation.
- You still need to print out the documentation for the examiner.

Here are some basic rules for the production of user guides:

- Always annotate your printouts.
- Test the guide yourself to make sure that it works.
- Make sure that someone other than yourself has tested the guide.
- The guide should be a separate document and not be included as part of the project documentation.
- The guide layout should be easy to follow and logical. For example, start with the main menu and cover all the options on a screen-by-screen basis, or you may choose to cover first input, then processing, then output. The choice is yours but it must be easy to use.
- Make sure that you have spellchecked the document – there are marks for written communication.

The various elements that you may choose to include as documentation are:

- a 'Getting started' guide
- a user guide
- a troubleshooting guide
- on-screen help.

'Getting started' guide

A 'Getting started' guide contains information for the novice user on how to start using the system. It will be only a few pages long. The guide should not begin with how to switch on the computer (unless there is some special reason why this needed), but should start with how to run your system and show its opening screen.

The 'Getting started' guide should contain a purpose of the software: what is it to be used for and where is it to be used. You should include all the initial information required to use the system, such as whether or not a username and password are needed, and if they are, where the user can get them etc.

It should be written for the novice user. This means that you should use as few technical terms as possible and include a glossary of terms used (e.g. defining 'mouse click' etc.).

User guide

A user guide is the most important of all of the guides. It should contain all the information needed to run the system on a day-to-day basis within one standalone document. When writing the user guide, you need to remember at all times that the audience of the document will range from novice to expert users.

You need to include in the user guide text on the following:

Entering data

This will include the data needed to be entered into the system and where to enter it. You must illustrate this with annotated screenshots which show examples of the actual data to be used wherever possible.

If there is more than one data entry point, each needs to be covered in separate sections.

Processing

All options must be covered. Processing includes anything that happens to the data: sorting, searching, updating, deleting etc. If there are several options that cover a similar item, such as four different methods of searching, they can be grouped together.

You need to cover every button/option. For example, you may have a main menu with lots of buttons, or there may be options on a data form to go to the first, last, next and previous records. All of these must be documented. However, if you have several forms with the same buttons on them, you only need to cover the buttons on one form, not all of them.

Output

There are likely to be three main methods of output: screen, disk and hard copy (paper). Each of the different outputs must be included in the documentation, covering what each is and how to produce it.

Back-up and recovery of data

You can document data back-up and restoration with a simple set of instructions and screenshots.

Security

Different systems will require different security options. You need to document how the end user can get through the security or, if appropriate, change security levels.

Reference material

The guide must contain an index, a glossary of terms and a table of contents – remember to add page numbers.

Professional user guides are written in many different styles. You can get some idea of how to write one by looking at user guides produced for applications by major software providers and independent companies. You will not be expected to produce a guide that is up to the same standard (although no one is going to stop you!), so long as you remember that it needs to be usable and helpful.

Different projects will have different types of end user. Some systems might have more than one type of end user. For example, a website with a back-end database is unlikely to have a guide in the form of a manual for the user of the site itself, but it will have a hard-copy guide for the use of the database part of the system.

When you collect images for a user guide, make sure they:

- are what the user will see
- have been cropped so there is no background
- have real data in them so the user can see what the are supposed to do.

Once you have collected the images, they must be positioned on the page so they can be easily annotated with text and arrows.

< Example >

Here is a simple example of how you might lay out a user guide.

This screen is for viewing and changing details about companies. You need to search through the companies by pressing the First, Next, Previous and Last buttons, until you come to the name and address of the company you want.

When you begin, some of the buttons will appear faded, for example the First and Previous buttons in the screenshot below. This is because the screenshot shows the first record and there is nothing before it. If you moved to the next record, the faded buttons would become active (i.e. the text turns black and you can click them).

You can edit the details and press the Update button to save your changes.

If you want to exit from the screen, press the Close button.

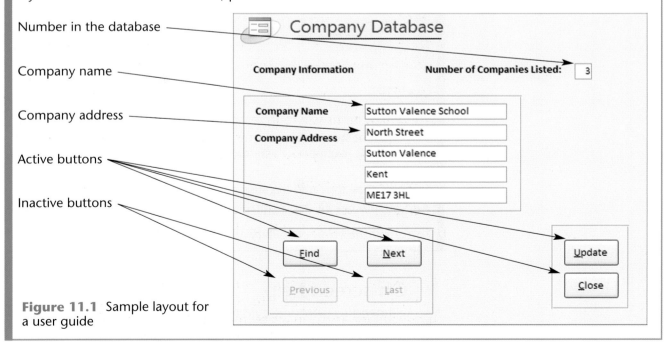

Figure 11.1 Sample layout for a user guide

Troubleshooting guide

A troubleshooting is a guide to likely problems with their solutions. You need to list all the different problems the user might encounter, what caused them and how to get out of them.

You must include any error messages the system generates. (If you have used the recommended format for error messages, with each message represented by a unique number, the errors can be sorted and presented by number.)

The troubleshooting guide is a collection of screenshots of the errors with explanatory text about each.

In general terms, you should include anything that generates an error message within your test plan.

The format for representing each error in the troubleshooting guide is:

- What screenshot evidence will the end user see to tell them they have an error?
- What does this mean? What has the user done to generate the error?
- What do they need to do to correct the error?

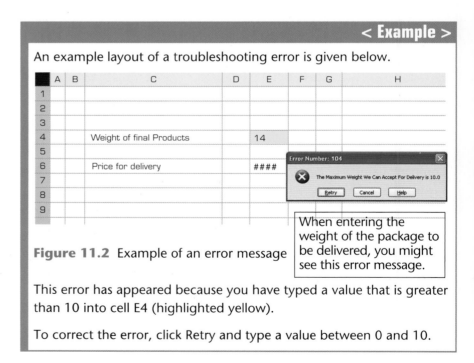

< Example >

An example layout of a troubleshooting error is given below.

Figure 11.2 Example of an error message

When entering the weight of the package to be delivered, you might see this error message.

This error has appeared because you have typed a value that is greater than 10 into cell E4 (highlighted yellow).

To correct the error, click Retry and type a value between 0 and 10.

On-screen help

You will need to print out evidence of this type of help because you are not allowed to submit disks. The on-screen help will depend on the package you are using. It could be web-based online help using HTML, or a collection of screen tips or a series of text files accessed by clicking a button.

On-screen help must be accessible and relevant. It is usually a collection of concise documents, the content of which will depend on individual requirements. You should again include table of contents, a glossary and index to help the user.

One of the most effective ways of providing on-screen help is to make it context sensitive. This means providing specific help for the screen that the user is currently on. The easiest way of providing context sensitive help is to create a Help button on the screen on which you want the help. The button links to an external file (this may be a pdf or a txt file) and when clicked the relevant help text appears.

< Example >

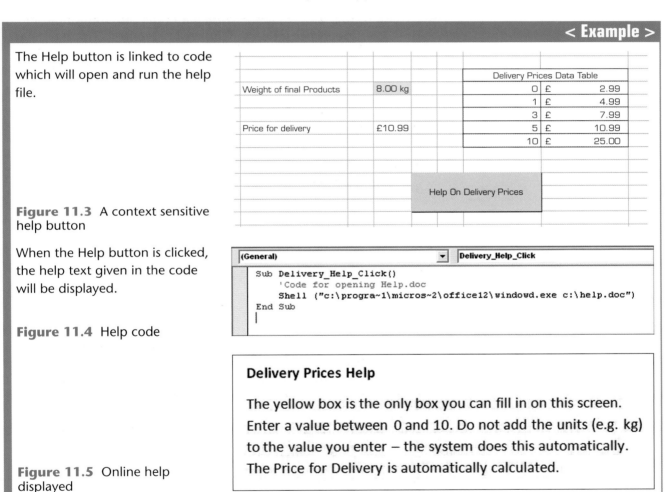

The Help button is linked to code which will open and run the help file.

Figure 11.3 A context sensitive help button

When the Help button is clicked, the help text given in the code will be displayed.

Figure 11.4 Help code

Figure 11.5 Online help displayed

Delivery Prices Data Table

0	£ 2.99
1	£ 4.99
3	£ 7.99
5	£ 10.99
10	£ 25.00

Weight of final Products — 8.00 kg

Price for delivery — £10.99

Help On Delivery Prices

```
(General)                                    Delivery_Help_Click

Sub Delivery_Help_Click()
    'Code for opening Help.doc
    Shell ("c:\progra~1\micros~2\office12\windowd.exe c:\help.doc")
End Sub
```

Delivery Prices Help

The yellow box is the only box you can fill in on this screen. Enter a value between 0 and 10. Do not add the units (e.g. kg) to the value you enter — the system does this automatically. The Price for Delivery is automatically calculated.

■ Marking

8–10 marks Candidates will produce detailed and accurate documentation. The manual will be presented in a well-structured and coherent format. Subject specific terminology will be used accurately and appropriately. The documentation will include a complete and detailed user guide covering all operations that the user would be required to perform. The on-screen guide should be well presented and easy to follow. There will be few if any errors in spelling, grammar and punctuation.

4–7 marks Candidates will provide clear documentation. The documentation will be well presented. There is clear on-screen help to support the end user. The supporting documentation and on-screen help is well presented and covers most aspects of the operations that the user would be required to perform. Some subject specific terminology will be used. There may be occasional errors of spelling, grammar and punctuation.

0–3 marks Candidates will provide a superficial documentation with weak supplementary user documentation covering few aspects of the operations that the user will be required to perform. The information will be poorly expressed and limited technical terms will be used. Errors of spelling, grammar and punctuation may be intrusive.

12 Evaluation

Introduction

There are a total of 6 marks available for the evaluation.

This is the final section of the project. By reading the first section (the analysis) and this final section, a moderator can get a good idea of the quality of your project: that is, what you have done and how successful you have been.

Overview

The evaluation of your project needs to be done by you and by the end user.

Your evaluation needs to tie in with the objectives given in the Analysis section, so without a good analysis (i.e. with poor objectives), you will not score any marks in the evaluation.

The evaluation by the end user requires any individuals you identified early in the project (in the analysis) to look at the system and given a written response.

The evaluation is an assessment of what the finished product you have created can and cannot do in relation to what it was required to do. It is not about how well you think you have done, or how much fun you have had doing it.

Honesty is the best policy with any evaluation. If something has not worked, then say so. Explain why and what you have done about it. If you try to cover it up, the likelihood is that evidence will be in the rest of your project to prove that it has not worked and you will be caught out. If you have lied here, how can the examiner be sure you have not lied elsewhere?

The section can be broken down into three main stages:

- An assessment of the final project against the requirements from analysis.
- Comments from the end user on the system that you have created.
- Identification of possible future extensions to the system.

Comment on the success in meeting the original objectives

It is not possible to achieve marks in this section unless you have completed the requirements specification earlier in the project. You need to take each objective listed in the requirements specification and comment on the degree of success you have had in meeting it.

What are the 'degrees of success'? There are four possibilities:

- An objective has been met completely.
- An objective has not been met in its entirety, but most of it has.
- Most of an objective has not been met, but a small part has.
- An objective has not been met at all.

Initially, you can note the success attained by referencing the requirements in the form of a table. This will give the examiner an immediate overview of how successful you have been in implementing the requirements specification. However, you will need to list the objectives and your evaluation of success more fully at some stage to prevent the examiner from having to flick backwards and forwards though the project.

< Example >

Requiement	Completely met	Mostly met	Mostly not met	Not met	Page number for evidence
Edit members' information	The system allows information for existing members to be edited.				65
List of overdue books sorted by date		The system gives a report of all books that are overdue but they are not sorted by date but by members.			66

Table 12.1 Format for visual reference for meeting objectives

There needs to be an element of description, rather than a simple 'yes' or 'no'.

The table is only an initial guide: on its own it will not get you any marks. To get marks, you must decide into which of the four success statements each objective falls. You must back up the objective with evidence, which may be from testing, a statement from the end user, or a printout of parts of the development.

You must comment on every objective and produce evidence to back up your assessment. You will lose marks if you miss out any requirements. You must provide evidence: the statement alone is insufficient to achieve the marks.

Where you have not completed the objectives, you must provide a reasoned comment saying why, what you have done to try and meet it, and what you could do in the future to meet it. The more honest you can be, the better!

You can still achieve full marks for this section even if you have not managed to fulfil all the objectives. It is, however, important that you give full and frank comments on the success of the project.

The evidence you need to produce can be page references to test run printouts or to specific areas of coding. If the objective you are producing evidence for is to do with the ease of use for different ability users, it might be appropriate to get a written statement from them.

If you have completed the full test plan in the development and testing section you will have gone through the requirements specification and provided screenshots to show that each one has been implemented and works. The page references you give in the evaluation will direct the moderator to this section to see the evidence of success.

Sometimes the evidence might not be in the system itself: you might have to go out and get it. This may require additional data collection, interviews or signed statements.

End user comments

The comments from the end user must be backed up with evidence.

There are two ways to get an end user's comments:

- By letter from the end user.
- By questionnaire.

You need to focus on getting the end users' comments in relation to the requirements, by asking if they are satisfied that the system does everything that it should do.

The end user is someone who knows and understands the underlying system: they know about the data and the results required, but may not necessarily be competent at using computers. You need to assess whether they can use the system, understand the screens, enter the required data and produce the results they want in a format understandable to them.

If the user thinks that the system does not meet the requirements, take on board the comments, re-design and re-test the system showing what you have done and the new results. This is perfectly acceptable.

Letters

Letters need to be sent from the end users to yourself showing that they have compared the system that you have developed against the initial requirements. If the end user writes that everything works then your tests should support this. An example letter is given below.

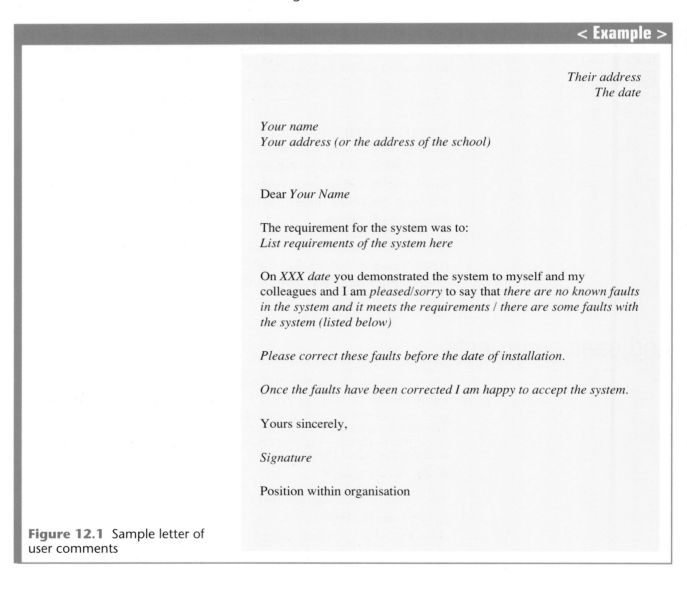

< Example >

Their address
The date

Your name
Your address (or the address of the school)

Dear *Your Name*

The requirement for the system was to:
List requirements of the system here

On *XXX date* you demonstrated the system to myself and my colleagues and I am *pleased/sorry* to say that *there are no known faults in the system and it meets the requirements / there are some faults with the system (listed below)*

Please correct these faults before the date of installation.

Once the faults have been corrected I am happy to accept the system.

Yours sincerely,

Signature

Position within organisation

Figure 12.1 Sample letter of user comments

Questionnaire

Part of a sample questionnaire might be:

< Example >

Question	Yes	No	Comment
Can you read the labels on the buttons?	✓		
Is the colour scheme appropriate?	✓		
Can you find all the options?	✓		Not initially obvious, but once found, ok.
Can you edit members?	✓		
Is the help easy to understand?	✓		Yes, if I use the glossary.
Can you produce a report of overdue books sorted by date due back?		✓	The report is easy to produce but it is sorted by Member.
Can you enter data accurately?	✓		The error checking works well.

Figure 12.2 Sample questionnaire to evaluate a system

Do not forget that you need to name and date every questionnaire. Include one blank and one filled-in questionnaire in the body of the project. You can summarise the results in the body of the text.

If there are any 'No' responses, you need to collect more information and evaluate what has gone wrong. If it is something simple, then correct it. If it is a fundamental problem, then evaluate and comment on it.

Range of possible extensions

There are four marks available for this section. There are two areas you must cover to gain marks in this section:

- Describe the necessary correction of shortfalls in the system.
- Describe possible extensions to the system and how they should be carried out.

Shortfalls

Shortfalls in the system are areas where you have not met the requirements specification and the system fails to achieve its objectives.

There may not be any shortfalls in your system, and if this is the case, then you can skip this section.

If there are shortfalls, then they need to be identified with methods of correcting them so that they are eliminated.

< Example >

Overdue books sorted by date

At present, the system sorts by Member and not by Date. To change the system to sort by Date, the date the book is due back needs to be identified as a sort field in the query the report is based on.

To ensure that this sort is made before the Members, the Date field needs to come before the Member field.

There is no requirement to carry out the correction.

Possible extensions

You must not only describe the possible extensions but give some idea of how to carry them out. This does not need to be a complete design, but a very general and rough description of what might be done to implement the extension.

This section requires you to use your imagination. You need to think about what you would do to improve the new system. Some ideas might be become evident as you develop your existing system, but don't be tempted to add them in as additions to your original specification. For other ideas, you will need to think further afield.

< Example >

Database	Spreadsheet	Web
■ Connect to external applications – spreadsheets, word processing. ■ Access to the system via the Internet. ■ Payment options – credit card etc. ■ Move to a partitioned system.	■ Replace the worksheet entry with forms entry. ■ Connect to external applications – databases, word processing. ■ Allow web-based applications to access the spreadsheet.	■ Connect to a database/ spreadsheet to store data. ■ Personalise the visit by storing customer information and profiles. ■ Add interactive elements – Web 2.0 etc. ■ Automatic display changes for different browsers/ resolution of screen.

Table 12.2 Example of extensions

Do not forget that there needs to be a brief description of the possible extension and how it could be achieved.

▨ Marking

5–6 marks   A detailed evaluation of the system which includes a description of whether the requirements specification was met, where the requirements were not met in the light of the end user's comments, why they were not met. A detailed description of how shortfalls could be achieved and a description of a range of possible extensions.

3–4 marks   An evaluation of the system, which may include a response from the client/end user. The report may lack specific detail but should include a description of whether the requirements specification was met in light of the end user's comments. The report should include identification of how shortfalls could be achieved and identification of possible extensions.

0–2 marks   Some material which attempts to evaluate whether the solution meets the requirements specification. There may be no or limited response form the client/end user and limited consideration will be given to the areas of the solution which have worked and those that have not. Possible extensions may be vague.

13 Presentation of report

Introduction

There are a total of 3 marks available for the report.

This is not a separate section. The marks are awarded for the presentation of your coursework.

The elements of the report that need to be present to gain full marks include:

■ Detailed and accurate means of navigation

There should be a title page to the project. This needs to be followed by a contents page. The contents page should map the sections and headings of the project so that it is easy for the moderator to work sequentially. Pages in the project documentation need page numbers. A contents page references these page numbers in order for it to be useful.

You are expected at this level to use an automated table of contents. This requires the use of styled section headings within the body of the text.

The project documentation should be fit for purpose – it is the report into a system's life cycle project for an A-Level ICT qualification. The presentation needs to be consistent, with appropriate use of font sizes and font styles.

■ Layout determined by the reader rather than the author

You, as the author, are not the intended audience of your report. The intended audience is the reader: in this instance, your teacher and the moderator. You must be aware of their needs when putting together the project. A system's life cycle project has a natural progression: analysis, design, development, testing, evaluation. This needs to be reflected in the project documentation. The user manual must be presented as a standalone document to gain high marks.

There should be very little need for the reader to flick backwards and forwards through the project: everything they need should be in the correct order.

Few spelling and grammatical errors

Most software provides spellcheckers and grammar checkers so there is no excuse for any spelling mistakes or grammatical errors in the project documentation. There should be appropriate use of technical terms and subject specific terminology.

Log of events

You cannot get more than one mark if you do not keep a dated log of events. The log should have been kept since the beginning of the project. See chapter 7, page 247 for more detail on the log of events.

Use of templates

There are two types of templates: task templates and document templates.

Task templates are templates that have been created to meet a specific task or purpose. For example, a test plan layout is a task template. There is a formalised structure to these documents and their use is common place within industry. The use of task templates is acceptable, encouraged and will not lose any marks.

Document templates are templates which set out the entire structure of a document. These include project documentation templates and user documentation templates. The use of these, while not forbidden, does have an impact on the marks. If you make use of a document template for the project report then you will not be able to achieve any marks for this section.

Marking

3 marks — The candidate has provided a detailed and accurate means of navigation of the report and has tailored the language used, both technical and non-technical, to the audience for which the parts of the report were aimed. Subject-specific terminology will be used correctly. A professional approach to the presentation will be expected and a clearly understandable, dated log of events will be kept. The information will be presented in an ordered and well structured manner. There are few if any errors of grammar or spelling.

2 marks | The candidate will produce a navigable report. The contents will be determined by the requirements of the candidate rather than the reader. A log of events will have been kept. The information is presented in an ordered fashion that maintains some coherence. There may be some occasional errors of grammar or spelling.

0–1 mark | The candidate has produced some material that explains part of the solution attempted. It will be difficult to navigate and will assume much knowledge of the solution that the reader will probably not possess. The information may be expressed without a structure. Errors of grammar or spelling may be intrusive.

Index